ALL THE BLUE BONNETS
The History of The King's Own Scottish Borderers

ALL THE
BLUE BONNETS

The History of The King's Own Scottish Borderers

Robert Woollcombe
Late K.O.S.B.

With a Foreword by
Brigadier F. H. Coutts, C.B.E.
The Colonel of the Regiment

ARMS AND ARMOUR PRESS
|London—Melbourne

To H.R.H. Princess Alice, Duchess of Gloucester,
for upwards of forty years Colonel-in-Chief.

Published in Great Britain by
Arms and Armour Press, Lionel Leventhal Limited,
2-6 Hampstead High Street, London NW3 1QQ;
and in Australasia at
4-12 Tattersalls Lane, Melbourne, Victoria 3000.

British Library Cataloguing in Publication Data:
Woollcombe, Robert   All the blue bonnets
1. Great Britain. Army. King's Own Scottish Borderers — History
I. Title 356'.11'0941 UA652.K52/
ISBN 0-85368-354-9

Cartography by Alexander Elder.
Edited by Michael Boxall.
Designed by David Gibbons.

Printed in Great Britain.

CONTENTS

LIST OF MAPS

FOREWORD

As the 27th Colonel of The King's Own Scottish Borderers, I feel very proud to introduce this history of the Regiment. The Regimental Trustees decided some years ago that there was a real need for a new history. It was felt that the earlier history should be re-traced and that there should be a comprehensive account of the past hundred years to complement the many admirable histories, mainly covering the two World Wars, already in existence. This book is, therefore, the first full history of The King's Own Scottish Borderers from our formation in 1689 up to the 1970s, as we approach our tercentenary.

We were fortunate indeed to find the ideal historian within our own ranks. Captain Robert Woollcombe served with distinction in the 6th (Border) Battalion during the Second World War, and he is the grandson of Lieutenant-General Sir Charles Woollcombe, who was Colonel from 1910 until 1923. As an author, Robert Woollcombe is best known within the Regiment for *Lion Rampant*, the story of the 15th (Scottish) Division, one of the most readable personal accounts of the war. We are greatly indebted to him for his research and for his dedication to the task.

Throughout these pages runs one common thread—a great sense of belonging to one Regimental Family; this is as true of the men of Leven's Regiment who rallied with such alacrity to the defence of Edinburgh in 1689 as it is of our very professional soldiers of today. The sense of belonging was greatly strengthened by our permanent affiliation to the six counties of the Scottish Border and it is a constant source of strength to the Borderers of the Regular Battalion, the Volunteers and the Cadets alike.

Today, the Regiment is one of only five Infantry Regiments of the Line to have remained unchanged and unamalgamated since their formation. For close on three centuries The King's Own Scottish Borderers have taken pride in their service to their Monarch and their country. I feel sure that the reader will sense this pride in Robert Woollcombe's History of the Regiment.

Colonel
The King's Own Scottish Borderers

ACKNOWLEDGMENTS

My first thanks must go to Brigadier Frank Coutts, C.B.E. for his great encouragement throughout the preparation of this book. I would like also to record my debt to Lieutenant-Colonel W. M. B. Dunn, T.D., who was Regimental Secretary throughout, for placing the Regimental records unreservedly at my disposal and for the help he gave me at every turn. My thanks go also to all those Borderers and others connected with the Regiment, with whom I have spoken or corresponded, for their ready assistance. Where I have quoted from their material it is acknowledged in my narrative; and in thanking them I cannot fail to remember Major-General E. G. Miles, C.B., D.S.O., M.C., Lieutenant-Colonel P. St C. Harrison, D.S.O., O.B.E., and Colonel G. G. M. Batchelor, H.N ' my great regret have not lived to see the book in print.

The resources of the Ministry of Defence Library, the National Army Museum Reading Room and the Public Record Office have also contributed to this book, and in particular I thank Mr William G. F. Boag, M.A., of the Scottish United Services Museum, who has been a mine of information on various historical points. I would also like to thank Mr. Alexander Elder, who took over the preparation of the maps. I am most grateful to Regimental Headquarters for compiling the index.

I wish to thank the estate of the late Major-General John Hay Beith and William Blackwood & Sons Ltd for permission to quote a verse from *The First Hundred Thousand*; Sir Philip Magnus and John Murray Ltd for permission to quote a passage from *Kitchener: Portrait of an Imperialist*; William Heinemann Ltd for permission to quote extracts from *The Indian Frontier War* by Lionel James; and Macmillan (London & Basingstoke) Ltd for permission to quote two passages from *The Relief of Chitral* by G. F. and F. E. Younghusband. Crown Copyright photographs are reproduced by permission of the Controller of H.M. Stationery Office.

ROBERT WOOLLCOMBE

Chapter 1

LEVEN'S REGIMENT

A few weeks before the outbreak of the Second World War, the Regiment marched through the City of Edinburgh. It was the culmination of the parade, held on 28 July 1939, to mark the Regiment's 250th anniversary. Headed by the Pipes and Drums of the 1st Battalion they marched past the saluting base at the Royal Scottish Academy and filled Princes Street from end to end: the Colour Party, and nearly 2,000 men of the recently doubled Territorial battalions, marching with bayonets fixed, followed by hundreds of old comrades who had assembled from all over the north. On the Glengarries glinted the Regimental badge, showing the city's motto, *Nisi Dominus frustra*, surmounted by the city's arms, the Castle, encircled by the words, *The Kings Own Scottish Borderers*. Two hundred and fifty years earlier, on Scottish soil, the Regiment had fought its first battle—in defence of Edinburgh.

This march past was rooted in 'the Glorious Revolution' of 1688 when William of Orange landed at Torbay, disembarked a Protestant army and, in the cause of the Protestant succession, marched on London to be proclaimed King of England. At that time, though, Scotland was divided. In Scotland there was the special grip of religion on politics. Kirk and the Covenant and the tyranny of a Catholic king exercised through a Privy Council contended for the allegiance of the State, while in the Highlands were the clans, a law unto themselves, where the heart of Jacobite sentiment lay.

Nowhere in the two kingdoms was turmoil greater than in Edinburgh when James II of England and VII of Scotland fled his realm. From England there came to the city at the end of February 1689, John Graham of Claverhouse, Viscount Dundee, the scourge of the Covenanters and the man responsible for a chill connotation to the word 'dragoon'. Major-General of cavalry in a Scottish force that had crossed the Border to help King James, he had been granted William's protection provided he returned to his home to live in peace; he was resolved, however, to raise the Highlands.

A few days later there came to Edinburgh a young nobleman aged twenty-eight, David, third Earl of Leven, who with his father, Lord Melville, had been living in Holland with other expatriates since the Rye House plot to assassinate Charles II. He had inherited the Earldom of Leven from his mother, through whom he was descended from the Scottish soldier of fortune, Sir Alexander Leslie, created first Earl. David, the third Earl, had raised a small corps of Scottish refugees in Germany and Holland, and took them to England in William of Orange's expedition. At the landing at Torbay on 5 November 1688, it mustered 25 officers and 257 rank and file, and it was sent to garrison Plymouth.

Leven had then been selected as the bearer of letters summoning the Scottish Estates. The corps he had brought from Holland remained at Plymouth and was soon dispersed, only the officers following Leven to Scotland, where by authority of the Estates he was to raise the Regiment that became The King's Own Scottish Borderers.

*   *   *   *   *

Edinburgh, in March 1689, was in a ferment. The Convention of Estates met on 14 March—the Lords of the Clergy, whose presence derived from Stuart enforcement of episcopacy, the Nobility and the Commissioners for Shires and Burghs. Leven was present and so was Dundee. A deputation was sent to the Duke of Gordon who still held the Castle in the name of King James, and whose cannon could at that moment have made life uncomfortable in the Parliament House. He was required to capitulate, but an unsatisfactory reply was received. Trumpeters and heralds went out formally to summon him, but the Duke of Gordon remained where he was.

Knowledge spread that Dundee was visiting the Castle, and he was believed to be persuading the garrison to hold out. On 16 March the Estates met again and a 'committee for securing the peace' was nominated. A temperate letter from William, conveyed by the Earl of Leven, was read out, as well as a highly intemperate one received by special messenger from King James in France. Uproar ensued. Dundee's appeal to the Scottish Cavaliers, the Jacobite party whose strength lay among the great nobles, has been romanticized by Sir Walter Scott in *Bonnie Dundee*:

'To the Lords of Convention 'twas Claver'se who spoke,
"Ere the King's crown shall fall there are crowns to be broke;
So let each cavalier who loves honour and me,
Come follow the bonnet of Bonnie Dundee". '

The Cavalier faction decided to make for Stirling, although already abandoned by some of their number. They intended to hold a rival Jacobite convention, but there was a delay. Their most influential figure, the Marquess of Atholl, who could call forth many clansmen, urged caution. Dundee, alone, with his troopers, was

away even as the Estates met for the third time, on Monday, 18
March. The alarm was raised:

'Dundee he is mounted, he rides up the street,
The bells are rung backwards, the drums they are beat;
But the Provost douce man, said, 'Just e'een let him be,
The Gude Town is weel quit of that Deil of Dundee.'

The news of Dundee's flight had been brought to the Parliament
House. Taking the road to Linlithgow and passing with his
troopers under the Castle rock, he had been seen approaching the
ramparts and holding a shouted exchange with the Duke of
Gordon. In the Parliament House there was uproar again. The
'Lords of Convention' then and there authorized the Earl of Leven
to levy a regiment of 800 men by beat of drums for the defence of
the city, and to assemble them in the Abbey Close. This was in fact
the first proposal of a report laid before the Convention on that
day by the committee for securing the peace, which can be seen in
Acts of the Parliaments of Scotland, dated 18 March 1689, and
which reads:

'The Committee doe offer it as their opinion that for secureing
the peace of the toune the Meeting of Estates may be pleased to
grant warrand to the Earle of Levin, with all expedition to levie
ane Regiment of foot consisting of eight hundred men, and to
beat Drummes to that effect, And that so soon as they are in
readiness, he cause them Rendevouze in the Abbey Close at the
sight of, and that from the tyme they are Rendevouzed there they
shall be taken into pay.'

This was at once approved. Leven immediately ordered the
drums to beat, and the Regiment sprang into existence. By the ruins
of the Abbey Church at Holyrood, 800 armed men were assembled
within the space of two hours, according to the *London Gazette*.
The entry headed *Edinburgh, 19th March*, reads:

'The Convention have since our last ordered a Proclamation to
be published, requiring all Persons from the age of sixteen to
sixty to be in readiness to take Arms, when the House shall think
fit to give further directions to that purpose.'

After reference to officers of Militia and to the appointment of
Sir Patrick Hume who 'came over with the King of England from
Holland,' the *London Gazette* continues:

'They ordered 800 men to be levied under the command of the
Earl of Leven, who likewise came over with His Majesty, which
were raised and armed in two hours time, and appointed to
guard the town.'

The memoirs of General Mackay, who was sent to Edinburgh by
William and reached the city on 25 March, relate that he brought
with him money to distribute to the troops that came with him, 'as

also to the Earle of Levin, to levie of 780 men, according to his Majesty's order'. 780 was the authorized strength of a regiment on the English establishment, which was thirteen companies of sixty men, including one Grenadier company. The Regiment was paid from the English establishment, and the *English Treasury Records* of 1689-90 refer to the pay of Leven's being computed for one colonel, one lieutenant-colonel, one major, nine 'other captains', twelve lieutenants, twelve ensigns, one 'chirurgeon and his mate', one adjutant, one quartermaster, one chaplain, 24 sergeants, 36 corporals, 24 drummers and 780 private soldiers.[1] In an order issued by the Convention they were described as sentinels:

'The Meeting of Estates doe ordaine that such Centinells as the Earl of Leven has levied be payed . . . att six shillings Scots per diem since the tyme of their respective enrolments, and that the officers be payed conforme.'

And as sentinels, with firelock and pike, and perhaps halberds and a variety of other naked blades, they kept guard in the city. At the same time, armed men from the west, Cameronian men, volunteered their services and began digging entrenchments around the Castle, to intercept its communications. Strong guards were set towards the West Port. The Cameronian men were stood down when General Mackay arrived with his troops.

The Convention's report from Edinburgh dated 21 March as published in the *London Gazette* contained the following:

'The Convention have been busied in putting the country into a posture of defence . . . The Viscount of Dundee is gone further westward . . . Several ships do appear in the Firth, in which, it's believed, is Major-General Mackay with the three Scotch regiments under his command.'

Dated 28 March, came another report:

'The 27th the Convention ordered that warrant be given to Major-General Mackay to beat drums through the Kingdom, for recruiting four regiments of Foot and one of Dragoons.'

Evidently the Earl of Leven was in overall command of the defence of Edinburgh, for the report states:

'An act approving the good service of such men from Argyle, Glasgow and the Western Shires as were in arms and kept guard in Edinburgh under the command of the Earl of Levin, since the meeting of the Estates, with an allowance to such of them as have not listed in the Earl's Regiment, to return with their arms to their respective homes, was brought in, considered and approven.'

---

[1] *The Lowland Scots Regiments*, edited by the Right Hon. Sir Herbert Maxwell, Bart. (1918).

Meanwhile, the man 'the Earl's Regiment' was to meet in battle at the top of the pass of Killiecrankie was outlawed. He made his way to Stirling, where his plan for a Jacobite convention came to nought, and when the Convention of Estates offered the Crown of Scotland to William and Mary, Dundee was in Lochaber to raise the clans.

* * * * *

Major-General Hugh Mackay of Scourie, who was commissioned to be Commander-in-Chief by the Scottish Convention, was a soldier of fortune. Aged fifty years, Mackay had served in Dumbarton's Regiment on the Continent under Marshal Turenne, and had then transferred his sympathies to the States-General of Holland. Mackay formulated the *Rules of War for the Infantry*, which was published in 1693, the year after he was killed in Flanders. Their substance was certainly intended to apply to the forbears of The King's Own Scottish Borderers at Killiecrankie, and the last rule, Number 22, may appeal to serving officers today:

'When the army is embattelled and the troops ready to march towards the enemy, all Commanders, Majors and Officers commanding Plotoons, ought to affect a cheerful countenance, speaking friendly to and encouraging the souldiers in the most touching expressions, and by the most persuasive arguments, as Religion, Liberty and Personal Honour and Safety, humbly depending upon their good behaviour, the Justice of the Cause, the Obligation of our Conscience to serve our Master faithfully, the Reputation of our Country, alleging the good examples of our Predecessours, and the like, which out of the mouths of Officers showing good examples of their own Persons particularly, if just to, and beloved of their souldiers, will be good effect to animate them to the Work.'

A Scots-Dutch brigade, raised in Holland, which Mackay brought with him to Edinburgh in March 1689, had been divested of its Dutch troops in England before it sailed for the Firth of Forth. These three regiments, Balfour's, Ramsay's and a regiment of which Mackay himself was Colonel, numbered but 1,100 men. With this meagre force, which it was intended to augment by further levies, Mackay took over the blockade of Edinburgh Castle, and reinforced by some cavalry from England, moved into the Highlands with a small expedition to apprehend Dundee. Despite the allegiance to the government of the formidable House of Argyll and the adherence of a few other clansmen, 'neare three months chicane with a very small parcell of forces', as Mackay described it,[2] showed him that he would never master Dundee by toiling through the mountains with exhausted men and horses. He decided it was necessary to put a strong garrison in the heart of the Highlands at Inverlochy in Lochaber, and smaller ones elsewhere, and had returned to Edinburgh to 'put life in the design of Inverlochy', when an emergency was caused by Jacobite movements in the Atholl country. The powerful Marquess, whose attitude throughout had been equivocal, had disappeared to England. His vassals declared for James and occupied Blair Castle. His eldest son, Lord Murray, declared for William, but was shut out of the ancestral seat. Dundee, apprised of events, marched with what force he could muster from Lochaber to Atholl. And for Leven's Regiment battle was at hand.

Mackay had fixed on Perth as the rendezvous for his forces. Irked by government delays in the provision of meal and horses, to Perth he at length sent his provisions. The force that he had by him he described in his *Short Relation* of events, written soon afterwards, as 'six good battalions of foot'. These were Hastings's regiment (later the 13th Foot, Somerset Light Infantry), Leven's regiment, Viscount Kenmore's levies, and a 'battalion' from each regiment of the Scots-Dutch brigade. Mackay in his memoirs used the word 'battalion' fairly indiscriminately with 'regiment'. Literally, a battalion was a body of men in battle array. The whole force, according to Mackay's account, numbered some 3,000 foot. There were also Lord Belhaven's and Lord Armandale's troops of horse, altogether about one hundred mounted men.

Mackay had given orders for more horse and dragoons quartered at Stirling to follow him to Perth, but at Perth there was no sign of their arrival, so he took a deliberate risk and marched without them from Perth on 26 July for the mountain defile that gave access to Blair Castle, the two-mile pass of Killiecrankie. He was in haste to forestall Dundee at Blair. He halted that night at Dunkeld, where at midnight he received an express message from Lord Murray informing him that Dundee had entered Atholl and that Murray's followers had retreated from the ground around Blair Castle. Murray claimed that his men were guarding the pass for the passage of Mackay's troops, but he was uncertain of their reliability.

At daybreak on 27 July, Mackay set out to march the eleven miles to the pass, having again sent back word to hasten the horse and dragoons which he hoped were following. As it happened, Dundee reached Blair Castle, two miles beyond the top of the pass,

---

[2] Quotations from Mackay in this chapter are taken from his *Memoirs of the War carried on in Scotland and Ireland* and from the letters in the appendix thereto, including his *Short Relation* of the Battle of Killiecrankie.

at almost the same hour as Mackay reached the foot of the pass.

*   *   *   *   *

The Viscount Dundee had troubles of his own. Something over 2,000 broadswords were all he had been able to muster from the disunity and rivalries of the clans for his march to Atholl. Macdonalds of Clanranald, of the Isles and of Glengarry; Cameron; Maclean, were those who came with him. With them was a contingent of 500 Irish which King James, who was now in Ireland, had sent to strengthen Dundee's hand. Dundee had with him also a body of horse whom Mackay viewed with some apprehension, knowing these were fervent Jacobite gentry, former officers who had all seen cavalry service, and that the remainder were Dundee's faithful dragoons.

General Mackay, having sent ahead 200 'fusiliers', the pick of his battalions, as an advanced guard to secure the top of the pass, reached the foot of the pass with his main body at 10 o'clock in the morning. In his Memoirs he wrote that even when he left Edinburgh he had begun to 'have very ill thoughts of the expedition in gross'. Approaching the entry to the pass, he came upon Lord Murray who told him that most of his followers had melted away to safeguard their cattle. Mackay sent ahead 200 men of Leven's regiment under their lieutenant-colonel, Arnot—one of several Huguenot officers who had landed with Leven at Torbay—to reinforce the fusiliers at the head of the pass. The other battalions fell out for a two-hour rest.

Then word came that the pass was clear. The battalions fell in and, in ragged file, began to climb up the mountain ravine through which tumbled the River Garry. The order of march of the regiments was Balfour's, Ramsay's, Kenmore's, Belhaven's troop of horse, then Leven's, Mackay's and 1,200 baggage horses, then Annandale's troop, with Hastings's regiment bringing up the rear. In the column were some petards for blowing in the gates of Blair Castle. The five leading battalions reached the top of the pass and halted in a field of corn, the River Garry on their left, to await the baggage and the rear of the column. The 200 fusiliers under their officer were sent ahead again and presently espied parties of Highlanders about a mile towards Blair, approaching slowly along the foot of a hill.

Mackay galloped forward and discovered the main body of clansmen now 'gaining the heights' to his right. He galloped back to his troops and ordered what he called a 'Quart de Conversion to the right' by battalions, and an advance, 'each before his face', up a steep brae. This manoeuvre brought the battalions into line at the top of the brae, on what Mackay judged to be a piece of ground 'fair enough to receive, though not to attack, the enemy on it'. It brought them into line in an order of battle from right to left that was the order of march reversed. Thus Hastings's regiment came up last on the extreme right, on their left was Mackay's, then Leven's, Kenmore's, Ramsay's, and Balfour's on the far left. 'Upon the left of all, on a little hill wreathed with trees,' were the fusiliers. Arnot and his men had evidently rejoined Leven's.

A short way ahead, on rising ground above the Lowlanders, and with a steep hill at their back, as was their customary way of fighting, the Highlanders drew up at about the same time by clans. One of the chieftains carried the royal standard of King James VII of Scotland. Military discipline as the Viscount Dundee knew it, and the tried tactics of European warfare, he had been unable to inculcate in them; and he had let them have their own way. They would advance in poor formation, discharging their firelocks ineffectively. If the day went ill for them, they would scramble back over the hilltop behind them. But if all went well the moment would come when they would throw aside their firearms and draw the broadswords for their wild charge.

Mackay adjusted his battle line, the men three deep, in half battalions. Among them were pikemen, probably in the proportion of about one in five, the pikes being carried by the strongest fellows. Between each half battalion was a small gap and in the centre Mackay formed a larger gap, in the rear of which he positioned his two troops of horse. He then made a speech of exhortation to every battalion, in the sense that he set down in his Rules of War. But he was anxious about the number of inexperienced, levied men, and in the knowledge that none of his officers and soldiers had previously encountered Highlanders. He warned his battalions that there was no alternative but to stand to it, for if they gave way there would be no escape from their half-naked pursuers who were so much the speedier of foot; moreover, the natives of Atholl themselves were in arms, 'ready to strip and knock in the head all runaways'. All asseverated that none would abandon him, 'which,' he adds with some bitterness in his Short Relation, 'most of them belyed shortly after'.

And so, for two hours on the sunny summer evening of 27 July 1689, General Mackay waited for what Dundee would do, and Dundee waited for what Mackay would do. Mackay dreaded, above all, an enemy night attack, but he had got himself into a position where the initiative was hardly his, for the Highlanders completely overlooked him. Indeed, from their vantage place they could make out quite clearly his person, and shots from their firearms were aimed at him wherever he went . . . Yet despite one skirmish, and the provocative firing by the Lowlanders of 'three little leather field-pieces', the two sides held back.

At last, half an hour before sunset, the Highlanders put aside their plaids and, stripped to their shirts and bare-footed, moved slowly down the hill in their rough formations, firing at random. Their pace quickened. Then with a yell their firearms were thrown down and out came the broadswords. There was a rush. With sword and buckler they swarmed forward. Dundee himself was at the head of his cavalry; his horsemen came straight towards the centre of the Lowlanders' line.

All was over in a few minutes. The ferocity of the charge was too much for the bulk of the Lowland levies. Officers commanding the battalions had been instructed to open fire 'by platoons' at one hundred paces. Those who stood their ground were still fumbling to fix their bayonets to the muzzles of their muskets to receive the charge when the clansmen were upon them.

At the same moment, a musket ball struck Dundee below his cuirass. Despite a warning from Cameron of Lochiel that he should guard his person, he had insisted that he must establish his courage in front of the clans and had placed himself at the head of his cavalry. Charging for the centre of Mackay's line, the clansmen then wheeled left towards Mackay's and Hastings's regiments. According to Macaulay's account, Dundee had raised his bonnet aloft (by another account it was his sword) to signal his cavalry to charge. At all events, none of the Lowlanders and few of the Highlanders saw him sink from his saddle, hidden by dust and smoke; and laid low was the bonnet of Bonnie Dundee.

'The battailon of Hastings which was ranged upon the right hand (and) that of my regement, my Lord Leven's, and Kenmore with the half of Ramsay's battailon, made pretty good fire,' Mackay wrote in his *Short Relation*. But his left gave way without firing a shot. On the extreme left, the lieutenant-colonel commanding the picked fusiliers was deserted by his men. Balfour's men fled. Balfour was killed. Mackay ordered his two troops of horse to take the Highlanders from both flanks, but they turned about. To shame his horsemen by his example, Mackay spurred his charger through a press of Highlanders, but none save a servant followed him. His whole line was now breaking up, and in a 'twinkling of an eye', as he wrote, victors and vanquished were out of sight, the vanquished to their hapless fate, the Highlanders to plunder the baggage down the pass. Mackay's brother, lieutenant-colonel of his own regiment, was among the slain.

In his Memoirs, in which he wrote rather engagingly about himself in the third person, Mackay described his attempt to rally his battalions:

'At which sad spectacle it may easily be judged how he was surprised to see at first view himself alone upon the field, but looking further to the right he espyed a small heap of red coats, whither galloping, he found it to be a parte of the Earl of Leven's regiment, with himself, his Lieutenant-Colonel, Major, and most of his officers upon their head, whome the General praised for their steadfastness; but seeing the men in confusion, there being some few of other regiments got among them, prayed the Earl with his officers to see to get them speedily in condition to receive the enemy, whom he minutely expected, while he galloped further to a parte of Hastings.'

In his *Short Relation*, written three weeks later to the Earl of Leven's father, Lord Melville, who had been appointed Secretary of State for Scotland, he wrote:

'In a very short tyme all did run except a parte of the Earl of Leven's regiment, which by the diligence and firmity of the saide Earle with his Lieutenant-Colonel, Major and other officers and a parte of Colonel Hastings regiment, which after they had lost ground the Colonel with his Lieutenant-Colonel and other officers brought up againe, and kept the field of battail . . . I could learn of no commanding officer that misbehaved, though I confesse that my Lord Leven, Colonel Hastings and their officers have distinguished themselves on this occasion above all others.'

Then, having formed into one body those of Hastings's and Leven's regiments who were upon the field, as dusk was coming on, and 'exhorting the officers to get their men in a condition to make at least one discharge if they were attacked,' Mackay reconnoitred and saw Highlanders gathering again. Avoiding the pass and the route to Perth, he withdrew the remains of his force down the hillside and across the Rivery Garry, the men being told to take 'special care to march off very softly'. And abandoning that hostile country with the staunchest of his beaten army, and some 150 'runaways' from Ramsay's regiment that he came across, General Hugh Mackay conducted his sorrowful retreat. Striking south across the mountains he came back to Stirling, and not until he arrived there did he learn of Dundee's death.

'My Lord,' he wrote to Lord Melville, 'your son hath behaved himself with all his officers and souldiers extraordinary well, as did also Colonel Hastings with his.' In his Memoirs, he ascribed the steadfastness of Leven's regiment partly to their being less numerously attacked than Mackay's own regiment on their right, who received a particularly savage onslaught from the Macdonalds; yet Leven's, the right-centre of the line, must have faced Dundee's cavalry. Mackay also ascribed their steadiness to their higher

proportion of officers than in the three Scots-Dutch regiments—
'and very good brisk gentlemen'.[3]

*   *   *   *   *

So ended a battle of long ago. The regiment of the Earl of Leven
did not climb the pass of Killiecrankie to easy glory. Had he lived,
John Graham of Claverhouse, Viscount Dundee, might have had
all Scotland at his mercy, but his death robbed his cause of the
moral effect of victory and of the leadership to pluck its fruits.
General Mackay, on his part, did not forget the charge of the
Highlanders and his fumbling ranks, borne down before they could
fix their plug bayonets into the muzzles of their muskets. Hence he
invented an historic attachment which hastened the departure of
the pike from the battlefield. It consisted of two external rings
which enabled the musket to be fired when the bayonet had been
fixed.

The Regiment's time-honoured privilege of beating up for
recruits within the City of Edinburgh without seeking permission of
the Lord Provost, as sanctioned by the City Magistrates, dates
from soon after Killiecrankie. After the battle the Regiment was
quartered at Edinburgh until it sailed for the Irish war, and on 13
February 1691 Bailie Grahame permitted the Earl of Leven, who
was Keeper of Edinburgh Castle and had the authority of Their
Majesties' Privy Council, to levy one company of foot for the
Castle, to beat his drums through the city and suburbs. It is the
privilege of the Regiment to this day, together with that of
marching through the city with bayonets fixed and Colours flying.

---

[3] They included a number of Huguenots from the Continent, but mostly bore
straightforward Scottish names. See Dalton's *English Army Lists and Commission
Registers 1661-1714,* in which there is a list of the officers of Leven's Regiment
compiled from the *Warrant Book for Scotland, May 1689 — February 1690.*

Chapter 2

THE 25th FOOT: KING'S OWN BORDERERS

In a letter to the Duke of Hamilton, President of the Convention, written immediately after the battle, Mackay had not minced his words on the subject of Killiecrankie:

'I had no regement or troop with me but behaved like the vilest cowards in nature, except Hastings' and my Lord Leven's, whom I must praise to such a degree as I cannot but blame others of whom I expected more.'

Leven's was retained on the permanent rolls of the British Army, and was for long regarded in Scotland as The Edinburgh Regiment. It was never so designated in the Army List, and was known officially by the names of its successive Colonels until the numbering of regiments was introduced. It then took its place as the 25th Regiment of Foot to be raised since the disbanding of the New Model Army. It is food for thought that of the twenty-four line regiments that preceded it in the Army List only four still exist. Leven retained the Colonelcy until March 1694.

The Regiment made good its Killiecrankie losses. Its immediate purpose now was to safeguard the Lowlands. 'The low country over all is guarded,' Mackay reported to the Duke of Hamilton on 11 October 1689; Leven's Regiment was at Leith and 'Canegate'. In 1690, the year when he established Fort William, Mackay wrote to Hamilton that Leven's, with certain other infantry, and the Royal Dragoons and the Horse Guards, 'all very good forces,' were to be ready to march to where the service most required it.[1]

In 1691 the Regiment embarked with other Scottish regiments for William's campaign in Ireland; then, in 1692, embarked for Flanders to fight in the war of the League of Augsburg, the alliance formed by William III against Louis XIV.

The wars of those days moved at a leisurely pace with their protracted sieges, lengthy manoeuvrings, and 'close seasons' when armies retired to winter quarters and kings to their palaces. The shock of pitched battle, however, came periodically, as the Regiment experienced at Steenkirk, where General Mackay was among the slain, and at Landen where the casualties on both sides amounted to 25,000 men. In 1695, under Colonel Maitland, the

[1] Mackay's Memoirs: letters on military affairs in Scotland, 1689-90.

Regiment took part in the siege and capture of Namur, and is recorded to have had twenty officers and upwards of 500 men killed by the explosion of a mine under the fortifications. These times were immortalized in fiction in Laurence Sterne's classic, *Tristram Shandy*, in which Uncle Toby, a comic character of Shakespearean proportions in his 'great ramillie-wig', was a former captain in a corps named as Leven's Regiment. He had been wounded in the groin at Namur, and his servant, Trim, a former corporal in Leven's, had been disabled by an injury to the knee-cap at Landen.

The Regiment returned from Flanders to Scotland in 1697 to recruit, and remained there for the next twenty years, which included the year of the Union, mostly garrisoning the Highlands.

*   *   *   *   *

The Regiment, therefore, took no part in the campaigns of Marlborough, but it fought in the other Continental wars of the 18th Century in which the United Kingdom was engaged; the War of the Austrian Succession (1744-48), the Seven Years War (1756-63), and the French Revolutionary Wars at the end of the century. Of all those battles, the victory at Minden in Germany, on 1 August 1759, is of special significance to The King's Own Scottish Borderers. Revisiting the site of the battle in later years, Prince Ferdinand of Brunswick, who had commanded the allied army of British, Hanoverians and Hessians against the French and Austrians, remarked, 'It was here that the British infantry gained immortal glory.' Six regiments of British infantry, the 25th Foot among them, mistaking the order of their general, had marched in line against 10,000 French cavalry massed opposite them, regardless of the flanking cannonade, had repulsed charge after cavalry charge with their musketry, and had broken the French centre. Reflected Marshal Contandes, French Commander-in-Chief, 'I never thought to see a single line of infantry break through three lines of cavalry ranked in order of battle, and tumble them to ruin.'

Hitherto, it had been thought unchivalrous to take true aim with the musket, which was discharged from the breast in the direction of the enemy. Minden was the first occasion when the British infantry put the butt into the shoulder and aimed along the barrel.

The tradition grew up that at Minden the men had plucked roses as they passed gardens or orchards; hence there was born, militarily speaking, the Minden rose, and The King's Own Scottish Borderers wear red roses on Minden Day. Contemporary accounts are silent about the rose, and indeed, the circumstances of the battle, which was fought on heath, make it unlikely that there were any roses to hand. It is more likely that the men put sprigs of green foliage in their hats—particularly laurel. The wearing of such sprigs is ancient in origin and became commemorative; paintings of the Regiment in Minorca (1769-75) show similar sprigs worn on headdress ceremonially. Be that as it may, the tradition of the rose was nicely observed in 1944 during the invasion of Normandy, when 6th K.O.S.B., actually making an attack on Minden Day, plucked the wild roses from the hedgerows and wore them in the netting of their helmets as they went into action.

Apart from the Continental campaigns, the Regiment garrisoned Ireland for a number of years, and was prominent in holding the Rock of Gibraltar for the British Empire. It was stationed there for two lengthy periods, totalling twenty years, and took part in both the siege of 1727 and the relief of 1782. The 25th Foot sailed for the Relief of Gibraltar in Lord Howe's flagship, *Victory*, Nelson's future flagship. The Regiment can also claim to have served in the War of Jenkins's Ear, the maritime confrontation with Spain, when it was sent to the West Indies (1740-43).

At the end of its first period in Gibraltar, in 1736, a great upheaval befell the Regiment. The entire body of private soldiers were drafted to North America, and the officers and non-commissioned officers were sent to Ireland to recruit ten new companies, presumably from the Irish Protestants. However, the Colonelcy was held by a Scotsman, the Earl of Rothes, and most of his officers were Scottish. In 1755 the 25th Foot recruited again in Scotland, and the Regiment returned to Scotland for four years in 1764. The Regiment was stationed in Edinburgh, 1780-82, during which time the flank companies attended a camp at Dunbar under the command of Colonel the Duke of Buccleuch. When the Duke ceased to have a footman running before his carriage he presented his runner's silver-headed cane to the Regiment, for the use of the Drum Major. Unfortunately the Drum Major left it behind on the Isle of Wight, 'by neglect', in 1799.

*   *   *   *   *

The Regiment fought at both the Jacobite outbreaks of the '15 and the '45. In 1715 it was withdrawn from the Highlands to fight under the Duke of Argyll at Sheriffmuir. Here, 4,000 Crown troops prevented the Jacobite army of about 9,000 men under the Earl of Mar from crossing the Forth. A month later James the Old Pretender stepped ashore at Peterhead in Aberdeen, without personal magnetism, and too late. Very different was the situation in 1745, when Bonnie Prince Charlie took Edinburgh and held court at Holyrood. The 25th Foot, with other British corps, was hurriedly brought home from the Continent and was present at Culloden on 16 April 1746, under the Duke of Cumberland. In all, the Regiment served the Hanoverians well, and is the only regiment in the British Army to have engaged the Highlanders at Killiecrankie, Sheriffmuir and Culloden.

The Regiment took the title of The King's Own Borderers in 1805 by command of George III, and thereby became a royal regiment: they were sometimes called the Royal Borderers. The uniform facings and the Regimental Colour were accordingly altered from yellow to blue. At the same time, George III commanded that the Regiment adopt the motto, *In veritate religionis confido*, 'I trust in the truth of religion'. This motto was incorporated into a new badge, approved by the King, in which the motto was surmounted by the White Horse of Hanover, and the Royal Cipher within the Garter, and the Crown. The motto also encircled the White Horse of Hanover on the shoulder-belt plate.

In 1828, when new Colours were being prepared, George IV approved the retention of this motto upon the Colours,[2] but the question of the insignia was still not settled, and in 1832 William IV permitted the Regiment to bear the arms and motto of the City of Edinburgh upon its Colours and appointments in recognition of the Regiment's origin. It had been assumed that *In veritate religionis confido* was a reference to the religious motto of Edinburgh, *Nisi Dominus frustra*, and the connection was now deemed to have been made manifest.[3] The Edinburgh arms and motto were placed in the centre of the Regimental Colour. William IV further commanded that the motto conferred in 1805 be placed beneath the royal crest of England in two corners of the Regimental Colour. The English crest is the lion *statant guardant*, Imperially crowned, standing upon an Imperial crown. According to the contemporary records of the Inspector of Regimental Colours at the College of Arms, the White Horse of Hanover was not shown on the Colours of the 25th Foot; these records were not completed until 1820, and there is some documentary ambiguity as to what was done in practice. At

[2] *Public Record Office*, WO 3/78, p. 263: Adjutant General to General the Hon. Charles Fitzroy, Colonel of the 25th Regiment. Horse Guards, 12 June 1828.

[3] 'His Majesty has been graciously pleased to permit the 25th Regiment or 'The King's Own Borderers' . . . to bear on its Colours and Appointments the Arms of Edinburgh with the motto *Nisi Dominus frustra*, also to retain the motto *In veritate religionis confido* which was authorized by His late Majesty King George the Third in reference to the badge and motto above specified . . .' *Public Record Office*, WO 3/84, p. 62: Adjutant General to Lieutenant-General Sir Henry F. Campbell, Colonel of the 25th Regiment. Horse Guards, 12 March 1832.

all events, King William IV also sanctioned the White Horse and it is emblazoned in the other two corners of the Regimental Colour.

In 1961, the badge of The King's Own Scottish Borderers came to the attention of Lord Lyon King-of-Arms, who perceiving it to be surmounted by the royal crest of England, advised that this should be altered to the Sovereign's crest of Scotland, a lion *sejant affronté erect*, Imperially crowned and holding sword and sceptre. This was the crest assumed by the House of Stuart in the 16th Century which, it appeared, should have been adopted in 1887 when the word 'Scottish' finally came into the title. The Colonel of the Regiment, Major-General J. Scott Elliot, took soundings on the subject within Regimental circles, but the retention of the crest of England was favoured by a large majority as more appropriate to the Regiment's history. Accordingly, The King's Own Scottish Borderers retain their English 'Dog and Bonnet', as the Regiment familiarly calls it.

*   *   *   *   *

As troops of a maritime power the Regiment has sailed many seas. It took part in combined operations with the Fleet in raids on the Spanish and French coasts, the first in 1719 against Spain at Vigo Bay, and twice was dispatched against the French coast during the Seven Years War. During the French Revolutionary Wars the Regiment was based at Plymouth and actually supplied marine parties, who during the years 1793-97 served afloat on His Majesty's ships in the Mediterranean, the English Channel and the North Sea. The marine detachments stood guard outside the captain's cabin and at the magazine hatchways and other vital parts of the ship; in action they took station on the poop, the quarter deck and the ship's gangways. The Regiment served under Lord Hood and Lord Howe. Its marine parties were present at the blockade of Toulon, and when the port was besieged by a republican army they engaged the French vanguard ashore at Ollioules, where the enemy artillery was placed under the command of Captain Napoleon Bonaparte. Detachments of the Regiment served with the Fleet on 'the Glorious First of June', 1794. In 1797 in the Mediterranean, the detachment of the 25th Foot on the 98-gun man-of-war, *St George*, effectively supported the ship's officers in putting down a mutiny. Earlier, the *St George* had captured a French privateer with her prize, a Spanish galleon worth one million pounds sterling; this yielded so much prize money that when the Regiment's detachment eventually disembarked at Portsmouth, the men paid for the church bells to be rung in every town through which they passed on their journey back to Plymouth.

Meanwhile, the younger Pitt's maritime challenge to France had sent the Fleet to the West Indies to take the French sugar islands. In 1795, after the revolt of the slave populations, the entire Regiment with the exception of those on marine service sailed to Grenada to secure the island from the insurgents. A second battalion was raised at Plymouth and sailed for the West Indies to be incorporated into the Regiment, but their ship was captured by a French corvette off Barbados. All aboard were transferred to the corvette, and the rank and file were put in irons. The officers attempted to seize the ship, but were betrayed and thrown into the hold. They were destined for a prison ship. The rank and file were transferred to another French vessel, but they were men to be reckoned with. Under one, Sergeant Leech, they overpowered the crew and forced the master to sail to Grenada, where they joined the Regiment. The 2nd Battalion included in its ranks mariners and landsmen of many nationalities taken off Dutch men-of-war confiscated in Plymouth Sound, when Holland had declared war; men who 'in general behaved themselves well and served faithfully', it is recorded, and certainly they must have done.

In Grenada, nearly six hundred men of the Regiment perished from disease in fifteen months. In 1796, the remnants of the 25th Foot returned to Plymouth to recruit, and in 1799 the Regiment sailed to Holland with the expedition which fought the unsuccessful Helder campaign. A Grenadier detachment of the 25th Foot under Lieutenant McDonald were the first troops ashore. The expedition, which included a Russian force from the Baltic, was under the overall command of the Duke of York, celebrated for marching 10,000 men to the top of the hill and marching them down again. The Regiment fought among the sandhills at Egmont-op-Zee, and as the star of Napoleon rose, it sailed again, in 1801, to take part in the siege of Alexandria which compelled the French to evacuate Egypt. For this, the device of the Sphinx and the word 'Egypt' is borne on the Regimental Colour.

After a period in Gibraltar, and then in Ireland, the 25th Foot returned to the West Indies for ten years, 1807-17. With the Fleet it took part in the capture of Martinique and Guadaloupe from the French, in 1809 and 1810. The rôle of the Regiment in the Revolutionary and Napoleonic era had thus been almost entirely of maritime significance.

A second battalion was raised again in 1804, when the army was being expanded to meet the needs of the war. It was formed at Penrith from volunteers from the Army of Reserve and Militia and from men raised by its own recruiting parties. The reserve which had been raised for the counties of Cumberland and Westmoreland was attached.[4] In 1813, the 2nd Battalion was part of a small force sent to Stralsund on the Baltic coast, at the request of the Crown Prince of Sweden, to free Swedish troops for service in Germany. The 2nd Battalion was then withdrawn and joined a force, composed almost entirely of second battalions, under General Sir Thomas Graham, which embarked for Holland from Harwich and other ports in January 1814. This force made a reconnaissance upon Antwerp, but its further proceedings were cut short by the abdication of Napoleon. The 2nd/25th Foot was disbanded in Ireland in 1816.

The composition of the rank and file of the Regiment between the years 1808 and 1816, as rendered to the War Department and compiled from bygone Regimental record books, was subsequently published as:[5]

	1st Battalion	2nd Battalion
Scots	344	576
English	613	639
Irish	506	288
Foreigners	37	8

In those days, long before regiments had become localized, regiments recruited where they could. Most of the Scotsmen in both battalions came from Edinburgh, the Lothians and the Border counties.

*   *   *   *   *

'It is unpleasant to think of the amount of physical misery and suffering that lies behind a simple remark such as 'the Regiment then went out to the West Indies where it served for ten years,' comments *A Short History of the King's Own Scottish Borderers*, issued to recruits in the 1920s; for conditions of service during the Napoleonic era were harsh in the extreme, and in the 18th Century they were brutal. The Mutiny Act of 1703 had at least regularized the systematic robbery that endeavoured to wring the army's subsistence out of its pay, which, was always in arrears, a type of national debt. But a standing army was still disliked, so deep had been the revulsion against Cromwell and his major-generals. The

---

[4] According to *Records and Badges of the British Army* (Gale & Polden, 1900), the 2nd Battalion of 1804 spent much of its service at Berwick-upon-Tweed, with detachments at Holy Island and Dunbar.

[5] *An account of the Scottish Regiments with the statistics of each, from 1808 to March 1861.* (Nimmo, Edinburgh, 1862).

net pay of the private soldier after deduction for subsistence was a grudging tuppence a day. It was easier for commanding officers to recruit from the gaols than to augment inadequate levy money from their own pockets, as bounty for recruits of higher standing. Except in time of war, enlistment was for life, which meant until a man was discharged, had deserted or was dead. Punishment could be a thousand lashes, and for cowardice a man was shot. Service in colonial stations, particularly the West Indies, was hated; there was no system of reliefs and before a regiment embarked there were usually many desertions. The troopships, so often battered by storms, were floating hells. Improvements came, though slowly, but the purchase of commissions — briefly abolished by Cromwell — remained as a guarantee that the army would never fall into revolutionary hands. In 1797, a soldier's daily pay was increased to the coin that was to become symbolic, the King's shilling, and nearly one hundred years later Kipling was writing in his *Barrack Room Ballads*:

'Shillin' a day,
Bloomin' good pay —
Lucky to touch it, a shillin' a day!'

Their hard lives built more than they knew, and when times were at their worst some men had stood out for the welfare of the soldier. In this respect, the memory of the influential General, Lord George Henry Lennox, Colonel of the Regiment, indeed a father to it, for nearly forty-three years from 1762 until his death in 1805, is honoured in the Regiment. He could be termed a Stuart. His grandfather, the First Duke of Richmond, was the natural son of Charles II and Louise de Keroualle, Duchess of Portsmouth. It was Lord Lennox who commissioned the six paintings of the Regiment in Minorca, recently donated to the National Army Museum by Lady Ponsonby, the widow of a descendant; and perfect copies of these exquisite paintings hang in the Officers' Mess of the 1st Battalion.[6]

Paradoxically, it was during the Colonelcy of Lord Lennox that the thread of the Regiment's identity might have been broken. To stimulate recruiting there was a scheme in 1782 to confer upon the foot regiments the names of English counties. The Scottish regiments remained unaffected, but as luck would have it, a recruiting party of the 25th Foot under a Captain Flint, was at that very time in Edinburgh and is said to have been prevented by the magistrates from beating up in accordance with the old privilege. It

---

[6] The copies were painted by the late Mr. Gordon Ellis, who also painted a fine reconstruction of the Battle of Minden for the Regiment.

is stated in the Regimental records that the magistrates of the city were interested in raising a new levy, and that Lennox, when he heard of it, took such offence that he asked his friend George III to make the county of his family seat, Sussex, the designation of the Regiment. The Third Duke of Richmond, who resided at Goodwood, was Lennox's elder brother. In fact, a few years previously the City Fathers had raised The Royal Edinburgh Volunteers, with the approval of the Crown, and in 1782 the Volunteers returned to Edinburgh from service in America. It is possible that they competed for recruits to the discomfiture of Captain Flint.

At all events, the Regiment became the 25th (Sussex) Regiment of Foot and was so designated for a period of twenty-three years until Lennox's death in 1805, a mere six weeks before the King conferred the title of The King's Own Borderers. Elsewhere in the Regimental records, it is stated that the application of Sussex in 1782 came from the Duke of Richmond. The Duke and Lennox were close, and the Duke was Lord Lieutenant of Sussex. However, this entry in the Regimental records, in contradiction to the one referred to above, adds that the Sussex title was much against the wishes of Lennox who never allowed 'the Scotch beats' to be discontinued. The 'Scotch beats', also known as the 'Scots Duty' as opposed to the 'English Duty', were the actual fife calls and drum beats peculiar to Scottish regiments, wherever they were stationed. From all of which it may be best to conclude that Lennox had initiated the matter in anger, and had his regrets. It was a characteristic of the Richmond family that they could be hot-headed. The Duke had many quarrels, and had once quarrelled with George III because Lennox had been passed over for promotion. Lennox himself had quarrelled with the Governor of Minorca about the quality of the wine served to the Regiment on the island; indeed, he achieved the distinction, unique in a Colonel of the Regiment, of being court-martialled for writing a letter deemed to be 'improper and disrespectful' to the Governor.[7] Lennox's son, who became fourth Duke, fought a duel with the Duke of York.

The exercise of the privilege of beating up for recruits in Edinburgh fell into abeyance, and in view of the 'Sussex' title, the more remarkable was an event in 1797 when the Regiment was at Plymouth. Troubles in the Royal Navy had evidently spread ashore and many attempts were made by unspecified people to seduce the

---

[7] *Public Record Office,* WO 4/88, p. 378. The King agreed with the Court, but did not confirm the sentence, and directed that Lennox should apologize before the assembled Field Officers in garrison at Minorca. The court-martial was in 1771.

military garrison from its allegiance. Declarations renouncing such attempts at sedition were circulated with apparent spontaneity by the troops of the garrison, which was commanded at the time by Lord Lennox. A loyal declaration signed by all the non-commissioned officers of His Majesty's 25th Regiment of Foot was issued, and was headed by the splendid royal motto of Scotland: *Nemo me impune lacessit* — No man with impunity attacks me, or, more colloquially, *Wha daur meddle wi' me?*

Chapter 3

BLUE BONNETS

A reasonable definition of a bonnet is that it is a round, flat cap of thick, blue cloth, formerly in general use in Scotland. Bonnets for military wear became 'cocked' or 'set up', evolved into famous shapes, and were adorned with feathers or badge. The dice-band is thought to originate from the threading of ribbon around the bonnet, tied at the back, to keep it on.

For very many years the Regiment had worn the same dress as English regiments of the line as did all regiments raised in the Lowlands. The espontoon or half-pike went out for officers, swords went out for the rank and file, and for most of its earlier history the Regiment shouldered the smooth-bore flintlock, 'Brown Bess', modified for the percussion cap in the 1830s, that served the British Army from shortly after Marlborough's campaigns almost up to the Crimean War. In the period around 1770, early in Lord Lennox's colonelcy, Scottish insignia appeared on headdress, but disappeared again until the mid 19th Century when Edinburgh Castle became a device on shako plates, which was transferred to the helmet plate when helmets were introduced in the 1870s. In 1864 the Regiment was given permission to wear the Kilmarnock forage cap, uncocked, somewhat in the shape of a 'pill-box', with red tourie and dicing, which gave way in the 1870s to the dice-bordered Glengarry cap. A smart peaked forage cap, with dice-band border, was also taken into wear and was worn with ceremonial dress by officers, warrant officers and senior N.C.O.s.

The conspicuous date for dress, for the Regiment, was 31 January 1882, when Queen Victoria approved that doublet and trews be worn in addition to the dice-bordered Glengarry already worn. At the same time, the officers were asked if they wished to wear the claymore. The Regiment made efforts to secure the right to wear the family tartan of the Earls of Leven, the 'Leslie' tartan, but these were not at first successful, and it was not until 1898 that the Commander-in-Chief was convinced that the 'Leslie' tartan was authentic and that one of Her Majesty's regiments could safely be clothed in it (see Appendix VII). Meanwhile, the dark green Government (or Black Watch) tartan had been issued, disrespectfully known at the time as the McChilders, after Mr Childers, Secretary of State for War.

The Regiment's badge of today first appeared as the Regimental-pattern Glengarry badge, sealed for the Regiment in 1871, and lacking only the word 'Scottish'. It had a Roman 'XXV' underneath, but with the army reorganization of 1881, numerals were discontinued, although they lingered in sentiment. The Glengarry badge was also worn on the peaked forage cap, and by the 1890s was worn on helmets as well. But that is to anticipate.

* * * * *

It has to be realized that before regiments were anchored territorially, which Cardwell began in 1873 and Childers completed in 1881, the 25th Foot, in common with all the line regiments of the British Army, was totally itinerant. There was no Regimental home. It recruited where it could, and overseas service in particular broke up its composition, for there was no system of providing overseas replacements on a regimental basis. The Regiment's only fixed point was that it had been raised in Edinburgh; but from this came the tenacity with which it held to its Scottish tradition.

The West Indies until 1817, and then Ireland, then the West Indies again, saw the 25th Foot, The King's Own Borderers. The Regiment served in South Africa, 1840-42, during the Boer insurrection in Natal, and then in the Madras Presidency of India. When the Regiment went overseas, depot companies were usually left behind, mainly in Scotland or Ireland; and it was in 1829, when the Regiment was in the West Indies, that its old privilege was restored to it through the initiative of the officer commanding the depot companies, which were then at Edinburgh Castle. He was Major Courtenay Chambers, a great name in the Regiment in those days, who purchased the Lieutenant-Colonelcy in 1830 and commanded the Regiment in cloud and sunshine for the next eighteen years. At Edinburgh Castle in 1829 he had received this letter from the Lord Provost:

Sir, I this day read your note to me of the 11th current to the Magistrates and Council; and I was authorized to inform you, that so far as they can restore the privileges of the 25th Regiment, they are most happy to do so; and therefore your men may beat up for recruits through all streets any day of the year, Sunday of course excepted. The Magistrates and Council hope also that your Regiment may soon be restored to its primitive name and honours;[1] and if they can in any way aid you to obtain them, it will afford them much pleasure.

I have etc.,

W. ALLEN, Lord Provost.

---

[1] Clearly a reference to the title, *The Edinburgh Regiment.*

Another milestone was reached in 1858, when pipers were
sanctioned for certain Highland regiments. It was discovered at the
Horse Guards that The King's Own Borderers had pipers, on whose
authority it was not known. It appeared that 'permission for these
men is lost in time', the Adjutant-General's Department reported
to the Duke of Cambridge, Commander-in-Chief, and it was ruled
that 'these men are to be on the footing of bandsmen and not of
drummers, as regards their being borne on the strength of the
Regiment, and also that the public is put to no expense for their
clothing as pipers'.

There were, in fact, three pipers. The Colonel's company would
have had a piper, and probably the two flank companies, the
Grenadier and Light Companies, which were abolished at this time.
No doubt there were always men in the ranks who could play the
bagpipes, although to class them as drummers would never do, for
the drummers were the élite soldiers; they beat the drum calls, they
beat up for recruits, they beat for marches and for parleys, and it
was they who used to carry out floggings under the eye of the Drum
Major. The bugle began to supersede the drum for calls, while the
pipers played on. The number of pipers grew, as a parallel develop-
ment to the regularizing of military bands, and by the 1880s, when
the Regiment had a 2nd Battalion, both battalions maintained a
sizeable number of pipers. Then the drums were included, to form
a marching band. Even so, it was not until after the First World
War that pipers were officially permitted to Lowland regiments;
before that, their extra cost, above that of their maintenance as
soldiers, was paid for regimentally. One of the paintings of the
Regiment in Minorca shows a piper who appears to be wearing a
kilt of the 'Black Watch' tartan, but later the pipers of the 25th
Foot adopted the Royal Stuart tartan, and indeed, may have done
so before that name was coined. They have worn it ever since,
although official sanction was not received until 1920.

The 2nd Battalion was formed, for the third time, soon after the
Regiment returned from India in 1855. The Regiment was stationed
at Manchester, where in 1856 four companies were formed into a
depot which joined a depot battalion, holding men from a number
of different regiments, at Preston. In 1857 the depot left Preston
for Pembroke Dock, South Wales, and in 1858 the Regiment went
to Gibraltar; but it was at Preston in 1859 that the 2nd Battalion
was embodied. This was part of a new expansion of the army
following the Indian Mutiny, in which the first twenty-five
regiments of the line became two-battalion regiments, and this time
the 2nd Battalion was to serve for eighty-eight years.

The 2nd Battalion went to Edinburgh in 1862. 'They are called
The King's Own Borderers,' a young man who was enlisting as a

private soldier wrote from Edinburgh Castle to his father, a crofter in Sutherland . . . 'There are two battalions and this is the second battalion. They are very well off as to clothing and rations. They get two pairs of boots per year, one Red coat, two pairs of trousers and light summer dress, and in fact everything they require, such as soap, black, whitening, shoe brushes, clothes brushes, shaving articles etc etc, together with their rations and washing, all for 8½ pence per day. Their rations are as good as I would wish to have. They have three meals per day, loaf and coffee at breakfast, potatoes, soup and beef at dinner, and tea and loaf to supper. They have breakfast at 8 am, dinner at 1 pm and supper when they want it. They have not to cook their rations but get it cooked, only one of the mess men has to go and fetch it from the cookhouse. They have very good beds, every man has his own bed which is about six feet long and three broad, the bedding comprises a mattress, a pillow, two coarse sheets and two blankets and bed cover.'[2]

The 2nd Battalion was presented with Colours in Edinburgh in 1863 and embarked for Ceylon for its first overseas tour.

*   *   *   *   *

The Localization of the Forces, effected by Cardwell in 1873, welded together the regular and reserve forces throughout the country. The system of two-battalion regiments, one battalion serving at home and the other overseas, was extended throughout the line by pairing the one-battalion regiments, and permanent depots were created, or planned, where the reserve forces were to be brigaded with their line regiments.

The full impact of this was not felt by the Regiment, which appeared in the Army List as the 25th (King's Own Borderers) Regiment of Foot, until the reorganization of 1881 carried out by Childers — which almost proved disastrous for the Regiment. That year saw the introduction of territorial titles and regimental districts which injected profound sentiment into a military epoch. Henceforth, the line regiments would be the territorial regiments of the British Army, a fabric which would serve the nation throughout two world wars, and which has been largely destroyed by the amalgamations of recent years. Unfortunately, this imaginative reform bade to ride roughshod over The King's Own Borderers, for the committee advising the Secretary of State on the formation of territorial regiments proposed to re-designate the 25th Foot *The York Regiment (King's Own Borderers)*, with its permanent depot

---

[2] The author is grateful to Mr Robert McIntosh for permission to quote the above extract from his grandfather's letter.

at York, and Yorkshire militia converted into its 3rd and 4th Battalions.

The proposal was regarded by the Regiment as a deliberate attempt to de-nationalize it, no less, and as one account has it, 'the heather was on fire'. Lieutenant-Colonel G. S. Hallowes, commanding the home battalion, the 2nd Battalion, then at Fermoy in Ireland after twelve years of overseas service, complained to the Adjutant-General. 'To be deprived of our title would be the most severe blow that could be inflicted on us,' he wrote. He cited the origin of the Regiment, and added that it was 'still recognized in Edinburgh as the only Edinburgh Regiment', and still retained 'all the privileges of the City'.[3]

There was disagreement within the War Office itself. The Adjutant-General, General Sir Charles Ellice, held that it was a 'geographical anomaly' that 'a Borderer [sic] regiment with Scotch traditions' should be located at York. He regarded it as 'highly desirable' that the Regiment should be located at Berwick-upon-Tweed, and pointed out that the south-eastern counties of Scotland would not otherwise be drawn on for recruits by any depot station. His view was that the case of The King's Own Borderers should be treated as an exceptional one, and that the Regiment should for the present be located at Berwick without militia. It should here be explained that the affiliation of local militia and Volunteer Corps to the line regiments had been fundamental to the Localization of the Forces.

The Director-General of Recruiting, Major-General E. G. Bulwer, uncompromisingly held that there were already too many Scottish regiments for the population, and he doubted if they could be filled. Scotland was 'over-regimented', as he later put it, and according to him, if the 25th Regiment were located at Berwick 'we shall be practically creating another Scotch regiment'.

The Duke of Cambridge, Commander-in-Chief, came down strongly on the side of the Adjutant-General, but for a time the Secretary of State had been obdurate, for all the other regimental districts had been completed. Mr. Childers saw too many difficulties over finding militia for the Borderers at Berwick, and took into account that Scotland as a field for recruiting was 'already quite full'.

Lieutenant-Colonel Hallowes had made another plea to the Adjutant-General, through an appropriate channel. In a letter dated 20 April 1881, he wrote:

---

[3] The author has drawn on the memoranda and letters on this issue at the Public Record Office, WO 32/6092: *Localization of the K.O.S.B., 1881-87.* Extracts, including the above, are quoted in this chapter.

'We hope that we shall still be included in, and take our place, amongst the Scotch regiments as we have always done, especially as we are almost the senior Scotch regiment and have always been much more connected with that country than many of those that are about to be located there. Everything connecting us with Scotland has always been and is still kept up. Our Regimental Games are on St. Andrew's Day and the Regimental Dinner on the same. Our Regimental Records printed and in possession of every officer, past and present, our Regimental plate, all our badges, our Pipers, our dice cap, point to our Scotch connections and the strong feeling still existing with regard to this.'

His letter ended: 'Could we only go to Berwick when the 5th Fusiliers go to Newcastle.'[4]

Meanwhile, powerful support for the Regiment came from the two Members of Parliament returned by Berwick-upon-Tweed in those days. Briefed by Major C. E. Hope, commanding the depot companies, Colonel D. W. Home, M.P. did all he could to get the Regiment to Berwick, and in May 1881, in the House, Sir Dudley Marjoribanks, later Lord Tweedmouth, asked Mr. Childers why York had been preferred to Berwick-upon-Tweed 'as the head-quarters of The King's Own Borderers, a regiment essentially Scotch in its privileges, history and origin'.

The Secretary of State replied that the Regiment had been localized at York since 1873, and that although he had endeavoured to make some arrangement 'more in harmony with the traditions of the Regiment, whose title is the Borderers, by moving them to Berwick,' the difficulty of making the necessary arrangements for the affiliated militia battalions, and of barracks, had led him to decide with great reluctance that it would be best to leave matters as they were. Nevertheless, a deputation went to Mr. Childers, and matters did not rest there much longer.

*   *   *   *   *

On paper, the Regiment had indeed been localized at York since 1873, after some curious paper migrations affecting the three senior Scottish line regiments. Originally it had been intended to locate the Borderers at Ayr, with militia from Ayrshire and Dumfriesshire affiliated.[5] Ayrshire, Wigtown, Kircudbright, Dumfries, Peebles,

---

[4] The Northumberland Fusiliers had a temporary depot at Berwick pending completion of new barracks at Newcastle.

[5] Memorandum by H.R.H. the Field Marshal Commanding-in-Chief on the proposal of the Secretary of State for War for the organization of the various Military Land Forces of the Country; and report of a Committee on the details involved therein. *Command Paper* 493, 22 February 1872.

Selkirk and Roxburgh constituted what was then known as the Sub-District, renamed Regimental District in 1881. The 21st Foot (later Royal Scots Fusiliers) were to be located at Edinburgh, and the 1st Foot (Royal Scots) were destined for London, with a depot at Greenwich. Subsequently, the 1st Foot were re-allocated to Edinburgh, the 21st to Ayr, and the 25th to York.[6] The Regiment appears to have accepted the latter arrangement with equanimity or indifference; possibly it was so accustomed to a roving depot that the full implications were not realized. The 2nd and 5th West York Militia were now affiliated, and the Regiment was earmarked to share a double depot at York with the 14th (Buckinghamshire) Foot, later The Prince of Wales's Own West Yorkshire Regiment. However, the York depot had yet to be built, and would not be ready until 1880. Captain J. T. Coke, King's Own Borderers, was posted to York as Adjutant, Brigade Depot, in 1875, and in 1878 when war between Russia and Turkey caused the militia reserve to be mobilized, some 400 Yorkshire militiamen were sent to the 2nd Battalion, King's Own Borderers, which was then at Plymouth. That was the sum of the contact with York, until the depot companies were ordered there in 1880. It was this event, and the threatened change of title, that evidently awoke the Regiment to its predicament.

It may be added that the depot companies spent a total of fourteen months at York, and although the Director-General of Recruiting described the Regiment as 'very popular in Yorkshire', it had been stated by Colonel Hallowes that the affiliated Yorkshire militia battalions gave no recruits to the line. Indeed, it was later pointed out on the Regiment's behalf that when the depot was at York the authorities were obliged to open every district in England and Ireland to it, to obtain the required number of recruits.

Needless to say, the Secretary of State was, in the end, persuaded of the Regiment's resentment. Major Hope received a telegram at York on 30 June 1881: '*It has been decided to locate the 25th King's Own Borderers at Berwick-on-Tweed as King's Own Borderers with no Militia or Volunteer battalions*'. The West York Militia, who were on parade, were dismissed and took off the dice-bordered Glengarries with which they had been issued. The Regiment, its militia still to be formed, took up its home in the grey town, buffeted by North Sea winds, at the mouth of the River Tweed, that had been disputed by the English and the Scots so frequently in the Middle Ages. The depot companies moved there on 29 July 1881.

[6] Final report of Committee on the organization of the various Military Land Forces of the Country. *Command Paper* 712, 21 February 1873.

Nowadays, Berwick has three bridges, but it still lives up to the old rhyme:

A bridge without a central arch,
A church without a steeple . . .

The barracks are among the earliest in the country. They were begun in 1717 and are attributed to Vanbrugh, Controller of the Office of Works at that time. They have an intimate character, and the fine Royal Arms over the gateway are a striking feature, being the Royal Arms of 1714-1801, which have quarterings: 1 and 2, England and Scotland impaled; 3, France; 4, Ireland; 5, Hanover.

The Regiment was now the 'territorial regiment' at Berwick-upon-Tweed, and appeared as such in the Army List. Berwick was the Headquarters of the 25th Regimental District, but the position was still far from satisfactory. The district was not defined. Having been moved to Berwick as a special case, the Regiment was allowed to recruit on both sides of the Border within a certain radius of Berwick, but it had no affiliated militia and Volunteer Corps, and no specific county connection to accord with the concept of a territorial regiment. The Regiment tended to draw on other regimental districts in Scotland and England for recruits, and above all, without a militia it had no militia reserve. Without this it would be almost impossible to complete the home battalion to war strength in the event of mobilization.

More than one bizarre solution was proposed at the War Office in an attempt to settle the militia problem, until at length the opinion, surprisingly enough, took root again that the Regiment's natural recruiting ground should be the Scottish Border, and that The Scottish Borderers Militia should be affiliated to The King's Own Borderers. This would put the Regimental District within the very region that had been intended when localization was first planned in 1872; for The Scottish Borderers Militia, a title dating from 1864, were a detached militia battalion with headquarters at Dumfries, where they were first assembled in 1798 as The Dumfriesshire Militia. Their area covered Dumfriesshire, Selkirk and Roxburgh. Since 1881 they had been the 3rd Battalion, Royal Scots Fusiliers.

The barracks at Berwick-upon-Tweed were considered inadequate as the depot of a full-scale regimental district, and it was proposed to move the depot from Berwick to Dumfries, in the centre of the new district, where new barracks would be built. However, the Commanding Officer of the militia battalion, Lieutenant-Colonel G. G. Walker, objected strenuously to any further change affecting his battalion. In his opinion, militia artillery in the Edinburgh area (Haddington) should be converted to infantry, a solution 'allowing The King's Own Borderers, as distinctively *the* Edinburgh Regiment [*sic*], as shown by their badge of the Castle, to recruit in their historical headquarters'.

Edinburgh, however, had become the territorial domain of The Royal Scots. Despite Colonel Walker's resistance the needs of army organization were overriding, and a key rôle was played by C. E. Hope, now Lieutenant-Colonel commanding the 2nd Battalion in Dublin, who sent a lucid memorandum to the Adjutant-General, General Wolseley, dated 19 January 1886, on behalf of his officers.[7] In the course of his memorandum he stressed the Regiment's considerable success at attracting the Scottish 'recruit class' since the depot had been at Berwick, and claimed The Scottish Borderers Militia as its 'natural militia battalion'. It was Colonel Hope, in this memorandum, who proposed that the two titles be interwoven to become *The King's Own Scottish Borderers*. And this graceful suggestion brought about a happy ending.

The new title took effect by General Order in 1887, when The Scottish Borderers Militia, late 3rd (Militia) Battalion R.S.F., became the 3rd (Militia) Battalion K.O.S.B. The Border counties of Dumfriesshire, Selkirk and Roxburgh, with Berwickshire and Kirkcudbright, were assigned as the Regimental District, and later Wigtownshire was added.[8] Funds were not available for building new barracks at Dumfries, so the militia battalion remained detached at Dumfries and the depot remained at Berwick-upon-Tweed.

The Scottish Borderers Militia, who were regarded as one of the finest of militia battalions, were officered almost entirely by the landed proprietors in the Border counties, or their sons. Their men without exception were native to the country of the Border reiver and the peel, where the knell of disaster at Flodden had once sounded, and from where the lament, *Flowers of the Forest* (Ettrick Forest), came forth. Their affiliation brought much to the heritage of The King's Own Scottish Borderers. So much so that it is difficult today to think of the word 'Borderers', within the context of the Regiment's title, as ever having had any other connotation than the historic border with England. Yet among an older generation in the Regiment the not unreasonable belief undoubtedly existed that the title conferred by George III implied a recognition of the Regiment's original purpose: the keeping of Edinburgh and

---

[7] *Public Record Office,* WO 32/6092.

[8] The affiliated Volunteer Corps were the 1st Dumfriesshire Rifle Volunteers, the 1st Roxburgh and Selkirk Rifle Volunteers (The Border Rifles), and the 1st Berwickshire Rifle Volunteers. The Galloway Rifle Volunteers were affiliated in 1899.

the low country from the Jacobites.[9] Be that as it may, Colonel Walker of the militia, like a good soldier, avoided the contentious when his battalion was presented with its new Colours by the Duchess of Buccleuch in 1888, and declared in his reply: 'We have the honour now of being linked in name and title with a grand old historic Scottish regiment, one whose fighting ground extends from Minden to Afghanistan.'[10]

*   *   *   *   *

When Alexander Leslie led the Scots over the Border in the Civil War, a march was played in the van:

March! March!
Why the devil do ye na march?
Stand to your arms, my lads,
Fight in good order;
Front about, ye musketeers all,
Till ye come to the English border . . .

It was known as *Leslie's March*, and at some time the music was adapted to the pipes. The tune was included in the first printed selection of pipe marches, *The Piper's Companion*, by Donald Macdonald, about 1830, by which time the magic wand of Sir Walter Scott had been at work. In 1829, Scott had published *The Monastery*, set in the Melrose country in 1547-57 after the Border warring of the Reformation. In the novel a song is sung: it is called *Border March* in Scott's collected poetical works, but is described in *The Monastery* as sung to 'the ancient air of *Blue Bonnets over the Border*':

Come from the hills where the hirsels are grazing,
  Come from the glen of the buck and the roe:
Come to the crag where the beacon is blazing,
  Come with the buckler, the lance and the bow.
    Trumpets are sounding,
    War-steeds are bounding,
  Stand to your arms then and march in good order . . .

There were no official regimental marches until 1881, but regiments had their favourites. The tune that had become *Blue*

---

[9] It is interesting to note that the old Stirling, Dumbarton, Clackmannan and Kinross Militia were renamed The Highland Borderers Light Infantry by Queen Victoria in 1855. In 1881 they became the 3rd Battalion, Argyll and Sutherland Highlanders.

[10] *The History of the 3rd Battalion, King's Own Scottish Borderers.*

Bonnets over the Border was certainly played by the pipers of The King's Own Borderers, and they played it when the train taking the depot companies to Berwick-upon-Tweed crossed the Border Bridge. To all intents and purposes it was also the march of The Scottish Borderers Militia. In 1881, all regiments were required to select a march as their own, and hence it was adopted as the Regimental March, with Scott's first verse as the customary words:

> March, march, Ettrick and Teviotdale,
>> Why the deil dinna ye march forward in order?
> March, march, Eskdale and Liddesdale,
>> All the Blue Bonnets are bound for the Border.
>> Many a banner spread,
>> Flutters above your head,
>> Many a crest that is famous in story.
>> Mount and make ready then,
>> Sons of the mountain glen,
>> Fight for the Queen and the old Scottish glory.

It has been played in many parts of the world, the march that tells that the Scots are coming. Preceding it, with no ascertainable historical relevance, but it came into use and sounds well, is the Regimental charge, *The Standard on the Braes o'Mar*.

Chapter 4

THE SECOND AFGHAN WAR,
1878-80

1st Battalion
The decade of the 1870s was a watershed in the history of the British Army, beginning as it did with the Cardwell reforms, the abolition of purchase, the introduction of short service engagements designed to provide a reserve, and most of the proposals which formed the basis for the changes effected by Childers in 1881. And conveniently the year 1875 can be taken as a starting-point for the modern history of the Regiment. In that year, the 2nd/25th Foot sailed from Bombay for 'the barren rocks of Aden', and in 1876 returned to the United Kingdom. In the 1875-76 relief season the 1st/25th Foot sailed to India in the troopship *Malabar*, and disembarked at Bombay complete with wives and children, the new valise equipment, and the Martini-Henry breech-loading rifle.

Since its last tour in India the 1st Battalion had been stationed in Gibraltar and Malta, and in 1864 went to Canada, where in 1865-66 it took part in quelling the Fenian raids from the United States.[1] Since then the battalion had been at various home stations. It now went to Fyzabad, in the former kingdom of Oudh, and here in 1877 a new subaltern joined, Lieutenant Charles Woollcombe, a future Colonel of the Regiment, who in later life wrote this description of his arrival:

'I arrived in Fyzabad on 25 November about 5 p.m. I had not warned the Regiment when I was to arrive, as I should have done, but I found a gharry at the station which conveyed me and my kit to the Mess. The first officer I met was Johnnie Nixon, afterwards General Sir John Nixon. He offered to put me up as Gordon who shared his bungalow was in Madras on famine duty.

In India there were no officers' quarters in the barracks as in England. The Mess and officers' bungalows are private property belonging generally to natives, sometime to Eurasians or retired Europeans. Two or more officers generally live together and share certain servants. Each officer has his bedroom, dressing room and bathroom, and possibly a sitting room or there may be a common sitting room. Close by is a row of servants' houses,

---

[1] The aim of the American Fenians was to act in support of the Fenians in Ireland. They were mostly disbanded soldiers from the Federal Army.

stables, etc. There is generally a garden, paid for by the Sahibs, but cultivated in the case of bachelor occupants for the benefit of the gardener.

It was nice and cool, but though it was nearly the end of November I found punkhas had only just been taken down. Nixon took me to see the hounds fed and there I met Dixon, 2nd Senior Subaltern, afterwards Brigadier-General Sir Henry Dixon whom at intervals I saw a great deal of and became a great friend of . . . There were about sixteen officers at Mess, and as I was a bit late owing to unpacking and a strange servant, I didn't realise who they all were. I was anxious to see which one was Dering, the Adjutant, as I felt I ought to apologize for not having formally reported myself, and when after dinner he came and spoke to me I was surprised to find he was, though only a subaltern, a rather stout elderly looking man whom I had put down in my mind as a major, and who had peacefully slept between the courses. I little anticipated as he talked to me that I should in less than seven years become Adjutant and hold the appointment for five years.

I had heard wonderful stories about drinking in India. I dare say there were some hard drinkers generally, and a good many officers would perhaps have been better if they had taken less, but with a few exceptions the officers of my regiment were very moderate in that respect. In the cold weather we mostly drank beer. I hardly saw whisky till some years later, and the alternatives to beer seemed to be light claret and brandy and soda. In the 2nd Battalion which had gone home before I joined there had been a very hard drinking gang, but most of them had retired or died. Their usual allowance was a bottle of brandy a day besides what they took in Mess. There was one left who was then in the 1st Battalion—a captain—a great friend of mine. I never saw him drunk or even the worse for drink, but he got through a wonderful amount. He commanded a battalion and died soon after retirement.

I had never smoked in my life or ever wished to. I was rather afraid I should be made to, but to my surprise I found that of the sixteen officers present my first evening, six besides myself were non-smokers. The question of who I was to live with cropped up in the evening. Jimmy Reid after a year with the 2nd Battalion at home had joined the 1st Battalion a week before I arrived and wanted a stable companion, and we agreed to set up house together and from that evening our life-long friendship started which only ended with his death in 1920.

Colonel Ruddell commanded the battalion. I was most kindly received by the officers. Richardson was my captain. My mother had discovered that Major Carwithen, afterwards commanding, was the son of an old friend of hers, and his father had written about me, and I found a very warm welcome awaiting me. Life was very peaceful and work not too strenuous, the only serious difficulties we had were coping with Colonel Ruddell's dress regulations. Sometimes we wore a sash, sometimes brown strap and helmet badge, and sometimes not, sometimes full dress etc. Richardson used to bring all his kit in his trap and when he saw how the Adjutant was dressed he used to retire to the Guard Room and dress like him.

I wasn't keen on polo, but I bought a polo pony which I used principally to hack, out shooting. Jimmy Reid started polo at once and very soon bought a second pony and was looked upon as very go-ahead. As is well known he became the best back in India, and by buying raw ponies and training them he made polo pay. Fyzabad was a sociable little place and one dined out a lot. We used to have afternoon parties in the Mess, tennis and dancing. In April from shooting in the sun I got a bad go of fever and was sent on sick leave to Naini Tal. The Regiment took a house there and all of us who came up (to the Hills) put up in it.'

Meanwhile, war was on the horizon. In Kabul the Amir of Afghanistan had received a Russian envoy with pomp and ceremony, but Britain regarded Afghanistan as in the British sphere of interest. It was demanded that a British Mission be admitted to the country, but its way was barred at the Khyber Pass. British invasion of Afghanistan followed, on 12 November 1878.

*   *   *   *   *

At Fyzabad the 1st Battalion, scarcely recovered from a cholera epidemic, was aware that regiment after regiment was being hurried to the frontier. However, the battalion heard with some misgiving that Army Headquarters proposed to send it to Dum Dum, near Calcutta. Through Major Terry, who was in temporary command, a plea was made to the Commander-in-Chief that The King's Own Borderers should not be passed over for active service. The plea was effective and on 18 October 1878, a telegram was received ordering the 1st/25th Foot to the front. Within three days the battalion was ready and on the evening of 21 October left its quarters full of enthusiasm. Except for a brush with the Boers in Natal it was to be the Regiment's first fighting for nearly seventy years. General Woollcombe described the journey to the frontier:

'Colonel Ruddell was on leave and fortunately for us Major Terry was in command and went to Simla, where he found the battalion was to go to Dinapore [sic], and but for his personal intervention we should have gone there. I remember about one hundred time-expired men, the pick of the battalion, had left for home and we started very weak in numbers. Khaki didn't exist in those days and we were ordered to get two white suits dyed. Each company had its own dyer and the battalion varied by companies from bright yellow to dark brown. One put one's hand in one's pocket and brought out a handful of mud.

I don't know how we managed it but we had a Guest Night the evening before we left. A wing of the 73rd, now 2nd Black Watch, relieved us, and dined with us, and Major Terry promised Pipe Major Macdonald he would give him his set of pipes if he played the battalion over the frontier — a promise he was able to fulfil.

In those days the railway only went as far as Jhelum and it took us three nights to get there. We travelled in two trains by half battalions. The first rest camp was at Bareilly where we were most hospitably entertained by The Queen's. The second halt was at Meean Mir (Lahore) and I remember the rest camp seemed to be all sand.

We got to Jhelum on the third day. It is impossible to describe the confusion that existed there. Troops were pouring in and the 5th Northumberland Fusiliers arrived just after us. Being shortly due home they were full of long-service men, they were enormous men and a splendid battalion. Colonel Rowlands who commanded them had been in the 25th. The 51st King's Own Light Infantry arrived at Jhelum after us, but they got transport and got away before us and were at the capture of Ali Masjid. We had an idea they did us over the transport. We were at Jhelum about five days. Hardly any of us knew anything about a march and Colonel Ruddell decided to begin with an afternoon start. We were of course late starting and it was dark when we got to camp, and we started next morning in the dark, and I wonder we didn't lose more things than we did. We had camel transport and no one knew anything about a camel. The days were very hot, but it was cold at night and very cold in the early morning. Rawalpindi is sixty miles from Jhelum and five marches. I remember the day we marched into Pindi seeing The Suffolk Regiment on parade, "marching past" — such was the training on the eve of war!'

Colonel Ruddell had rejoined from leave at Bareilly. Rawalpindi was reached on 1 November, where there was a halt of over two weeks before the battalion marched on, across the Indus at Attock, to Peshawar:

'To our disgust we were ordered to go into barracks at Rawal Pindi, but having taken them over we were ordered on to Peshawar, a hundred-mile march. I shared a small tent with my captain, Lloyd. We had to halt a few days near Attock and I had my first experience of an earthquake. Lloyd and I were sitting on our camp beds and our Colour-Sergeant was standing talking to us when there was, as we thought, a tremendous shaking of the tent and Lloyd shouted out. Looking out, the ground seemed to be rolling away in a series of undulations. Another incident of that camp I have never forgotten — we had a captain called Curtis, a rather peculiar sort of man. He had smallpox at Fyzabad and soon after the war he retired, married and became a clergyman. Curtis and I one afternoon left camp together, he with a gun and I with a fishing rod. We separated and I fished for some time without any luck and returned to camp. I had heard several shots, and when Curtis returned he was covered with blood and feathers. He told us he had missed several snipe and at last had shot them. We asked what he had done with them and he said he had cooked and eaten them, and on being asked how he had managed to do so he said, "Oh, I had a box of matches."

We reached Peshawar. We stopped there only a day and were played "over the border" across the frontier to Jamrud. While at Jamrud our work consisted generally in taking convoys up the Khyber as far as Ali Masjid and sometimes to Landi Kotal, a wearisome day's work. The convoys consisted of camels and bullock carts. Camels got along fairly well, but carts were painfully slow. The pass was picquetted and I personally never had any trouble. It was bitterly cold at Jamrud and we had heavy rain.'

The invasion of Afghanistan was conducted in three columns. In the north, the Peshawar Valley Field Force occupied the Khyber Pass and Jalalabad. In the centre, a force under Major-General Roberts advanced through the Kurram Valley. In the south, the Southern Afghanistan Field Force under Lieutenant-General Sir Donald Stewart occupied Kandahar. The King's Own Borderers formed part of the Peshawar Valley Field Force, and the battalion was brigaded with two native regiments, in the 2nd Division commanded by Lieutenant-General Maude. The Peshawar Valley Force was under the command of Lieutenant-General Sir Samuel Browne who gave his name to the famous belt.

$$*\qquad*\qquad*\qquad*\qquad*$$

It was at the end of December 1878 when the 1st/25th Foot reached Jamrud, which had been fortified in days past by the Sikhs when they were masters of the Punjab. On New Year's Day 1879, the battalion was inspected by General Maude, and shortly afterwards four companies took part in the Bazar Valley expedition. They formed part of a small column from Jamrud which included some cavalry, two guns of Royal Horse Artillery and twenty-eight elephants. Similar columns set forth from Ali Masjid and Landi Kotal, the whole expedition totalling 3,000 men.

The tactics on the frontier were to command the heights by picquets, and the picquets went up and constructed stone sangars, and the main body advanced through the valleys and the passes. The tribesmen sniped, ambushed, or swept down with the knife where they could. To be taken prisoner by them meant a merciless end. The troops toiled to their camps, where they constructed perimeter defences of stones, stone walls from which semi-circular picquet posts projected, so that the perimeter was covered by enfilading fire. At night the tribesmen marauded, or fired shots into the camp, or maybe only the jackal howled. By day, much of the work consisted of the punitive blowing-up of the towers of the fortified mud-walled villages.

The tribesmen of the frontier mountains lived in *khels*, or clans, and the Bazar Valley lay south of the Khyber in the hostile country of the notorious Zakka Khel who fired on the force by day and night.

'The object of the Bazar Valley expedition,' the Regimental diary stated, 'was said to be to punish a certain portion of the Zakka Khel who were still refractory and had obstinately refused to give up the telegraph wire that had been carried off in the pass, but more especially to survey the country through the Bara Valley and on to Tirah, which has hitherto been terra incognita. At the same time, to impress the inhabitants of these regions with an idea of the British Power and the feasibility of entering their territory when desired.'

A limit of ten days had been fixed for the expedition, after which the troops returned to their line of communication in the Khyber. The 1st/25th Foot was then ordered to Landi Kotal and remained there until May 1879, when the Treaty of Gandamak was signed. The battalion then returned to India, reaching Peshawar on 1 June exhausted from long marches. Two men had died of cholera on the road. General Woollcombe wrote:

'After the Peace of Gandamak was made we returned to Peshawar and did it in two marches, 30th and 31st May. We got to Ali Masjid very early on the 30th, but the march from there to Peshawur, about eighteen miles, was very trying, the heat being intense. I carried the Queen's Colour all the way and bits of silk dropped out of the case, and I collected and kept them. They were in an envelope in my despatch box for forty-two years.

We had not been in Peshawar more than a few days when

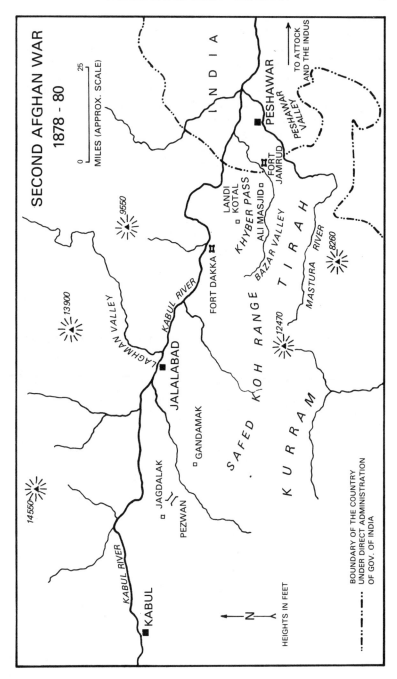

SECOND AFGHAN WAR
1878 - 80

MILES (APPROX. SCALE)

0   25

cholera broke out. Two camps were established outside the place. I went with my company to a nice camp but intensely hot. We had some cases and had to move, but eventually we got back. The battalion lost over fifty men.'

Later in the year, the battalion suffered severely from the fever prevalent in the Peshawar Valley; among its victims was the Commanding Officer, which was to have consequences. Major Ramsay took over the command of the battalion, shortly before orders were received in December 1879, to return to Landi Kotal in the Khyber, hostilities having been resumed.

*   *   *   *   *

The resumption of the war had been caused by the murder in Kabul of the British envoy, Sir Louis Cavagnari, together with his entire escort, in September 1879. The Peshawar Valley Field Force had been broken up, following the treaty, and the force in the south was in distant Kandahar, leaving only General Roberts in the Kurram Valley able to take swift action. His force was now designated the Kabul Field Force, and in October it occupied Kabul.

At Landi Kotal the 1st/25th Foot formed part of the 2nd Division, Kabul Field Force. In January 1880, the battalion took part in a fight to dislodge a large force of Mohmand tribesmen who had crossed the Kabul River and cut communications between Landi Kotal and Fort Dakka in the Jalalabad plain. Two hundred bayonets from the battalion paraded for the operation at 3.30 a.m., and a march was made in darkness in extended single file along a mountain goat track. Mules fell to their deaths over the khud and ammunition boxes had to be retrieved and slung on poles. Two other companies of the battalion, on detachment at Fort Dakka under Captain Dixon, marched with another column which co-operated from that place, and by early afternoon, assisted by mountain guns, the enemy's sangars had been carried. The men spent the night without baggage or food, and such was the difficulty of the terrain that the last of the baggage mules did not come up with the rearguard until two nights later, although the distance from Landi Kotal was only twelve miles. The scale of baggage per man was two blankets and a waterproof sheet.

The battalion was then ordered forward through Dakka to Jalalabad, of sombre memory from the First Afghan War of 1839-42. Here, Major Terry returned from duty elsewhere and took command, and at the end of January 1880, the battalion took part in the Laghman Valley expedition, crossing the Kabul River on rafts, while the guns were taken across on elephants and the cavalry forded the river. The objective in the Laghman Valley was the fort of a tribal chieftain, Futteh Mahommed Khan, but the fort was found to be deserted, and reconnaissance and road-making became the work of the expedition until the Laghman was evacuated.

'It was very cold and wet, and we were on half scale of baggage, two in a shelter, but we got lots of straw and plenty of food,' General Woollcombe wrote. The battalion was then moved up the line of communication towards Kabul:

'Soon after our return to Jalalabad we moved on through Gandamak to Pezwan, with two companies at Jagdalak. I returned to Peshawar with Dandredge to help him to take over the depot, and coming up again I brought up a draft of the 72nd Highlanders, all very young. I was attached to a Madras regiment on the way up. At Ali Masjid a few shots were fired in the night and I heard a great commotion, and found that the Colonel of the Madras regiment had turned out his regiment. The Adjutant came to me to find out why I had not turned out my draft. I advised him to let his men go back to bed, which he did after a short time.

On reaching Pezwan I found myself made Station Staff Officer. We were frequently fired into, and one night quite a determined attack was made on the post. There was a colonel in the Royal Engineers there, a very stout man. Someone asked him what he did when firing began, and he said, "I get out of bed and lie flat on the ground!" One night Corporal Wakefield, afterwards my Orderly Room Sergeant, called me and said there was a mass of tribesmen trying to pass through the camp. The picquet he was in command of had fired and wounded a man, but the tribesmen would not go away. I went to the place and saw they did not mean to attack us. Wakefield said, "Sir, if you will go out to them we will follow." I was climbing over the wall when something touched me on the thigh. This was Wakefield's bayonet, and in the moonlight I saw he had his finger on the trigger. As soon as an interpreter turned up we saw the people were friendly tribesmen wanting to pass through the place. The wounded man was brought in, shot in the stomach, and he died next day.'

The battalion had reached Pezwan, a pass at 5,000 feet, about fifty-seven miles from Kabul, in April 1880. By this time the 2nd Division had been separated from the Kabul Field Force and re-named the Khyber Line Force. The rôle of this force was to keep open the communications from Kabul to Peshawar. The battalion remained at Pezwan until the end of hostilities, together with small detachments of Bengal cavalry and native infantry. Meanwhile, on 26 June 1880, there had occurred the Maiwand disaster in the

south, where the Afghans defeated a British force, killing close on
1,000 men, and invested Kandahar. This caused General Roberts's
historic march from Kabul to the relief of Kandahar. At Kabul a
massed assault of the tribes had already been broken, and the
forced march to Kandahar, in which 10,000 troops covered 313
miles in twenty days, ended the war. It appears that the Borderers
would most likely have been included in that march, but for the
lack of a Commanding Officer.

First Roberts had to select his regiments and organize his
column, and among the regiments under consideration for the
march were The King's Own Borderers. Woollcombe's memoir
continues:

'The Maiwand disaster occurred while we were at Pezwan, and
one day Sir Frederick Roberts came down to see the Regiment
with a view to taking it to Kandahar. I rode with Sir Thomas
Baker.[2] Both were delighted with the appearance of the Regiment
and no doubt we should have been taken, but we were doomed to
disappointment. We had no colonel, Colonel Ruddell having
been invalided home. Terry and Ramsay, the two majors, had
quarrelled since they were subalterns and they could not serve
together. They had fallen out again at Pezwan and Ramsay had
been sent to command at Jagdalak. The result was that we lost
our chance of marching to Kandahar.'

The section of the Khyber Line Force forward of Gandamak was
withdrawn, and in August the battalion left Pezwan en route for
India. In an Approbationary Order dated 16 August, the Brigadier-
General commanding III Section, Khyber Line Force, declared that
the campaign had been one 'calculated to test the highest attribute
of a soldier, namely the patient endurance of hardship.'

'Preparations had to be made for the return to India,'
Woollcombe wrote. 'Among other things at Pezwan we had to
buy and stack enough grass for the animals coming down from
Kabul. Afghans brought it in and got their money on the spot. A
commissariat sergeant and a Babu weighed it and had a box of
rupees which they paid out. A bank note was worth a lot of
money, there was a lot of swindling and rupees were difficult to
carry. I remember a corporal who was acting as commissariat
sergeant died, and his kit was found full of rupees. When it
was estimated we had enough grass the purchase was stopped
and that night the enormous stack was burnt and the whole thing
had to be begun again.'

The battalion reached Peshawar on 28 August 1880:

---

[2] Brigadier-General T. D. Baker. He commanded one of the brigades on the
march to Kandahar.

'I was made acting Adjutant and there was a lot of work in getting the battalion into shape again. Major Terry was in command. He was a good friend to me and a good soldier, but he had a way of fighting with the General and Staff, and the everlasting row between him and Major Ramsay never ceased. Colonel Ruddell had retired and Colonel Harvey came out and took over command.'

At the start of the 1881 hot weather the battalion marched to the convalescent camp of Cherat, in the Khuttuck Hills which divided the Peshawar District from the Kohat District. There, at a full parade, Sergeant John Hamilton was presented with the Distinguished Conduct Medal for gallant conduct near Jagdalak in the previous June, when a convoy was attacked and four sepoys cut down. Sergeant Hamilton had rallied the guard, and seizing a commanding point, had overawed the enemy until assistance came. The D.C.M. was the only decoration for bravery in existence at that time apart from the V.C. As for Major Terry, he retired in 1881, but the next year he was unofficially present at Tel-el-Kebir. He also served as a trooper in the Bechuanaland Expedition. A Lieutenant-Colonel on the Reserve of Officers, he offered his services for the South African War, but was refused on account of his age. Back he came and volunteered for the First World War, with the same result. In London, at the Armistice Day parades in the 1920s, it was he who laid the wreath on behalf of the London and Southern Counties Branch of the Regimental Association. He died in 1933 aged 94. He was an extraordinary link with the past: his father had joined the Regiment in 1799 on the morning of Egmont-op-Zee.

The Queen was graciously pleased to permit the 25th Regiment to bear the word 'Afghanistan 1878-80' on its Colours and appointments, and in due course Pipe Major Macdonald was presented with a silver mount for his set of pipes, the gift of Colonel Ruddell and the officers of the 1st Battalion.

In 1883, the old Colours of the Scottish regiments were ceremonially deposited in St Giles Cathedral by H.R.H. The Duke of Cambridge, Commander-in-Chief. The Colours of the 2nd Battalion were among them, but for the time being the 1st Battalion had signified through its Commanding Officer that 'the present set of Colours were of the few that were carried by Regiments in the recent Afghan War, and the large number of officers and men now wearing that medal have no wish to part with their old Colours.' They had been consecrated in 1856, when the fragments of the set then retired had been parted among the officers.

Chapter 5

VARIOUS WARS

2nd Battalion: The Sudan, Suakim Field Force, 1888
The 2nd Battalion was at Aldershot in the Golden Jubilee year of 1887, when the final change was made in the title of the Regiment. One evening after tea the officers were playing croquet on the lawn in front of the Mess when the Commanding Officer came out. He was Colonel Charles Errol Hope, ripe with thirty-three years service.

'Gentlemen,' he said, 'lay down your mallets and come inside. I have important information for you.' The officers laid down their mallets and entered the Mess, to find that the Mess Sergeant had opened the best champagne.

'Gentlemen,' said Colonel Hope, 'I have received the news that we are no longer The King's Own Borderers. We are The King's Own Scottish Borderers.' They did not continue their croquet, but drank champagne.

*   *   *   *   *

On its return from Aden in 1876, the 2nd Battalion had been stationed first at Shorncliffe, then at Plymouth, and then in Ireland at Fermoy, Kinsale and Dublin. At Aldershot the battalion took part in the impressive Golden Jubilee reviews, and in May 1888, was complimented by the Commander-in-Chief, who declared that its drill and appearance was the best at Aldershot and that it was a 'magnificent battalion'.

In July 1888, the battalion embarked for Egypt, and was quartered in the Citadel at Cairo, Lieutenant-Colonel J. Talbot Coke commanding.

The debts of the Khedive had placed France and Britain in control of Egyptian affairs, but after the riots of 1882, when the British Fleet bombarded Alexandria and Sir Garnet Wolseley's expedition landed, France had surrendered her part, leaving Britain in sole control. Meanwhile, in the Sudan, nominally under Egyptian rule, there arose a Messiah. In the fastness of the Nubian Desert he proclaimed himself Mahdi, and with his militants of the faith, the Dervishes, he set the Sudan on fire. The British Government abandoned the country and General Gordon was sent out single-handed to evacuate the garrison and civil population of Khartoum. The Mahdi himself died of smallpox shortly afterwards, but he had a successor, the Khalifa, and there was no real peace.

Late one night at the end of November 1888, nearly four years after Gordon's death, the 2nd Battalion received orders to proceed on active service, to the Red Sea port of Suakim in the Sudan. When the belated attempt to relieve Gordon had been made, it had been intended that a railway be built from Suakim to the Nile for the reconquest of the Sudan; British troops had landed, and had been attacked by the Mahdi's lieutenant, Osman Digna. The British force was later withdrawn, and Suakim, the last outpost in the Sudan, was held by a garrison of Egyptian and Sudanese troops.

In 1888 Osman Digna was again investing Suakim. Trade with the interior was stopped to prevent the Mahdists obtaining money for arms, for their known intent was to attack Egypt, and Osman Digna at length opened trenches in front of the Suakim Water Forts, threatening the town's water supply which came from nearby wells. It was decided that for the safety of Suakim the Dervishes must be driven from their entrenchments. The task proved to be beyond the local garrison, and in Egypt the Sirdar, Major-General Sir Francis Grenfell, was placed in command of an expeditionary force, The Suakim Field Force which, at almost the last moment, had a British element added to it.

2nd K.O.S.B. left Cairo with the same enthusiasm to see active service that had animated the 1st Battalion ten years before. After an uncomfortable journey down the Red Sea in Khedivial postal steamers, the battalion assembled at Suakim on 8 December for the defence of the town and port, and took up lines in the fortifications. Forty N.C.O.s and men furnished a detachment of mounted infantry, and marksmen were sent daily into the Water Forts to fire at the Dervishes who were at a distance of about half a mile. By night the Dervishes brought out a gun in advance of their works and shelled the battalion's lines, which were about 1,500 yards on the Suakim side of the Water Forts. Between the two Water Forts ran an embankment, twenty feet high, and the battalion moved up and spent a day under fire converting the embankment to a parapet for musketry, while marksmen in the forts gave covering fire. When the parapet was completed, the whole battalion was brought into action on the embankment and swept the Dervish trenches and the bush beyond with sectional and company volleys.

Then, on 20 December, at 5 a.m., the Borderers paraded for a battle. Heavily laden, they marched out to the embankment again, each with 140 rounds of ammunition, rations for the day, greatcoats rolled on their waistbelts, haversacks, water bottles, and five sandbags. One man in three carried an entrenching tool. Reaching the embankment without attracting enemy fire they lined the parapet and fired company volleys at the Dervish lines. Marksmen were again posted in the forts. Also in position were 1st Welsh Regiment and an Egyptian battalion. At 7.30 a.m., Grenfell and his Staff arrived at Fort Gemaiza, the southern Water Fort where a signalling station had been set up to direct operations.

Out of the bush on the northern flank, two brigades of Sudanese and Egyptian troops led by British officers now attacked the Dervish trenches. There was a lot of heavy fire, and in the words of General Grenfell the Dervishes 'showed a good front' and seemed about to charge, but eventually their trenches on that flank were taken at the point of the bayonet. One of the attacking brigades was commanded by an officer who was making an unusual mark in the Service, Colonel Herbert Kitchener.

Grenfell then ordered the Borderers to advance from the northern Water Fort, Fort Shaata. The battalion moved round the fort and emerged into the open, in column, conspicuous in scarlet doublets, and marched forward into a brisk fire from the Dervish centre. By a remarkable stroke of good fortune only one casualty was sustained, for it turned out that the Dervishes had removed the backsights from their rifles in the belief that they could shoot straighter without them.

Gradually forming double column on the march, the battalion formed square on nearing the northern section of the enemy trenches. Reaching the trenches the Borderers halted, still in square, and set to work to form a *zariba*, a defensive enclosure made by hacking down thorn-bushes. The Sudanese battalions had now obtained possession of the remaining Dervish trenches, the retreating enemy were being shelled, and to the Borderers' right front, cavalry were warmly engaged. By 8.15 a.m. the battle was won. At least 1,000 enemy had been put to flight from their skilfully prepared trenches, as well as horsemen and several hundred spearmen in the bush behind, at a cost to themselves of about 500 dead.

The Dervish was an enemy to be reckoned with, and all information pointed to him counter-attacking. To withstand this the Borderers erected their *zariba* at a speed that was a feature of the action. The front rank men stood to their arms, while the rear rank men and two companies which had been kept in reserve within the square worked without stopping. In two hours the work was all but done, but to the battalion's disappointment the counter-attack never materialized. It was thought that a Naval demonstration a little further up the coast had kept Osman Digna on the defensive. And so ended the spirited action of Gemaiza, named after the southern Water Fort where Grenfell had his command post.

On 27 December, not three weeks from their disembarkation at Suakin, the Borderers re-embarked for Cairo, and in his dispatch Sir Francis Grenfell reported:

'The King's Own Scottish Borderers in the field fully upheld the high reputation with which they left Aldershot; a more handy, intelligent Battalion I never met, and the careful volleying both of their marksmen in Shaata and of the Battalion on the embankment, assisted in keeping down the Dervish fire and contributed greatly to the severe loss of the enemy. They were ably commanded by Lieutenant-Colonel Coke, who appears to have communicated his own ready resource and great energy to the men of the Battalion under his command.'

* * * * *

By June 1889, the Khalifa was, nevertheless, ready to invade Egypt. A Dervish army outflanked the forts at Wadi Halfa and advanced through the desert. Despite skirmishes with the Egyptian Frontier Force, the Dervish array established itself close to the Nile at Abu Simbel, and it was decided to form a brigade of British troops without delay at Aswan. The advance party of 2nd K.O.S.B., three companies, left Cairo by rail for Asyut, 250 miles upstream, and there transferred to the Thomas Cook river steamer *Cleopatra*. The steamer towed a barge containing men of the Royal Irish Rifles; the barge leaked and twice had to be run ashore and bailed out for the leaks to be repaired. On 3 August they reached Luxor, shortly followed by the main body of the battalion in another Cook's steamer. However, the Borderers' hopes of further action were dashed when a telegraphed order to proceed no further south was received at Luxor, when the advance party was within twenty miles of Aswan. The Sirdar had inflicted a terrible defeat on the Dervishes at Toski, 10,000 of their number being captured or slain. The Borderers returned to Cairo.

A few years later the name of Kitchener was carved across the Sudan, but The King's Own Scottish Borderers were no longer present in that part of the world. On 2 January 1890, the 2nd Battalion went by rail to Suez to embark for Bombay. The 2nd Battalion diary gives the strength as: 25 officers, 2 warrant officers, 28 sergeants, 14 drummers, 37 corporals, 750 privates, 3 officers' ladies and 5 children, 22 women and 36 children.

In due course, those who had been at Suakim were granted the Sudan Medal with clasp *Gemaizah*, and with the Queen's assent also wore the Bronze Star conferred by the Khedive. When they left Cairo, a testimonial signed by members of the British community was presented to Colonel Coke and the officers in recognition of their hospitality and in remembrance of the many friends they had made in Egypt. On the back was lengthy verse, specially composed for the occasion, which included the lines:

Yes, who is that with genial smile
Enjoying every joke?
Who makes each stranger feel at home?
'Tis *Colonel Talbot Coke.*

In 1889, the Regiment celebrated its bicentenary, and the entire 2nd Battalion were photographed standing, most aptly, on the Sphinx.

1st Battalion: Burma, Chin Lushai Expedition, 1889-90

The story of the 1st Battalion must be resumed from the time it was at Cherat in the 1881 hot weather. This was the year when the Regimental Sergeant-Major, the Trained Bandmaster, and School-masters of twelve years standing, became Warrant Officers. The same year saw the abolition of Drum, Trumpet, Bugle and Pipe Majors throughout the army, and those personages became Sergeant Drummer, Sergeant Piper, and so on; but the old designations died hard and were eventually brought back. 1881 was also the year when the Colonelcies of regiments became honorary appointments, with the result that officers commanded battalions for a few years in the rank of full colonel instead of lieutenant-colonel. Shortly, however, the one regimental Colonelcy, albeit honorary, was re-established and commanding officers were again lieutenant-colonels.

In the 1881-82 trooping season, the 1st Battalion left Cherat for the foothills of the Himalayas, proceeding by route march across Northern India. Across the Punjab they marched, to Rawalpindi, and down the Grand Trunk Road through Jhelum, Ludhiana and Ambala, and thence to the hill cantonment of Dagshai at 6,000 feet, near Simla, a total distance of 520 miles. The day's march usually began at seven o'clock in the morning, and ended at about eleven o'clock, sometimes earlier, an average of about twelve miles per day being covered. Occasionally the distance covered was much less, but day after day the march continued, the five rivers of the Punjab were crossed, and ten lesser streams and two canals, by bridge, bridge of boats, ferry, or ford. The only days when the men remained in camp were an occasional Sunday, Christmas Day, one day of rain, and five days at a camp of exercise at Ambala. The total duration of the march was four months.

After three years at Dagshai the 1st Battalion moved down to Meerut in the plains. Drafts came, and drafts of time-expired men went, with the trooping seasons. Then in October 1889, the 1st

Battalion left Meerut for Calcutta, Lieutenant-Colonel Carleton now commanding, there to embark for Rangoon and active service in Burma.

Burma was of natural political concern to the Government of India, and the so-called Third Burma War of 1885 had completed the annexation of the country, which had begun when the East India Company annexed all the Burma shore of the Bay of Bengal, and Lower Burma. In 1885 the British force had merely steamed up the Irrawaddy to Mandalay and deposed the notorious King Thibaw. Upper Burma was annexed, but its pacification by columns pene-trating the jungles to subdue claimant princes, guerrilla leaders, and the bands of dacoits which sprang up everywhere, continued for several years. Among these pacification measures was the Chin Lushai Expedition.

The battalion disembarked at Rangoon on 3 November 1889, and Headquarters and four companies selected for the expedition entrained at once for Prome. The remaining companies went into barracks in Rangoon. At Prome, the half battalion embarked on the Irrawaddy and was taken by steamer upstream towards Mandalay, to Pakokku, where it went into standing camp.

The force of which the Borderers formed part was known as the Burma Columns, and totalled about 3,500 men. Its object was to punish and subjugate the tribes of the Chin Hills between the Assam border and the Chindwin, whence the Chins raided British territory. The force was divided into Northern and Southern Columns, each composed of one British and two or three Indian battalions, and Sappers and Miners. The Northern Column was already in the Chin Hills at Fort White. The Borderers were with the Southern Column whose objective was Haka, to the south of Fort White. The troops were as lightly equipped as possible and had been issued with summer scale of clothing. In the case of British troops this included one blanket and a waterproof sheet, ammunition boots and one pair of puttees.

The march of the Southern Column to an advanced base at Kan, 165 miles through totally unknown country, was made in detach-ments of 200 men, with followers, the Borderers reaching Kan on 10 and 11 December. Treasure chest, Quartermaster's stores and tents, had been left behind at a base two days' march from Kan, the entire distance from Pakokku taking two weeks. Only tents for field hospitals were now taken forward. The followers consisted of the transport or baggage natives, cooks, grooms, servants, coolies, the camp followers that always accompanied British marches in the East. Supplies were built up by river, being taken up the Chindwin by steamer to Kalewa, and thence poled up the Myittha, work greatly hampered by the unreliability and desertions of the

Burmese boatmen. Cattle disease in the valleys killed thousands of bullocks, adding to the difficulties of the commissariat and transport officers, while troops and coolies succumbed in their hundreds to malaria and dysentery. The sick were evacuated to Kalewa, and from there by steamer to base hospital.

The rains were late that year and many supplies, including flour for the bread, were destroyed in the waterlogged boats on the swollen Myittha. The rations were unfortunate; the tinned meat was uneatable for sick men, the preserved compressed vegetables little better, and biscuits were found to be mouldy when the boxes were opened. By the end of January, the rivers had at last subsided and the Myittha was shallow, and supplies were sent by road from Pakokku to Kan, a track along which carts were hauled and pack-bullocks trudged. Particularly burdensome work was sick-convoy duty, with the coolie-bearers themselves falling sick. As though the climate were not sufficiently adverse, it rendered the telegraph inoperable through current leakage from the uninsulated wire hanging on wet trees. Visual signalling was largely impracticable because of cloud and mist, but the signallers of 1st K.O.S.B. provided this service for the Southern Column until sickness removed them.

It had been estimated that the advance of 64 miles from Kan to Haka would take ten or twelve days, but the tangle of steep jungle hills and ravines made for slow headway and it took the head of the column sixty-six days to get through, the construction of the mule road taking seventy-seven days. The Southern Column employed 1,000 mules, nearly 600 ponies, and 69 elephants. One by one the tribes encountered on the way submitted, but Second-Lieutenant Foster of 1st K.O.S.B. was at this stage killed, one of the Southern Column's only two casualties at the hands of the Chins. With the Surgeon-Major and another subaltern he had strolled from camp, along a path which coolies and convoys had been using daily, when they were ambushed by some Chins and fired at. The burning of the nearest Chin village was ordered in reprisal.

By the middle of February 1890, the Borderers had reached Haka, at the heart of the high watershed of the Chin Hills. Camp Haka was established, and a permanent outpost was constructed on a spur above the village. Over this country, with its ranges of hills, the full force of the monsoon would sweep, but now in February the dry winds were bitter and the temperature at night was below freezing. The Borderers took part in two lengthy reconnaissances which were part of the exploratory work of the expedition. Lieutenant Stevenson with 25 men and a party of Gurkhas, meanwhile struck fifty miles westwards in four marches and met the advance party of a force from Chittagong. The Chittagong party

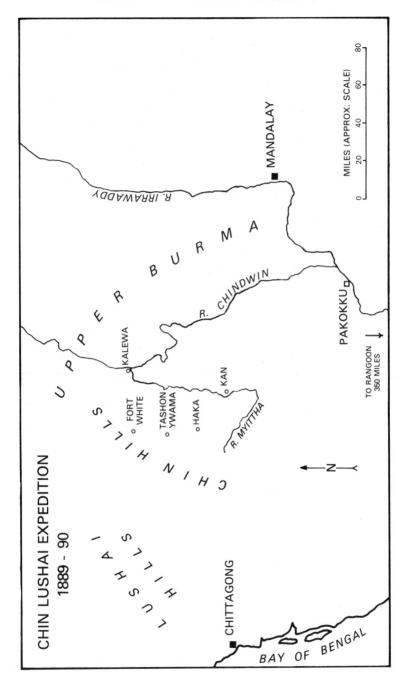

then came right through, with the returning Haka party, and the mule road from Bengal to Burma came into Haka a few weeks later. This was the most conspicuous success of the season's operations.

Although there was virtual non-resistance on the part of the Chin tribes, the Political Officer of the Southern Column was to report a little testily: 'With regard to the general attitude of the Chins, I may remark that they show no signs of having been subjugated. In fact they all seem to look upon us as being in their hills more on sufferance than by right of superior force.[1] The Chins also displayed the happy trait of drunkenness to a marked degree. 'They are perhaps about as drunken a race as any on earth,' declared the official report on the expedition. They obtained both small beer and strong spirit from millet, but their aggressiveness, when confronted by troops, varied by tribes. Some built stockades, or laid a small ambush. Others beat drums at a distance. On 9 March, the Borderers, at a strength of only 100 men, took part in an advance to the north, on Tashon Ywama, to link up with a column from Fort White; and the submission of the Tashons, the largest and most powerful of the tribes, was enforced.

By now, the troops were becoming greatly weakened by sickness, yet transport was only just able to ration them and it became necessary to reduce the strength of the columns in the hills to enable supplies to be built-up for the rains. The men came down in batches as transport became available. On 21 March, 60 Borderers and 137 coolies, all more or less unfit, came down from Haka to Kan and Pakokku, and thence to Rangoon. They were followed by another 25 rifles, and the last detachment of 45 men came down at the end of April. Of 14 officers and 502 men of 1st K.O.S.B. who served with the Southern Column, 21 men had died of sickness, and six officers and 273 men had been invalided, including two successive commanding officers. Major Stoney, who had succeeded Lieutenant-Colonel Carleton, did not recover his health and died in Europe later in the year.

Her Majesty granted a medal and clasp, and although few shots had been fired in anger, the Chin Lushai Expedition of 1889-90 was a feat of its kind. Mule roads had been blazed, troops had been kept supplied, the sick had been evacuated, unknown country had been charted and its inhabitants brought within the pale of the Empire. Captives whom the Chins had taken on their raids had been yielded up, and permanent outposts had been established.

In December 1890, the 1st Battalion embarked at Rangoon for

---

[1] *The Third Burmese War.* Period V. *The Chin Lushai Expedition* (*Burma Columns*), compiled under the orders of the Quartermaster-General in India. The author has drawn on this report in writing the above account.

Bombay and England, and many years were to pass before The King's Own Scottish Borderers returned on active service to the jungles of Upper Burma.

Chapter 6

THE RELIEF OF CHITRAL, 1895

2nd Battalion

The 2nd Battalion disembarked at Bombay on 15 January 1890, and went to the hill station of Sabathu, near Simla. At the camp of exercise at Ambala in 1891 they were inspected by the Commander-in-Chief in India, Sir Frederick Roberts, who found them to be 'a nice-looking set of men who turned out clean and smart, they drilled steadily, they are well behaved, and a good spirit pervades all ranks'.

In the 1893-94 trooping season, the battalion moved from Lahore to Rawalpindi, where in March 1895, Lieutenant-Colonel Henry Dixon arrived from England to assume command. Dixon had been with the battalion six days when he received a telegram:

'Your battalion is directed to mobilize in view of operations in Bajaur via Swat. Field Service clothing summer scale to be obtained in bulk but not to be issued to individuals without further orders.'

The Borderers entrained for the North-West Frontier, or as it was then called, the Punjab Frontier,[1] and at Hoti Mardan near Nowshera joined the force designated the Chitral Relief Force.

*   *   *   *   *

The small state of Chitral lay at the extreme north of the Frontier, sandwiched between Afghanistan and Kashmir, in the shadow of the snows of the Hindu Kush, the Pamirs, and the northern ramparts of the Karakoram range. In 1892 its ruler was murdered, and dynastic feuds broke out. Under the Durand Agreement of 1893, the Indo-Afghan frontier was re-defined, a belt of quasi-independent tribal territory under British political control was recognized, and the Amir was pledged not to interfere in Chitral. Nevertheless, Afghan intrigue was at work, and eventually a Pathan chief, Umra Khan, invaded Chitral and besieged the fort at the capital itself. Within, was the British Political Agent who had been sent from Kashmir, and five British officers, with a detachment of the 14th Sikhs, a few hundred Kashmir Imperial Service

---

[1] The North-West Frontier Province was created in 1901.

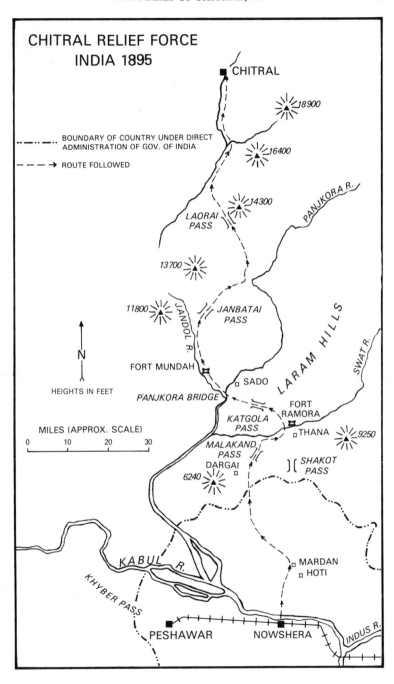

CHITRAL RELIEF FORCE
INDIA 1895

— ·· —— ·· —— BOUNDARY OF COUNTRY UNDER DIRECT
ADMINISTRATION OF GOV. OF INDIA

— — — → ROUTE FOLLOWED

troops, and a handful of local levies, clerks, servants and followers, totalling 543 persons. They had about 300 rounds of ammunition per man, and on half rations could last two and a half months.

Accordingly, the Chitral Relief Force was assembled, based on Nowshera, consisting of three brigades under the command of Lieutenant-General Sir Robert Low. The Borderers formed the 2nd Brigade with the 1st Gordon Highlanders, 4th Sikhs, and the Guides Infantry. Ahead lay a northward march of 150 miles across mountain passes and rivers in spate.

A general advance was made from Hoti Mardan on 1 April 1895. As there was not enough transport, the troops marched without tents and without the full field-service scale of kit. Personal baggage allowed was 80lb for Staff Officers, 53½lb for other British officers, 40lb for Warrant Officers, 32lb for Native Officers, and 16lb for British and Indian N.C.O.s and men. The British regiments were armed with the .303 Lee-Metford, the first magazine rifle. The troops marched with twenty days' supply of rations, and all the baggage in its due order; first and second reserves of ammunition, entrenching tools, cooking pots and utensils, sick litters and riding ponies, field hospitals, kits and spare animals.

First, the frontier hills had to be crossed, then the Swat Valley. Information indicated that several thousand Swati tribesmen were determined to resist an advance through their country. On 2 April, the 2nd and 3rd Brigades marched to Dargai, a village about four miles from a rugged entrance to the hills, the Malakand Pass. Heavy rain had fallen during the previous night and throughout the early morning, but morale was high and the men seemed indifferent to exposure. At Dargai they bivouacked under waterproof sheets in a ceaseless, drizzling rain. From the bivouacs could be heard the click and snap of breech actions as the men prepared their weapons for the morrow, while officers passed the whole night in discussing plans and in trying to sift the truth from a mass of information the Intelligence Department had produced on the movements of the tribesmen.

Meanwhile, it having become clear that all the passes would be contested, an intended advance of the 1st Brigade to the Shakot Pass, about seven miles distant, became a feint to make the Swatis divide their forces, and on the morning of 3 April General Low's Chief of Staff, Brigadier-General Bindon Blood, accompanied by the Political Officer, made a reconnaissance to the foot of the Malakand Pass. Large parties of men in white clothing were seen on the tops of the hills in the distance, waving white flags, and there were rumours that a large number of fanatical mullahs were lying not far away.

At 7 a.m. the order was given to the 2nd Brigade to advance, reinforced by mountain batteries and Bengal Sappers and Miners. 'It was a beautiful morning, clear and fresh after the rain,' wrote Major W. G. Hamilton, D.A.A. and Q.M.G. to the 2nd Brigade. 'A number of quail and partridge got up as we advanced and their calls were heard on all sides.'[2] The troops advanced up a level, fertile valley which gradually narrowed northwards and curved to the north-east, the advance following the dry bed of a watercourse which made a rough, natural pathway, leading up to a ravine. At the bend in the valley, high hillsides on its westward side dropped with immense steepness into the pass. The hill crests on that side were lined with men, and down all the main spurs the tribesmen had constructed stone sangars, each commanded by the one above it. Prominent on a crest at the end was a native village, a small group of stone huts. Beyond this, the end of the western hill plunged to the valley in a virtual precipice. A formidable position had been revealed, and it was afterwards estimated that the pass had been held by at least 10,000 tribesmen, of whom about half had firearms while the remainder acted in supporting rôles, recovering killed and wounded, carrying water, and hurling rocks.

The storming of the Malakand Pass began at 8.30 a.m. when the Guides Infantry moved up the centre of the valley to reconnoitre. At the point where the valley narrowed they immediately came under fire. The Guides were then ordered up a very steep 'Khud' on the left, so that when they had scaled it and reached the highest part of the hill, they could take the enemy in enfilade. The 4th Sikhs were sent up a spur on the Guides' right, and Guides and Sikhs began slowly to force their way up, under enemy fire and a barrage of rocks. Soon a Maxim gun opened fire, and then the guns of the three mountain batteries opened fire at the hilltops, but the range was too great. At 10 o'clock, C Company of the Borderers under Major Mayne pushed towards the village with the battalion's Maxim gun, the single-barrelled machine-gun which had superseded the old handle-operated, multi-barrelled Gatling. They were ordered to retire again; then the mountain batteries were briefly turned on to the village area, where the tribesmen had their main positions, while the Sappers worked on the mountain track, covered by Maxim fire.

General Low's intention had been to turn the flanking heights before launching a frontal assault, but the scaling of the heights was proving slow and difficult, and he feared that if a frontal assault were delayed, the Guides and the Sikhs would find them-

---

[2] *Journal of the R.U.S.I.,* Vol XL (1896): *The 2nd Brigade in the Chitral Relief Expedition.* The author has made general use of this excellent account.

selves outnumbered. At the same time, it became apparent that where the head of the pass rounded the almost vertical drop at the end of the western hill, it was entirely blocked by great boulders, and that the way ahead slanted upwards over the heights, a climb of about 1,000 feet through the enemy's main positions.

At midday a frontal attack was ordered. The batteries had now moved to within 1,000 yards of the enemy positions and their fire was becoming very accurate; nevertheless the tribesmen remained firm enough to face the bayonet.

The Borderers were given the centre spur of the hillside, the Gordon Highlanders the spur on their right, and the men of the two regiments began to climb upwards through thick scrub under a heavy, but erratic fire. Lieutenant McAlester directed the Borderers' Maxim gun. It was the only Maxim in the brigade that fired .303 cordite ammunition, and had a carriage designed by McAlester himself which had been made in the Rawalpindi railway workshops. The constant fire of the two mountain batteries and the Maxims covered the advancing bayonets as each sangar was rushed and often only carried after hand-to-hand fighting. The men then came under the fire of the sangar above; but fortunately, although these stone defences had numerous lateral slits which commanded every turn in the mountain path, the enemy had not reckoned on a frontal attack straight up the steep slopes. They had overlooked the construction of vertical slits.

'It was a fine and stirring sight,' wrote Captain George Younghusband, who was serving on General Low's staff, 'to see the splendid dash with which the two Scottish regiments took the hill. From the valley to the crest at this point the height varies from 1,000 to 1,500 feet and the slope looks for the most part almost perpendicular. It was this very steepness which partly accounted for the comparatively small loss suffered from the enemy's fire and the shower of huge boulders which were hurled upon the assailants; but the chief reason for this happy immunity was the wonderfully spirited manner in which the men rushed breastwork after breastwork and arrived just beneath the final ridge before the enemy had time to realise that the assaulting columns were at their very feet.'[3]

Leading the first company of K.O.S.B., Captain D. A. Macfarlane, later Colonel of the Regiment, was severely wounded. Second Lieutenant E. S. D'E. Coke was shot through the hip and received a sword cut in the leg. The Borderers lost two men killed, and fourteen other soldiers wounded.

[3] *The Relief of Chitral* by Captain George Younghusband and Captain Frank Younghusband (1895).

Younghusband, whose own regiment was The Queen's Own Corps of Guides, recruited from these same frontier mountains, wrote of the bravery of the enemy:

'One leader, carrying a large red and white banner, called on his men to charge the Scottish Borderers when they were half-way up the hill. The charge was made, but all his followers gradually fell, till the leader alone was left. Nothing daunted he held steadily on, now and again falling, heavily hit, but up and on again without a moment's delay, till at last he was shot dead close to the line . . . Again, one of the enemy's drummers, not content with taking his fair share of risks, persisted in mounting to the roof of a hut, where he showed up clear and conspicuous against the sky line, and thence cheered on his comrades. Every now and again a bullet would find him out, and he would drop to dress his wounds and then again mounting recommenced beating his drum. At last a bullet got him through the heart, and he fell headlong a hundred yards down the cliff, and there lay stark dead, but with his drum round his neck, and his arms ready raised to strike it.'

The 1st Brigade had been deployed to support the attack, and by an extraordinary chance the 60th Rifles, directed up a re-entrant on the left of the K.O.S.B., came upon an ancient and hitherto unsuspected Buddhist pathway. Following the path, it brought the Riflemen unexpectedly level with the leading K.O.S.B. companies. There was now a pause below the hill crest, to allow the many small groups which had been struggling up the khuds to reassemble and recover their breath. Then the bugles sounded along the line. There was a great cheer. With bayonets fixed the three regiments together stormed the crest, the Gordons on the right, 60th Rifles on the left, and 2nd K.O.S.B. in the centre. They gained the top almost simultaneously. The final charge on the enemy's village was made by the Borderers, led by Captain Wigram. After a five-hour action, the Malakand Pass had been taken.

*   *   *   *   *

'After the fighting was over, for some almost inexplicable reason the Regiment had to march all the way down the hill again to Dargai,' remarks the 2nd Battalion diary. What had happened was that the 1st Brigade had been ordered into the lead and the 2nd Brigade had been ordered to return to Dargai. Owing to the 2nd Brigade having its rations with it and its baggage coming up, while the baggage and rations of the 1st Brigade were farther to the rear, there was confusion as the transport columns and hospital doolies struggled to pass each other on the mountain path. One brigade went without rations and the other had to endure an extra march.

Next day the Borderers moved up through the Malakand again and bivouacked in the Swat Valley, and then advanced to Thana on the Swat River. Orders were issued for the crossing. It was a characteristic of the mountain tribesmen that they feared the power of the horse, and as the Guides Cavalry and Bengal Lancers appeared in the valley, the enemy, although massed in numbers, showed little heart for disputing the river crossing. At first, from good positions on the far bank in rocky and hilly ground, their fire was too uncomfortable for bridging operations. Then 2nd K.O.S.B. and the 4th Sikhs were moved up, and under their covering fire the 11th Bengal Lancers crossed by a ford. The Borderers followed, wading through the current with the water up to their armpits. The river, swollen by melting snows, was half a mile from bank to bank, flowing in a number of separate channels and still rising, but several thousand transport mules and camels forded it without loss before a trestle and pier bridge had been erected. On 8 April, the Borderers lay at a small fort, Ramora, on the north bank, near where they had forded, and here they ate their first cooked meal since leaving Nowshera.

The rigours of the relief march continued. They crossed the Katgola Pass through the next range of mountains, the Laram Range, which rose to 7,000 feet, and entered a narrow rocky valley through which flowed the treacherous Panjkora River, susceptible to the snows and liable to become a deep roaring torrent within hours. They were now approaching Umra Khan's own country. On 12 April, the Guides Infantry crossed by a rough footbridge constructed of logs and telegraph wire with raft piers, a little downstream of Sado. As the Guides marched out of the brigade bivouac, the pipers of the K.O.S.B. and the Gordons marched at their head, and in a spontaneous demonstration the British soldiers lined the path, cheering their Indian comrades. Across the Panjkora the Guides formed a bridgehead and burned some villages in reprisal for enemy sniping at our transport and working parties. The bridge behind them was then swept away by great logs being carried down the river, now in flood. Records the diary of 2nd K.O.S.B.:

> 'The destruction of the villages [by the Guides] aroused the whole country and the Guides were ordered to retire, which they did in the most perfect order, covered by the 2nd Brigade with guns and Maxims from the other side of the river. The Guides were then ordered to entrench themselves.'

It had been touch and go as the Guides fell back, fording a tributary stream, the Jandol, which flowed into the Panjkora at a point nearby, and carrying the dead body of their commanding

officer across the last stretch of open ground. Wrote
Younghusband:

'Standard bearers with reckless gallantry could be seen rushing to
certain destruction, falling perhaps within ten yards of the
invincible line of the Guides. Nay, sometimes men, devoid of all
fear, and having used up the whole of their ammunition, rushed
forward with large rocks and hurled these at the soldiers,
courting instant death . . . Even after the Guides had crossed the
Jandol stream and the enemy were under a severe fire from The
Gordon Highlanders and The King's Own Scottish Borderers,
they dashed into the stream, where each one stood out clear as a
bull's eye on a target, and attempted to close again. But not a
man got across, so steady and well directed was the flank fire of
the British regiments.'

The Guides held their bridgehead throughout the night. Star
shells fired by a mountain battery discomfited the enemy
sufficiently to prevent an onrush, and the Guides' medical officer
wrote in his diary: 'After a weary night of anxiety and watching,
the dawn at length approached, and just before, we heard the music
of pipes on the hills.'[4]

The 4th Sikhs then went across the Panjkora on rafts, but the
rafts disintegrated and a suspension bridge was built of telegraph
wire and beams stripped from native dwellings. It was completed
within forty-eight hours and had a span of 100 feet, and it took the
weight of all components of the Chitral Relief Force. On 17 April,
the Borderers crossed, in a general advance up the Jandol Valley,
and the campaign was as good as ended. Umra Khan, himself, had
been obliged to come down from Chitral with his picked warriors,
leaving the siege to a Chitrali confederate, Sher Afzul, while he
hastened to raise the tribes; but brushing aside a disheartened
resistance, the Relief Force reached his mountain stronghold at
Mundah, further up the Jandol, on 18 April, to find that Umra
Khan had disappeared. He was reported to have fled into
Afghanistan to seek asylum from the Amir.

Among the abandoned cannon, the scattered grain, books,
papers and general litter found at Fort Mundah, according to
Younghusband, was the writing of a mullah from the heights at
Malakand before the storming of the pass. The words began:

'We see the infidels, the sons of pigs, encamped down in the
plains below us. There are very few of them, and we shall easily
send them all to Hell.'

Ahead lay another mountain range, and the Janbatai Pass at
over 7,000 feet, and finally the snow-capped mountains through

[4] See *The Chitral Campaign* by H. C. Thomson, press correspondent (1895).

which Tamerlane had invaded India six hundred years before, where the Laorai Pass at over 10,000 feet gave access into the Chitral Valley. It was believed that the little garrison had supplies to last until 22 April. Then came Intelligence that Sher Afzul, too, had fled. A few hundred Indian Pioneers and Kashmiri levies under one Colonel Kelly actually got through to the garrison on 20 April, through the towering mountains from Gilgit in Kashmir. This was shortly after a dramatic sortie by the beleaguered company of the 14th Sikhs; but it was the actions fought by the main force at the Malakand Pass, the Swat, the Panjkora, and the capture of Fort Mundah, that had counted.

The Borderers remained at Mundah, while other troops crossed the Laorai Pass, and when the latest news was received, proceeded by easier marches unopposed into Chitral. The magical telegraph wire which the British had brought to India flashed the news of the relief to Peshawar, to Government, to the Empire. From Her Majesty came a gracious message, published in Divisional Orders, and tranquillity was restored in Chitral.

The Borderers moved to the Janbatai Pass at about the time the leading troops entered the Chitral capital, and tents and spare kit came up. Asked what had kept the troops so unusually immune from sickness, a Brigade Commander replied: 'Plenty of work and very little rum.' On that score the 2nd Battalion diary records: 'The heat became very trying but the battalion was kept busy with fatigues and became the most healthy regiment on the expedition.'

A man in the battalion wrote to a friend in Berwickshire:
'Outpost work has been heavy and I reckon many have had quite enough of it to last them all their lives. I don't see anything to grumble at as regards the Commissariat. All things considered the rations have been good, but "Tommy" has longed very much for his proverbial quart. Some of the regiments have managed to get a supply of country ale but our fellows seem to do very well without it. I hear that ours is the healthiest regiment in the force, and I believe also, the best behaved. This has been a good break-in for those who want to go teetotal, and the money deposits have been swelling enormously weekly. Great credit is due to the colonel, Colonel Dixon, whose previous experience has been of great service to the battalion. He has an eagle eye for sanitary matters, water, properly cooked food etc, not forgetting manual labour with the pick and shovel, and I feel sure not a few owe their young lives to his forethought, energy and sound advice.'

The battalion diary reports only two men wounded between Malakand and Mundah, but there was a small cemetery left in the mountains at Janbatai, wherein were buried men of The King's Own Scottish Borderers who had died from one cause or another.

It was a bleak enclosure without a blade of grass, marked out by boulders. The graves were bordered by sticks and stones, and the soldier's name and a horizontal cross were set out in pebbles. Long ago the winds of time have doubtless obliterated those rough respects to once bronzed, hardy men who fought and marched to the relief of Chitral . . . F. Ridler . . . Lance-Corporal Furness . . . E. Coles . . . W. Sims . . . Lance-Corporal W. J. Hyland of the Drums . . . J. Watson; and a soldier of The Gordon Highlanders. And simply 'Pte Buckner', who had an epitaph written in the pebbles, *Gone but not forgotten.*

Chapter 7

TIRAH, 1897

2nd Battalion

In August 1895, the 2nd Battalion left Janbatai and returned to Rawalpindi. It remained there for the next two years, with detachments in the Murree Hills. The 1st Battalion, since its return home, had been stationed at Devonport, York, and Aldershot successively, and was on ceremonial duty in Edinburgh with its Band and Pipes for the visit of the Czar and Czarina of Russia in 1896. The 1st Battalion lined the streets in the vicinity of Buckingham Palace at Queen Victoria's Diamond Jubilee. The 2nd Battalion, on the other hand, in 1897 mobilized again.

*　　*　　*　　*　　*

That year was one of great unrest on the North-West Frontier of India. No less than four major and two minor punitive expeditions were mounted as the result of the Pathan revolt of that year, when tribal attacks and British counter-measures ranged over two hundred miles of frontier, from the Swat Valley north of Peshawar, across the Mohmand country, the Khyber, Tirah, to the Tochi Valley of the Waziri tribes away to the south-west of Kohat.[1]

The first intimations of trouble came in June 1897, when the 2nd Battalion was in the Murree Hills, and by the middle of September the battalion had been concentrated at Pindi and was ordered to draw mobilization stores. Orders soon followed to mobilize for the Tirah Field Force. This was the largest of the several expeditions and was composed of two divisions under the Commander-in-Chief designate in India, Lieutenant-General Sir William Lockhart. The battalion travelled by train to the railhead on the Indus, then by route march to Kohat, Lieutenant-Colonel Dixon again commanding.

The Tirah expedition was caused by the rising of the Afridi tribes to the south and west of the Khyber, who included the Zakka Khel, known to Borderers of twenty years before, and the simultaneous rising of their neighbours to the south, the Orakzai

---

[1] The four major expeditions in chronological order were the Tochi, the Malakand, the Mohmand and the Tirah Field Forces.

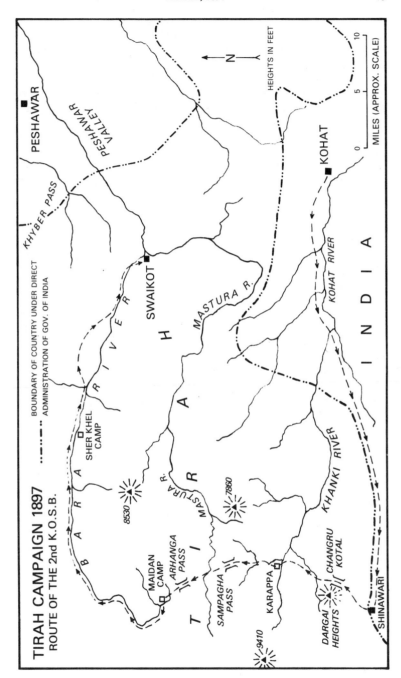

TIRAH CAMPAIGN 1897
ROUTE OF THE 2nd K.O.S.B.

BOUNDARY OF COUNTRY UNDER DIRECT
ADMINISTRATION OF GOV. OF INDIA

HEIGHTS IN FEET

MILES (APPROX. SCALE)
0   5   10

N

PESHAWAR

PESHAWAR VALLEY

KHYBER PASS

SWAIKOT

KOHAT

KOHAT RIVER

MASTURA R.

B A R A R A

T I R A H

SHER KHEL CAMP

8530

MAIDAN CAMP

ARHANGA PASS

MASTURA R.

7860

SAMPAGHA PASS

9410

KARAPPA

KHANKI RIVER

CHANGRU KOTAL

DARGAI HEIGHTS

SHINAWARI

I N D I A

tribes. Between them the two tribal groups could muster quite
50,000 fighting men, and their mountain domains covered many
hundreds of square miles on either side of the high plateau that was
Tirah. The Afridis had overwhelmed the Khyber forts, and after
looting arms and ammunition most had returned to their homes.
The Orakzais had then followed suit and attacked outposts in the
Kohat region, and it was fortunate that there was no co-ordination
between the two tribal groups. Nevertheless, we had temporarily
lost the Kyber forts, and a memorandum issued from Army
Headquarters, Simla, began:

'The general object of this expedition is to exact reparation for
the unprovoked aggression of the Afridi and Orakzai tribes on
the Peshawar and Kohat borders, for the attacks on our frontier
posts, and for the damage to life and property which has thus
been inflicted on British subjects and on those in the British
service. It is believed that this object can best be attained by the
invasion of Tirah, the summer home of the Afridis and Orakzais,
which has never before been entered by a British force.'

The Borderers were to form part of the 4th Brigade, in the 2nd
Division. From Kohat there was a march of forty-five miles into the
hilly country to the west, to Shinawari, where the main force had its
base camp. A few miles to the north lay the heights of Dargai,
shortly to be the scene of the most important action of the Tirah
campaign.

The Dargai heights, not to be confused with Dargai village near
Malakand, commanded a pass, the 5,500-foot Changru Kotal,
where British road-making parties had been harassed. On 18
October 1897, the 2nd Division attacked the heights.

A flanking movement by the 3rd Brigade started as early as 4
a.m., but such were the razor-like spurs with which the troops had
to contend that by noon there was no sign of the flank attack
developing. The 4th Brigade, meanwhile, attacked the Dargai bluff
by the direct route; this rose about 1,000 feet above the Changru
Kotal, and during the morning increasing numbers of tribesmen
had been appearing on the crest. Supported by mountain batteries,
the 1st/3rd Gurkha Rifles, followed by 2nd K.O.S.B., moved up a
sharp ridge which led from the kotal (pass) towards the heights.
They kept to the reverse slope away from the cliff-face. The
Gurkhas then came to a saddle, about 500 yards from the crest,
which led directly towards the precipices. There was no other way
but to cross this saddle, about 200 yards of open ground exposed to
enemy fire from all along the crest, and particularly from sangars
directly above. 'The Borderers and the Gurkhas had brought
themselves up to this by sheer climbing power,' wrote Reuter's
special correspondent, who was present with the campaign. 'The

Gurkhas were ordered to fix bayonets and carry the position, while the Borderers, who had behaved splendidly, covered their advance by "close up" volleys.[2]

The Gurkhas charged across this danger zone in company rushes, then gained dead ground and a steep mountain track. It was more like a rough-hewn staircase, but it provided the only sure footholds to the crest of the heights, and up it in single file scrambled the Gurkhas followed by the Borderers. They reached the top practically unopposed, because once the steel of their bayonets had crossed the open saddle the enemy lost heart and began to retire, partly prompted by the appearance about a mile away of the Gurkha scouts of the flanking 3rd Brigade.

Corporal Edward McKeown of the Borderers wrote in a letter to his parents in Newcastle:

'At about 800 yards our bullets took effect, and we poured volleys into them. I was in charge of No. 3 Section and opened fire at 750 yards. The enemy's fire coming over our heads made me a little excited, but I gave the commands all right except the command "Fire" which I gave too quick for the first two volleys, the men not having enough time to aim. After these two volleys I was all right, I had sixteen men and each fired nineteen rounds, myself and men were calm and collected and having the right distance we scattered the enemy. All then had to rush the position. We could not run, we didn't go up at ordinary walking pace, we were tumbling all over the place. I think nearly all of us had some scratches and scrapes, I having my right knee and wrist skinned.'

At the top, four companies of Borderers under Major Mayne occupied a commanding point, but the troops had not been equipped for holding the heights, eight miles from their camp at Shinawari. Nor was there water for a considerable distance. A difficult retirement was made, therefore, involving a long traverse by the flanking brigade, the 3rd Brigade, and covered by B and H Companies of 2nd K.O.S.B. who held positions on the heights until it was almost dark. They were pressed hard by the tribesmen who, inevitably, had returned to harass the retirement, so much so that several companies of Gurkhas and Gordon Highlanders were sent to reinforce them, and there were a number of casualties. Next day, 4th Brigade Orders issued by Brigadier-General Westmacott contained the following:

'The thanks of the whole 3rd and 4th Brigades are due to Captains MacLaren and Sladen and Haig, Lieutenants

---

[2] Lionel James, whose reports from the Mohmand and Tirah expeditions were published in book form in 1898 as *The Indian Frontier War*.

Wolfestan and Keyes[3] and Surgeon-Captain More, and B and H Companies of The King's Own Scottish Borderers, for their tenacity in holding the crest of the ridge and steadiness in covering the retirement of both brigades.'

The withdrawal from the heights incurred criticism at the time, for when a general forward movement into Tirah was ordered on 20 October, the Dargai heights had to be attacked all over again. The tribesmen had massed in greater numbers. It was believed that 12,000 of them were now in the area, both Orakzai and Afridi, although only a small part of that number were actually posted on the crest of the formidable bluff. The second attack, which cost over 200 casualties, was memorable for the heroic charge of The Gordon Highlanders across the open saddle after three battalions had been brought to a standstill.

Corporal MacKeown, who had operated as a marksman during the withdrawal after the first attack, concluded his letter to his parents:

'The Brigade commences marching through the country next Thursday. If I am spared I will let you know everything. When you receive this letter it will be nearly all over, you will also know the correct news from the newspapers, and will have seen the K.O.S.B. mentioned. I am entitled to a medal and bar now. This has been my ambition since I enlisted. If I am spared I will be content with doing my eight years. The enemy are a very bad lot, if they get the chance they mutilate the bodies of our men, cutting pieces off and sticking them in their mouths. They are well armed with Martinis and outnumbered us by thousands, but they have no idea of order in their fighting. I am now called away to build sangars.'

*   *   *   *   *

After the capture of the Dargai heights the Orakzais never again made a resolute stand, preferring to follow up our movements and to harass. The Borderers and the 1st/3rd Gurkhas were rearguard to the 2nd Division during the second attack, and among the baggage problems was that posed by the transport ponies themselves. These wretched animals had been allocated at Kohat and were of such poor quality that they were continually collapsing under their loads.

'The baggage of the Division was going slowly out of camp all day,' relates the 2nd Battalion diary, 'but it soon became evident that the rearguard would not move that night. Accordingly the

---

[3] Keyes, attached to 2nd K.O.S.B.

1st/3rd Gurkhas and four companies 2nd K.O.S.B. were sent forward to picquet the road on which the baggage was blocked during the night.

About 11 a.m. on 21 October the remaining four companies of the Borderers moved out of camp, still leaving a certain amount of baggage behind. The transport belonging to the battalion proved absolutely incapable of getting up the hill, but luckily on the previous day arrangements had been made that the battalion should take over the Gwalior Imperial Service transport, which coming along on the 21st picked up the dropped loads and brought nearly everything into camp. This transport remained with the battalion during the remainder of active operations and proved invaluable.'

Reuter's special correspondent described the camp at Shinawari, with its thousands of troops and their camp followers and stores, as 'like a teeming city in the shadow of the hills'. He wrote of the army of non-combatants and followers and the multitude of transport animals, 'an array which would strike a Continental soldier dumb with amazement'. On the day of the first attack at Dargai there were, he reported, 43,810 transport animals attached to the Tirah Field Force:

'General Lockhart was called upon to take this undisciplined multitude across mountains where there was not even a vestige of a goat-track, along river-beds strewn with boulders where the only path was knee-deep in icy water, through gorges where two animals abreast closed the passage, up gradients which in their initial stages defeated even mountain battery mules, down descents which were almost precipes; through barren places where food there was none, and into extremes of climate which destroyed the weaklings and consequently increased the loads of the more robust.'

The advance into Tirah continued, through the Changru Kotal and into the next camp at Karappa in the Khanki Valley, and is described prosaically in the pages of the 2nd Battalion diary:

'During the next few days the 1st Division [following the 2nd Division] came slowly across the pass. The camp was heavily fired into at night. . . . On 26 October the battalion with The Gordon Highlanders and one battery, under Lieutenant-Colonel Dixon, went on a foraging expedition back towards the defile, and being ordered to assist in the convoy did not reach camp until 7 p.m. . . . On 29 October the attack on Sampagha Pass was made . . . The force moved down into the Mastura valley, the chief valley of the Orakzais, 4th Brigade leading, and formed camp. No baggage came into camp except one blanket per man, and the men had to do their best on what food could be found in the villages, consisting chiefly of Indian corn and beans, as no rations arrived until late on the afternoon of the 30th.

On 31 October the Arhanga Pass was attacked, the 4th Brigade leading. The battalion was in the attacking line, but only a very feeble resistance was offered and the pass was taken without any casualty in the battalion. The battalion at once moved down and occupied a hill in the Maidan Valley opposite the pass, and was therefore the first battalion into Afridi Tirah.'

An officer wrote in a letter:

'We are all very fit except a few colds. It is hot by day and cold by night. We are as usual on 40 lb kits, and tents made with our waterproofs. I have a tiny tent, but my air bed makes it quite comfortable sleeping on the ground. Our faces are dark red, brown noses, and lips cut by sun and wind.'

Villages were burnt in a valley of the Zakka Khel, and the battalion diarist noted that one day in H Company 'two men had their bayonets broken by bullets, and three others had bullets through their clothes or accoutrements.' Much of the work was picquet duty and giving cover to forage parties, and although danger to life and limb at the hands of the enemy was small compared to what the Regiment's ranks faced in bigger wars, the demands on the sheer physical endurance of the troops in those days of limited means of supply was probably often greater. The men got little rest, and there was always the possibility that at any turn the quick-eyed Pathan might try his marksmanship—and the wounded could never be allowed to fall into his hands.

One day 'Second-Lieutenant Broadbent had his head grazed while looking through his field glasses, and Sergeant D. Watson had a bullet through his helmet at the same time.' Another time, when G Company were going out to reinforce the day picquets, 'they were suddenly fired on and lost one man killed and two dangerously wounded'. After a reconnaissance in force down a river gorge, 'no blankets or food came into camp that night and all ranks spent a miserable night, having been thoroughly wetted by constantly having to ford the icy water'. Another night, the enemy crept through the scrub close enough to throw stones into Captain Macfarlane's sangar. They made three attempts to rush it, and killed two men in Sergeant Watson's sangar. This had followed an action fought by the advance guard of the 2nd Division to secure a picquet line, and Reuter's special correspondent wrote of 'the magnificent hill skirmishing of the Borderers'. Another account [4]

---

[4] Colonel H. D. Hutchinson. *The Campaign in Tirah 1897-98* (1898). Hutchinson, who dedicated his book to General Lockhart, wrote of 'the Borderers, under Colonel Dixon, one of the finest regiments in the Force'.

of the campaign quotes a letter by one of Captain Macfarlane's officers, describing how Macfarlane's company rushed the position, with pipes playing:

'When it got dark the Afridis began to fire at us, but we didn't reply. Suddenly one of the sentries called out, "Stand to! They're on us!" We all sprang to our posts and opened fire independently on a mob of men who were charging down with loud shouts. Some of them were within twenty yards. Our fire checked them and they drew off. We could hear groans, and the noise made by bodies being dragged and carried away. One dead man was left within ten yards of our wall.

They now established themselves under cover all round us within very short ranges, fired frequently, shouted abuse in Hindustani, and threw stones, by which several of us were hit. We took no notice, by Captain Macfarlane's orders, but waited to give them the bayonet should they come on.'

* * * * *

General Lockhart had vowed that the arms of the British Raj should be visited upon every valley in Tirah, and although this was in the main achieved, winter with snow on the hilltops and temperatures falling to near zero brought a somewhat inconclusive termination to the campaign. The Field Force was not equipped for a winter in Tirah, and troops and tribesmen alike sought the main valleys. It was decided to move the base of the Field Force from Shinawari to the Peshawar Valley, and down the Bara Valley to the Peshawar Valley the troops withdrew. The withdrawal was made entirely through the territory of the Zakka Khel, 'the thieves of the thieves', feared even by their confederates, and, interpreting the withdrawal to British India as a retreat, this warlike tribe pressed the troops hard.

The 2nd Battalion diary records it as an affair of advance guards and rearguards, the customary pattern of warfare on the North-West Frontier, in which it was not a good thing for troops to be caught by darkness when still on the line of march:

'On 11 December the march was resumed, the battalion forming the rearguard. The work was very heavy owing to the transport straying into the wet fields near the river bed and becoming bogged. Kahars and drabies[5] left their baggage and went to warm themselves at fires they had lighted, and the men of the battalion had to carry several wounded Sikhs and Gurkhas nearly the whole march, who had been deserted by their doolie bearers.

[5] Native doolie bearers and transport drivers.

It was about 5 p.m. before the rearguard reached Camp Sher Khel. The advance guard of 3rd Brigade was close behind, but owing to the baggage having become entangled in the wet fields the rearguard of 3rd Brigade could not reach camp. About 9.30 p.m. the battalion was ordered to fall in, as some of the baggage of 3rd Brigade was reported to have been attacked by the enemy. Eventually only H Company was sent out, it saw no sign of the enemy but many followers and ponies were found about one mile from camp, and were driven into camp.'

The rearguard had spent the night cut off, closely invested in a village an hour's march from camp. Next day there was a halt, the two brigades changed places and the 4th Brigade took over rearguard to the Division. When the march was resumed again there followed the sharpest fighting since Dargai:

'The advance guard left camp at 7 a.m., but it was obvious that the rearguard would not be able to leave camp before 11 a.m. at earliest. It soon became clear that the enemy meant to attack in force as all the picquets were engaged from an early hour, and the baggage of the battalion was loaded under a considerable fire, from which two followers and five ponies were hit. Lieutenant Sellars was also grazed on the head by a bullet.

About 11 a.m. the last of the baggage was clear of the camp and the picquets began to withdraw. F and G Companies were on picquet and their retirement was covered by B and C Companies. The picquets got in without loss, but each of the covering companies had a man wounded before being clear of the camp. Private Forsyth, B Company, was nearly captured by the enemy as he was wounded in the village without being noticed by anybody, but he managed to run in just before the enemy reached the village. He had a very bad wound on the face and two others in wrist and thigh.

The rearguard was very heavily pressed from the start, and some of the 3rd Gurkhas and C Company K.O.S.B. ran out of ammunition within three miles of camp. About three and a half miles from camp the path left the river and ran through thick scrub intersected with nullahs over a low kotal. At the point where the road left the river bed the baggage got blocked and the rearguard had to hold fast for about half an hour before the retirement recommenced. It was at this point that a great many of the casualties in the battalion occurred.

From here the retirement went on steadily until dark, when General Westmacott decided to hold a ridge west of the kotal for the night. Just as the sun went down the enemy crept close up to the position through the scrub and made an attempt to attack.'
It was a moment for steady troops. The Afridis leapt forward in

yelling swarms, their loose garments white in the fading light. Once more discipline prevailed. The field of fire was poor, but a storm of musketry crackled out, and as the bullets whipped and cracked down the slope the Afridis were halted, their charge wavered, then they broke, and except for random prowlers were heard of no more as darkness came on:

'The troops of the 4th Brigade were by this time reduced to 110 Borderers, about 100 Scots Fusiliers, 100 Gurkhas and 200 Sikhs, and lined the ridge for the night, which passed quietly. There was no water obtainable, but some rum and tinned meat were obtained and issued. The casualties in the battalion were two men killed, and one Colour Sergeant, one Sergeant, and eleven men wounded.

It was again 11 a.m. on 14 December before all the baggage was loaded and away. About 11.30 a.m. the rear line which was being occasionally fired at from the adjoining heights retired at the double on a given signal.'

There followed the last day's march, into camp at Swaikot, where the hills of the Afridis bordered the Peshawar Valley and British India. For the past thirty hours the men had gone without water. 'As a military achievement this march of Lockhart's 2nd Division will live in the military history of the century,' wrote Reuter's special correspondent. 'Nobody who was not there can conceive what was asked of the troops, British and Indian, in that terrible march.'

Swaikot was already picquetted by a column that had marched out from Peshawar. The whole Tirah Field Force had now withdrawn, its other division having already passed through. Except for operations in January to drive the Afridis and their cattle from the plain, 2nd K.O.S.B. remained uneventfully at Swaikot until April 1898, when the 2nd Division began to move back to India. In an eloquent farewell order to the 4th Brigade, Brigadier-General Westmacott recalled that from the heights of Dargai until the final operation in January, 'the Brigade has been in action twenty-three times, and has on every occasion nobly upheld the traditions of the army'.

The 2nd Battalion diary notes eight men killed, and five officers and thirty-eight men wounded, and refers to a 'great many' unspecified casualties on the penultimate day of the march to Swaikot.

*   *   *   *   *

The India Medal 1895 was awarded for both the Relief of Chitral and the Tirah campaign, with appropriate clasps, and the words

'Chitral' and 'Tirah' appeared on the Regiment's Colours and appointments. Captain Sladen became the second officer of the Regiment to be awarded the D.S.O., which had been instituted in 1886.[6]

The 2nd Battalion moved to Cawnpore, where on 1 April 1900, trews of Leslie tartan were issued to the battalion. One of the sergeants had sent a Christmas Card home to his brother, designed by Sergeant Hopkins, serving with the battalion, which showed a Scottish Borderer wearing the tartan. So the Regiment crossed the threshold of the 20th Century in the process of changing to the green and blue, with the red and white overcheck, of the family tartan of the Earls of Leven. Many years later the then Earl of Leven, when a guest at a Regimental Dinner, told of how he had been walking in Inverness, wearing his kilt, and had overheard two soldiers of the Regiment who were walking behind him. One said to the other, 'Yon felly's wearing oor tartan.'

'I think,' said the Earl, 'I swung my kilt a little more proudly for that remark.'

When that story was told, much water had flowed under the bridge since the time when the good sergeant in Cawnpore had written to his brother, in a letter enclosed with the Christmas Card:

'I am sorry the Authorities can't see their way to sending us to South Africa and there are no signs of them sending the home battalion either. It is altogether too bad. I suppose nearly every other regiment in the Service is represented by at least one battalion, but there are to be *no Borderers*. Who is to be blamed for this apparent oversight on the part of the Authorities?'

As it happened, the sergeant need not have worried.

[6] The first, who was among the first list of recipients in 1886, was Captain A. C. P. Haggard, formerly of the 2nd Battalion and a relative of Rider Haggard, the novelist. He won it in the Sudan in action against the Dervishes. He was one of the original nucleus of British officers who founded the Egyptian Army.

Chapter 8

THE SOUTH AFRICAN WAR, 1900-02

1st Battalion
In 1898 the 1st Battalion took part in manoeuvres on Salisbury Plain. A large detachment was then sent to Berwick-upon-Tweed where they were addressed and banqueted by the Mayor and Corporation before making a Border March for recruiting purposes. The 1st Battalion then proceeded to Dublin, where, in December 1899, it mobilized for active service in South Africa and returned to Aldershot. 1st K.O.S.B. embarked for South Africa on 5 January 1900, Lieutenant-Colonel Godfray commanding.

In the ranks was Private William Fessey, who came from Warwickshire, a Maxim gunner, whose diary of the South African War is preserved among the Regimental records.[1] He had completed nearly twelve years with the Colours when his battalion embarked:

'Reveille at 3 a.m.,' he wrote. 'Marched to the station, Aldershot, and got the train for Southampton at 8.15 a.m. and arrived at Southampton about midday. The very first thing I noticed was large cards stuck about the station, and on them was the Absent-minded Beggar,[2] and there was small stalls about the platforms, and we could hear them cry out now and again— Tommy Atkins can have what he likes free, either notepaper or cake or coffee. We had to move all Regimental baggage and us Tommies had to work like niggers to get all baggage on the boat.

Well, now I shall have to say goodbye to Old England. Talk about war, we chaps never thought about war or what was in waiting for us, but we found that out for ourselves later on. We had orders to get on the boat which we found out to be a good one. It is called the S.S. *Braemar Castle* . . . I must say that there was not another corps could have had a better reception from the public, leaving the harbour.'

Among the 1st Battalion officers on board was Lieutenant Chandos Leigh, who also kept a diary now preserved by the

---

[1] The author is grateful to Mr. W. J. Fessey, and to Mr. F. G. Fessey, late K.O.S.B., for permission to quote from their father's diary.

[2] An evident reference to the Absent-minded Beggar Fund, launched by means of Kipling's latest verses to raise money for the soldiers' families.

Regiment.[3] He was on leave as the old century drew to a close:

'When I went on leave in November 1899, I had very small hopes of getting out to South Africa, but the week before Christmas, after the successive defeats at Magersfontein, Stormberg and the Tugela, the wire from Dublin arrived to rejoin my Regiment at once, who were under orders to mobilize at Aldershot prior to embarkation for South Africa. Needless to say I was delighted, particularly as there was a hard frost at home which looked like lasting, and in consequence hunting prospects looked very bad. Perhaps if I could have had the smallest idea of the duration of my stay in South Africa the feelings I should have experienced on receiving that little yellow envelope might have been considerably modified if not altogether altered.'

Lieutenant Leigh arrived at Berwick-upon-Tweed on Christmas Eve to collect 150 reservists, 'all more or less drunk', and to take them by train to Aldershot. There, a young man of connections, on the eve of embarkation he dined at Government House where his sister was staying:

'We had a large party to see us off at Southampton, old and present Borderers and sisters and mothers galore, who lunched with us on board. Our ship is the *Braemar Castle*, she is not a particularly fast boat but very comfortable and roomy. We sailed at 5 p.m. amidst much weeping, cheering and playing of the pipes. I was rather thankful to have no relations to see me off as it is rather trying.'

The battalion embarked at a strength of 28 officers and 1,082 other ranks.

* * * * *

The British Army in South Africa was obliged to put into the field a quarter of a million men, including contingents from the Empire, and nearly 200,000 volunteers and non-combatants on the lines of communication, against an opponent very different from the Pathan tribesman and the Fuzzy-Wuzzy. To the Boer—the Dutch word for farmer—it was second nature to ride and shoot. In this way had he staked out his place in the sun. He was fighting, moreover, for his nationhood, and was so effective with his swift pony and German rifle that he engaged British regular forces whose numbers exceeded the entire Boer populations of the two republics of the Transvaal and the Orange Free State. After initial

[3] Extracts are quoted, and two of the drawings in the diary are reproduced in this book, with the kind consent of his nephew, Lieutenant-Colonel Sir Rupert Hardy, Bart.

humiliations, when British troops were besieged at Kimberley, Mafeking and Ladysmith, Field Marshal Lord Roberts was sent out at the age of sixty-seven to bring the Boer to book, with Kitchener as his Second-in-Command, styled Chief of Staff.

'In those days there were no automatic weapons,' wrote Second-Lieutenant W. F. Graham, who embarked with the 3rd (Militia) Battalion, K.O.S.B. 'The only machine-gun was the Maxim, a thing on wheels that had to be carried about on a mule and which took quite a time to assemble before use. There was also a gun known as a Pom-Pom that fired bursts of five half-pound shells. Its moral effect was greater than its physical. Cavalry still rode horses, infantry slogged on their feet, and generals could not move a step without a bugler and a trooper with a pennon. The infantry carried their ammunition loose in pouches on their belts. There were no clips of cartridges, but mounted men wore bandoliers. An officer was supposed to carry a carbine and a lot more equipment, but in practice he only carried a stick. The lines of communication were long and a large number of troops was required to guard them. This was mainly a job for the Militia, and 3rd K.O.S.B. was embodied in February 1900, went to Belfast, and later embarked from Queenstown . . . The men were nearly all old soldiers — professional militiamen — and about as tough and drunken a lot as one could wish to see.'[4]

The militiamen can be imagined when they held their concerts in South Africa, at which a parody written by one Captain Stewart of Shambellie and his daughter used to be sung by the Pipe Major and was very popular. It had been sent to the Commanding Officer, Lieutenant-Colonel James Maxwell-Witham, and the first verse went thus:

'To his numerous girls 'twas the Colonel who spoke —
"Ere I see you again Kruger's head will be broke,
So let each bonny lass that likes flirting with me
Cry "Good luck to brave Jim and his K.O.S.B.".'

At the same time, a volunteer service company was formed from volunteers of the 1st Roxburgh and Selkirk (Border Rifle) Volunteer Corps, the 2nd (Berwickshire) and 3rd (Dumfriesshire) Volunteer Battalions. After a short course of instruction at Berwick-upon-Tweed they embarked at Southampton.

Meanwhile, on 26 January 1900, the 1st Battalion disembarked at Cape Town, and entrained for the Orange River where it came

---

[4] The author is grateful to Miss Anne Graham for permission to quote from her father's memoir of the South African War. The 3rd Battalion was embodied on 25 January 1900; one hopes they had a merry Burns Night.

under the 7th Division, and marched to Paardeberg in pursuit of
General Cronje. After one of the harshest of marches, 1st K.O.S.B.
were present when Cronje surrendered to Lord Roberts at the
Modder River.

The Mounted Infantry company left the battalion before the
march began to form, with other companies from the 7th Mounted
Infantry Regiment. Chandos Leigh wrote in his diary:

'I shall never forget the day we took over our mounts. In the
first place not one of the officers had any previous Mounted
Infantry experience, and the few of our men who had were men
who had served many years ago in one M.I. section in Egypt. The
rest were chosen from men who were supposed to have a knowledge of horses, viz. any man whether he had been an officer's
groom, driven a milk cart or a hansom cab or even sold cats'
meat, would according to himself be eligible. Therefore, when
we proceeded to draw our cobs, all fat underbred looking
Argentines, there was chaos. Every man went for the cob he
liked the look of best, these beasts being all more or less wild
resented being bridled and still more being backed. In five
minutes the whole place was a mass of loose ponies flying about
with bridles round their legs, and Tommies vainly endeavouring
to mount bareback and being put off. I was shot off myself the
moment I tried to mount.'

After a few days of schooling, 'We invaded the Orange Free
State.' Soon they found the Boers occupying a long line of hills and
Leigh's company dismounted and lay in extended order, being
sniped from the kopjes while their horses were shelled behind them.
Then they marched that night, and the next day, and the day after.
There followed an action at Waterval Drift, a ford over the Riet
River, where a convoy of 180 wagons and its escorts were under
attack by the Boers. The Mounted Infantry were ordered to draw
the enemy fire, supported by the 1st Battalion, K.O.S.B., but at
length an order came from Lord Roberts to leave the convoy and
press forward with the march to Paardeberg:

'With no forage or rations we marched all day on 17 February
and all night, with just a short halt now and then to water and
graze our wretched horses. I found it all I could do to keep awake
on my horse and whenever we halted nearly every man was at
once off his horse asleep with his reins through his arm or round
his leg.'

Corporal C. Turner of G Company of the 1st Battalion, a
Reservist, wrote of the convoy action:[5]

[5] His diary of the South African War was presented to the Regiment by his
grandson who has kindly given permission for it to be quoted.

'Under cover of the artillery fire the Mounted Infantry had to retire at the gallop and out of order through us, but we advanced to the convoy under a heavy rifle and artillery fire from the tops of kopjes. When we got to the convoy we found it so much damaged that we could not shift it until we got fresh wagons.' At 3 a.m. Lord Roberts's order came to abandon the wagons. 'We had to march to Jacobsdal with empty stomachs as we had received nothing since the morning before. We had one biscuit a man but we ate our emergency rations. We got back to the rest of the column about 11 a.m. all about done up after about forty hours marching and knocking about among the kopjes, I can tell you. We were not very much use that day but we moved to Jacobsdal that night and General French [Cavalry Division] moved to the Klip Drift on the Modder River about nine miles from Kimberley on the morning of 16 February.

General French marched from Klip Drift at 1.30 for the relief of Kimberley which took place that day[6] and we marched from Jacobsdal at 5 a.m. for the Klip Drift with French's provisions and convoys for Kimberley. From the time French had left Klip Drift to the time we got there Cronje and his force from Magersfontein had passed through, but our Mounted Infantry got in touch with his rearguard.'

This was at the height of the South African summer:

'We had no meat for three days, only coffee and biscuits.' wrote Fessey. 'The next day we started on a little march, only lasted for thirty-six hours.' Arriving at Jacobsdal: 'We remained there till Sunday night we moved off again, to the Modder River, where we heard of General Cronje being hemmed in on the river bed. We marched all night long until 6 a.m. then we had our breakfast and rested for two hours after marching nineteen miles. We started again the same evening and got to where General Cronje was in the river bed, marched another sixteen miles up the side of the river, making a total of thirty-five miles.'

They had reached Paardeberg Drift.

The Regimental diary records:

'The troops reached Paardeberg in an utterly exhausted condition which was accentuated by the absence of food, the baggage with rations being far behind. Emergency rations were used at Paardeberg for the first time. We had marched thirty-six miles in nineteen hours.'

'Our General said we was far enough,' wrote Fessey. 'We had better lie down till daybreak with our rifles fully loaded, for we

6 Turner was one day out with the date; the cavalry left Klip Drift for Kimberley at 9.30 a.m., 15 February.

knew that we was close to the enemy and I can tell you this much, I was nearly starved to death with the cold (*sic*). So when daybreak came we got up and took our blanket back to the wagon when all at once the enemy opened a tremendous heavy fire on us, about 700 or 800 yards off us. Cronje on our left in the river bed, and the old famous de Wet on small kopjes on our right, he was trying to reinforce Cronje but he failed.

We found out that we was so near the river bed Major Mayne gave orders to the right half battalion to retire further out of range, so we commenced to move. We got a smart reception, they opened fire on both sides of us at the same time, we could not tell where they was coming from, they fairly rattled into us. So we thought the best thing to do was to lie down for a bit, so we got on to our stomachs and we blazed away at one another for three and a half solid hours . . . We had several of my corps hit but I do not know who they are at the present moment, but shall know at roll call. We had orders to retire, twenty paces interval. We got under good cover . . . but now our artillery comes and starts shelling them. My word they soon felt them. I could see them retiring in full haste but we kept sending a few pills into them for an hour or two, then my corps advanced to a farm close by, where they had been on the kopjes. We started at the kopjes and chased de Wet for his life as well as giving his troops a doing, the best cutting up that he ever had as yet, the Borderers did.

So we occupied this farm, Osfontein. We stayed eight days here. While we was here we received orders that we must stand to arms early in the morning, and that we would be attacked at daybreak. So we was prepared for them. It would be about 4 a.m. when the sentry saw some of the enemy on the move on the veldt. On reporting it to the officer, he had a look through his glasses and found out they were the Boers. He ordered the Maxim to get ready at once which we was all ready to move at a moment's notice. We went out and saw them coming rather thick, so we came into action at 1,730 yards, but it was a bad position for us, their Pom Pom was playing at us for a while so we shifted to a place where we could see them.

We let them come within 300 yards of us and then we started, and rattled into them with Maxim and vollies all we were worth. We emptied belt after belt and I could see them fall and I am sure they suffered heavily. We could see their horses fall by scores and running about riderless, they got a surprise. They made a rush for a kopje where one of our companies were, and the Boers were driven back with very heavy losses three times that morning. We was lucky on our side, we had only five men wounded and one officer.

24 February: Reveille 4 a.m. We started to build a sangar all round the farm in case of being attacked but there was no signs of them.

25 February: Reveille 4 a.m. Still building sangars. We worked about six hours a day on a biscuit, it was pure starvation. Went on night outpost 5 p.m. Remained on outpost all night.

26 February: Still on outpost. We came across a bag of Indian Corn, we call it maize at home. We got it from a Kaffir Kraal so you can guess how hungry we was. We started to roast the corn then smash it up and boil it.'

On 27 February Cronje surrendered and Fessey's entry for the day reads:

'We was standing to arms and there was very heavy firing going on around us all the night. We had heard that Cronje tried to escape but was repulsed and surrendered unconditionally and all his men numbering 4,000. Great rejoicing in our camp that morning I can tell you. The next morning, 28 February, we all went down to see his position that they had held for the nine days and nights. We could not have stopped him if it was not for our big guns firing Lyddite shells into them, and when I saw it I was surprised. Bags of flour and tobacco was left in the trenches, us soldiers had our eyes on it and off with it we went and had a good feed or two, and a pipe or two.'

'The battlefield,' wrote Kitchener's biographer, 'presented the extraordinary spectacle of the Boer laager, like a bulls-eye, encircled by a British army which was ringed, in its turn, by a number of Boer commandos of unknown strength.'[7]

Corporal Turner wrote this account in his diary:

'We have been standing to arms since one hour before daylight but no appearance of the Boers today. I think the loss they had yesterday has been too many for them so we are just resting in peace today and watching the naval guns blazing away at old Cronje. All his transport are on fire and they are making every shot tell along the river bank. He cannot possibly stand much longer now.'

On 26 February Turner wrote:

'The naval guns keep at him again and again . . . We are expecting a strong attack tomorrow as it is the anniversary of Majuba Hill, but we are ready for them, all the artillery and cavalry are coming in to our support tonight, if it only keeps fair we will give them a warm time of it for their breakfast.

'*27 February*: We are standing to arms at 3 o'clock a.m. ready to receive them this morning, but instead of receiving another

---

[7] *Kitchener, Portrait of an Imperialist,* by Philip Magnus.

visit from Cronje's relieving column we see Cronje's white flag flying and all his force collected round it, prepared to surrender. You should have heard the welcome cheer. Majuba avenged . . . Now Kitchener and an escort is away to receive all the prisoners . . . General Roberts meets Cronje and shakes hands with him and passes the remark: He is pleased to have the pleasure of receiving so brave a general as he has been, under his charge and a prisoner of war. Cronje's reply to General Roberts: I am sorry that I am compelled to surrender but I must come under on the plains [sic], but if I could have made my way to the kopjes I think I could have out-generalled you for some time yet. Roberts: Perhaps, but I think you have had your only chance now. Then he invited him to breakfast while he consulted with his Staff what would be the best way to get him to Cape Town.'

*   *   *   *   *

On Roberts's great march through South Africa, 1st K.O.S.B. entered Bloemfontein on 14 March 1900. The men were still on half rations, and troops and transport animals alike were exhausted with the whole-day marches.

'We did another little tramp, twenty miles,' wrote Fessey of one of the days: 'it was so very hot and we only had a pint of water per man per day, that was our allowance and the officers expected to see some of that left when we got to camp, but sometimes when we got to camp there would be a field of water melons there. We readily helped ourselves to them till we was fed up with that diet.'

At Bloemfontein there was a welcome halt, then at the end of March the Borderers took part in the capture of a ridge of hills to the north, and formed the most advanced outpost of the army. Dislodging the Boers from the hills, with other troops, the battalion had fought its most disastrous action of the war, the action at Karee Siding, in which it had eighty-three casualties. Private W. Walsh wrote in a letter home:

'This was a terrible day for our battalion. We were within about 100 yards of the enemy, when we got the word to fix bayonets and the Boers fled as soon as they saw the steel glittering. They are proper cowards when you get to close quarters, for they won't stand their ground but gallop away on their horses, and all we can do is to fire at them until they get out of range. They are all right behind a big rock, but they are no good as soon as you drive them out of cover.'

An officer killed outright at Karee was Captain A. C. Going, described as 'a dapper little officer, full of fun'. He had for long

been in demand at concert parties, where he excelled in putting over
a song, and many in Berwickshire were to remember the refrain of
his favourite song:

'We dont want the bullets' rattle in the battle,
And we don't want to hear the cannons roar any more.'

At the end of May, 1st K.O.S.B. crossed the Vaal River, were
present at the surrender of Johannesburg, and on 4 June 1900, were
present at the reduction of the southern forts of Pretoria. Records
1st K.O.S.B. diary: 'All that night we lay on the hills, hungry and

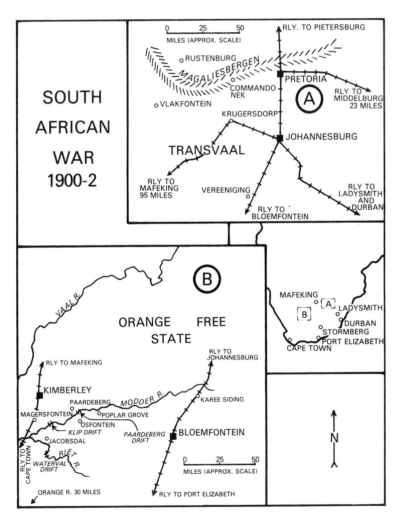

cold, with the twinkling electric lights of the town below us.' They entered Pretoria on 5 June, over 300 miles distance from Paardeberg Drift.

The volunteer service company had now joined the battalion, while in March 1901, a second volunteer service company from the Border Volunteer Corps, including the Galloway Rifle Volunteers, had embarked for South Africa.

Obtaining a commission in the line and transferring from the 3rd (Militia) Battalion, Second-Lieutenant Graham joined the 1st Battalion after the capture of Pretoria. 'Not a soul knew about my having been gazetted to them, but everybody was very kind and nice,' he wrote in his memoir; 'Mayne was in command, the C.O., Godfray, having been given a job in Bloemfontein. Amos was adjutant, and the whole outfit was a very happy family.' A little earlier Graham had seen a sunset he was not to forget:

'It was while I was at Pretoria that I saw one of the most wonderful sunset effects imaginable. All day long a stream of wagons had been going towards the north and the air was full of fine dust. The sun shining through this produced the most beautiful effect. The town, hills and plain all seemed to be enveloped in a glowing mist of crimson, orange, and rose pink. The only things that stood out in their natural colours were the dark green-blue gum trees and weeping ash trees. Wherever a white wall showed, it was tinted with an almost limelight effect.'

He described the veldt:

'It was fascinating in the early morning on the veldt. Everything was so fresh and clean, and you could smell the vivid scent of the veldt which can be experienced nowhere else. Then to start by moonlight and watch the day breaking, the curling mist roll away from the hollows as the sun came flashing over the tops of the mountains was a sight to remember. It was wonderful how bright the morning was, the air was so wonderfully clear and the horses were always aware of the freshness of the early hours. Until you have ridden tired horses in the heat of the day you do not know what that means.'

Graham later joined the Mounted Infantry and his latter remark was no doubt an allusion to his experience there. The Mounted Infantry had a lot of work to do, with constant skirmishing, and Chandos Leigh, who served with the K.O.S.B. Company throughout all the operations of 1900, records in his diary no less than forty-five engagements fought by the 7th Mounted Infantry Regiment and a total of 945 miles of treks in that year. He rode thirteen successive horses.

From the Eastern Transvaal, where the 1st K.O.S.B. were in small detachments garrisoning the railway between Pretoria and

Middelburg, Private Fessey's diary entry for 15 October 1900 was brief: 'Five men of ours was fetched into camp speechless drunk and they got a Field Court Martial.' No matter. The sieges of Kimberley, Ladysmith and Mafeking had been raised, and Baden-Powell had been relieved at Rustenburg. In the latter operation, 1st K.O.S.B. had marched with the relief force into the Western Transvaal and held Commando Nek. Above all, the capitals of the two Boer republics had been captured. Kruger, himself, had gone to Europe to seek help, and Lord Roberts returned home the victor towards the end of 1900. Kitchener succeeded as Commander-in-Chief, to conduct the final but drawn-out phase, the subjugation of the Boer 'bitter-enders' who waged guerrilla warfare under their daring commando leaders. He set about this systematically, evolving a strategy of cavalry sweeps, barbed wire and block-houses until he had literally rounded them up.

'We was rather too hot for them at the small stations', wrote Fessey. 'We was well entrenched all round the camps so they could fire away at our positions as long as they liked and do no damage whatever to us, and we would lay in wait for them to come as close as ever they dared so we could have a proper go at them. So I witnessed good smart work like this done at these small stations while the bulk of the British army was out in small columns for the purpose of driving the enemy into one another.'

In May 1901, the battalion joined a mobile column in the Western Transvaal, commanded by a well known old Borderer, Brigadier-General Henry Dixon, who, according to Graham's memoir, found it difficult not to resume his former rôle of Commanding Officer. 'He was constantly with us, and playing bridge at night when we wanted to sleep,' a habit which so aroused the jealousy of the other units of the column that the K.O.S.B. became known as 'Dixon's pets'. The first action fought by Dixon's column was a sharp one. Wrote Graham: 'Brother Boer in great force was met at a spot called Vlakfontein. He lit the veldt, advanced under cover of the smoke, drove in the Yeomanry outposts, captured our field guns and turned them on the camp. There was quite a lot of excitement.' It was described by Corporal T. A. M. Ayton in a letter:

'The Boers, however, were desperate, as they meant to have the guns. Rush after rush they made, and finally succeeded in getting possession of two of them. But they were owners of them only for a short time. The Volunteer Service Company of the K.O.S.B., in extended order on the left, and D Company of the Regiment on their right, on open ground, with great coolness pushed forward, delivering volley after volley into the Boer horsemen. But the Boers were as active as us, sending shell after shell from the captured guns through our thin line. But they were not timed properly, so went into the ground raising great volumes of dust around us. Still the Volunteers pushed on, driving the Boers over the crest of the ridge. The remaining artillerymen and Derbys, seeing us playing havoc among the Boers and driving them back, again charged the guns, recapturing them at the point of the bayonet. Our men, seeing this, rushed up cheering wildly, and they could be heard right down the valley. At the same time, along with our Maxim gun, they poured a terrible fire into the retreating Boers.'

Soon after, wrote Graham: 'We were told to burn farms in the line of march, a beastly job, as the women and children had to be collected on ox-wagons and brought along, some howling, but most of them cursing. Ultimately they were sent to concentration camps.'

About this time, Lieutenant G. H. B. Coulson, K.O.S.B., adjutant of the 7th Mounted Infantry, who had been trekking the length and breadth of the Orange Free State, in a rearguard action some miles south of Bothaville rode towards the enemy in an attempt to rescue a dismounted N.C.O. whose horse had been shot. He took the man on to his own horse, but Boer fire brought them down after a short distance, and Coulson told the N.C.O. to get along as best he could with the wounded horse. Coulson remained behind to look out for himself. Another N.C.O. rode back for him and took him up, but the enemy picked off both men. Coulson's would-be rescuer, severely wounded, managed to reach the carts on foot, but Coulson, who had fallen off a little earlier, was not seen again. He was posthumously awarded the Victoria Cross, the first Borderer to win the supreme decoration.

In the Western Transvaal the 1st Battalion continued to hunt the enemy among the ravines, ditches and watercourses of the Magaliesbergen, the command of the column being taken over by Colonel Kekewich, the defender of Kimberley. In September 1901, the battalion moved to blockhouse lines west of Krugersdorp, and in May 1902, a number of Boer commando leaders came into the battalion's line on their way to discuss peace terms at Vereeniging. They were escorted as far as Krugersdorp.

'If you were a "keen soldier" everybody laughed at you,' wrote Graham. 'The great thing was to pretend you knew nothing and were completely bored by the war. One pretended not to know or care a thing about one's men, but in reality one did, and the men knew it. It was a queer form of affectation, put on, in a way, to hide one's real feelings. It used to puzzle colonials very much. As a matter of fact, if you had taken things seriously you could never have stuck out the three years of what we went through. So much of it seemed aimless, and the hardships were real and prolonged — far worse than the actual fighting.'

*   *   *   *   *

Second-Lieutenant Graham was transferred to the arduous life of the Mounted Infantry at the beginning of 1902, but was hurt in an accident with his horse and was sent to hospital, and home to the United Kingdom. He reached Southampton on 5 June 1902, to hear that peace had been proclaimed.

Corporal Turner had fallen sick shortly after Paardeberg; he went by sick convoy to Kimberley and thence back to hospital, and sailed for the United Kingdom in April 1900.

Chandos Leigh was promoted to Captain, fell sick in April 1901, and sailed for the United Kingdom in July of that year. 'As I steamed out of Cape Town and saw the gigantic Table Mountain gradually disappearing,' his diary ends, 'I hoped I might never see it again. But it doesn't take long for that sort of feeling to wear off. Now that I have been home some months I begin to hope that I shall go back some day, though I am in no great hurry, to the country where I spent the most thrilling, not the most comfortable, and perhaps, I'm not quite sure, the best part of my life.' Alas, a grimmer destiny awaited him.

Private Fessey was awarded the Distinguished Conduct Medal. Time-expired, he joined the Johannesburg Police in 1901 for a year. Then, his diary ends: 'I made up my mind to come back to merry old England the land of the best, for I have been in the lands of Egypt, India and South Africa serving under dear old Queen Victoria, also finished up under King Edward VII. Now all is over, back in England, settled down I expect for the future after serving fourteen long years for King and Country. I now have to work hard for my family and myself.' He fired, so he noted in his diary, 8,235 rounds of Maxim ammunition in South Africa.

Chapter 9

1914

The total deaths including those who died from disease, in 1st K.O.S.B. for the period of the South African War numbered 97.

'Father Christmas, please give me a drum and a box of soldiers,' a small boy was writing before the troops came home from South Africa. 'Please Father Christmas bring me down a stocking of sweets and will you please bring me a pencil case and a toy knife, and a large gun not a pop-gun.' In due course the boy went to Sandhurst, to follow his father's footsteps into the Regiment, and his first term's report dated December 1913, summed-up his characteristics: 'Keen, hardworking and nice mannered; plays games; promises well.' Within a year his parents received one of those terrible telegrams, O.H.M.S. War Office, that began to fall across homes throughout the land like the autumn leaves: '*Deeply regret to inform you that 2nd Lieut . . . K.O. Scottish Borderers has been killed no further details received Lord Kitchener expresses his sympathy.*'

6,859 Scottish Borderers of all ranks gave their lives in the Great War of 1914-18.

*   *   *   *   *

The decade which preceded 1914 must now be traced. The 1st Battalion disembarked from South Africa at Queenstown, County Cork, in February 1903, and went into quarters at Victoria Barracks, Belfast. There, the Duke of Connaught, commanding the forces in Ireland, distributed South African medals, and the Colours were received back from Berwick-upon-Tweed where they had been kept while the battalion was in South Africa. The words 'Paardeberg' and 'South Africa 1900-02' were emblazoned on them soon afterwards.

In 1903, the Regiment discarded the incongruous Prussian type of spiked helmet which had been the full dress headdress since shortly after the Franco-Prussian War. At home stations, this helmet was now superseded by the cocked Kilmarnock bonnet with blackcock feather, which survived as headdress for the drummers until recent times. The return from South Africa was also marked by the issue of Leslie tartan trews to the 1st Battalion.

Overleaf: The Royal Arms of 1714-1801 above the Barracks Gates at
Berwick-upon-Tweed. (Crown Copyright)
Above left: An officer of Leven's Regiment, 1689. *Above right:* A private
in marching order. (Both plates from watercolours by R. Simkin.)
Opposite page, top: Lady Lennox, wife of Lord George Lennox,
Colonel of the 25th Regiment, Minorca, c. 1770, from a painting
commissioned by Lord Lennox. *Right:* The Barracks at
Berwick-upon-Tweed, from a photograph taken when the
Lowland Bonnet was worn. (Picture Post)

Above: Part of Fort Dakka in 1880, during the Second Afghan War.
Below: The Master Tailor, 1st Battalion, Aldershot, 1897.

Below: With the Chitral relief force, 1895. 'E' Company (Captain C. L. Woollcombe), 2nd K.O.S.B.

Above: The 1st Battalion Colours, consecrated in 1856 and laid up in
St. Giles' Cathedral in 1919.
Opposite page, top: Militiamen of the 1890s. *Below:* Fashion plates from
the South African War, drawn by Captain Chandos Leigh, K.O.S.B.
Company, 7th Mounted Infantry Regiment.

on Plates.

Capetown   & the Veldt

Left: "The Piper of Loos" — Piper Daniel Laidlaw, V.C., from the painting by Caton Woodville, A.R.A. *Above:* The Watch on the Rhine, 1919.

Above: The Colonel-in-Chief takes the salute at t
Regiment's 250th anniversary parade, Edinburgh, 28 July 1939. (The Scotsman Publicatio
Limited)

Left: Waiting for D-Day, 6 June 1944; with the 1st Battalion somewhere in England. (Imperial War Museum)

Opposite page, top: "Th Green Hills of Tyrol"; t 1st Battalion Pipe Band i Korea.

Right: The Commanding Officer on his arrival in Korea, April 1951. Lieutenant-Colonel J. F. Macdonald with his Intel gence Officer, Lieutenan A. B. Cran, and escort. (Crown Copyright)

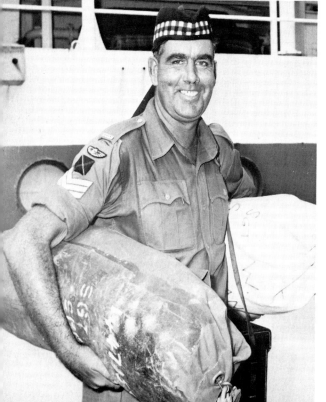

Above: The Commandin‹ Officer, Lieutenant-Colo› A. M. Thorburn, in Ade‹ 1962-64.
Left: Sergeant W. Speakman, V.C. (British Army Public Relations)
Opposite page, top: At h installation as 88th Governor of Edinburgh Castle, Lieutenant-Gener‹ Sir William Turner, K.B.E., C.B., D.S.O., Colonel of the Regiment 1962-70, is presented wit‹ the Keys of the Castle by ‹ son, Lieutenant W. S. Turner, 1st K.O.S.B. On the right is Sergeant W. Speakman, V.C. (The Scotsman Publications Limited)
Below: The Buccleuch Tartan. (The South Wal‹ Evening Post)

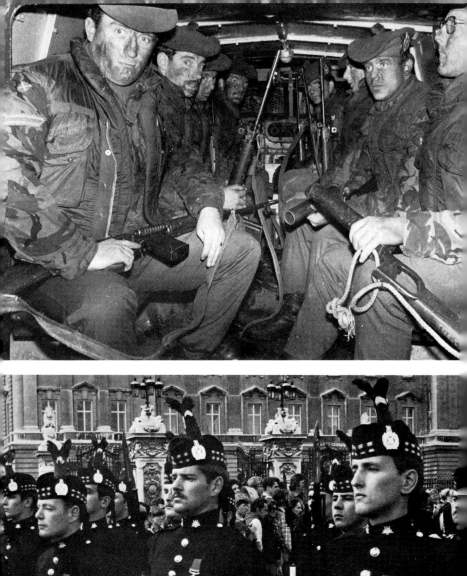

Opposite page, top: Northern Ireland. (The Scottish Daily Express)
Left: Changing Guard at Buckingham Palace, September 1977.
(Crown Copyright)
Above: Brigadier Frank Coutts, C.B.E., Colonel of the Regiment 1970-80.
Overleaf: The Colonel-in-Chief, H.R.H. Princess Alice, Duchess of
Gloucester. (The Scotsman Publications Limited)

In 1904, 1st K.O.S.B. moved to Newry, and in 1905 to Colchester. In 1906, the memorial on the North Bridge, Edinburgh, to the officers and men of the Regiment who had fallen in action in the six campaigns, Afghanistan, Egypt, Chin Lushai, Chitral, Tirah and South Africa, was unveiled, and the 1st Battalion provided the Guard of Honour shortly before proceeding overseas again, to Cairo. In 1908, 1st K.O.S.B. moved to Khartoum, and in 1911 embarked at Port Sudan for India.

The 2nd Battalion had moved from the Allahabad military district in India to Burma in 1903, to be stationed at Maymyo and Mandalay. In the 1905-06 trooping season the 2nd Battalion went to Aden, and in the following trooping season sailed for home and Maryhill Barracks, Glasgow. There was at this time surprise that for more than a quarter of a century the Regiment had never garrisoned Edinburgh Castle. A Press cartoon appeared, showing the Castle as lodgings, and a soldier in Glengarry, doublet and trews with a kitbag marked 'K.O.S.B.' who is saying:

'I was born here, Sir, and I would like to stay in my old home occasionally.'

The landlady, whose face is that of the War Minister, Mr. Haldane, retorts:

'You cannot get in; there is no reason, but you cannot, that is all.'

In 1910, the 2nd Battalion went to Belfast, to Palace Barracks, Holywood, and was on duty in Dublin in July 1911, for the state visit of King George V, when the King presented new Colours. The old Colours were ceremonially deposited in St Giles's Cathedral in 1912. After the ceremony the new Colours, which lasted the 2nd Battalion until its disbandment in 1947, were unfurled, as was the Regiment's privilege, and, escorted by the detachments of the Regiment with their bayonets fixed, were marched over the North Bridge, down Princes Street and up the Mound to the Castle.

In 1913, infantry battalions were reorganized into four companies instead of eight, and the two Colour-Sergeants, hitherto on the strength of a company, became Company Sergeant-Major and Quartermaster-Sergeant respectively. The Maxim gun, slightly modified, was now the Vickers gun. The S.M.L.E. rifle, whose handling at Mons, Le Cateau and Ypres was the greatest feat of British musketry, had been issued to home battalions in 1906. But the two great changes that marked the decade were the creation of the General Staff in 1907, and the Territorial Force in 1908, both carried through by Haldane.

The creation of the Territorial Force from the existing Volunteer Corps brought into existence, in 1908, the 4th (Border) and the 5th (Dumfries and Galloway) Battalions, The King's Own Scottish

Borderers. The 4th Battalion was drawn from 'the Borders', historically the region where there is a land border with England, but regimentally excluding a small part of Dumfriesshire, and was formed from the Roxburgh and Selkirk (Border Rifle) Volunteers and the Berwickshire Volunteers. It happened that Colonel Sir R. J. Waldie-Griffith, Bart., of Hendersyde Park, Kelso, who became Honorary Colonel of the 4th Battalion, wanted a Border design for the kilts of his pipers, and looked for something more distinctive than the universal check of the Border shepherds' plaid. Hence, by a happy inspiration there was invented the blue overcheck, and the design was named after the great House of Buccleuch. The 'Buccleuch' tartan was worn exclusively by the pipers of the 4th (Border) Battalion.[1]

The 5th Battalion was formed from the Dumfriesshire Volunteers and the Galloway (Kirkcudbright and Wigtown) Volunteers, in that wide area, with its own character and separated from the Borders by a divide of hills, that is almost twice the size of the Borders, although not of significantly higher population.

The Regiment, which was native to both regions, was in those days peculiarly a family one, in that, broadly, the officers came from the landowning class and the men from their tenantry. The 3rd (Militia) Battalion in particular was officered by the Border lairds, as it always had been. At the same time, the creation of the Territorial Force brought about a change in the rôle of the militia. The old militia was adapted to become the Special Reserve, and it was possible for an officer to obtain a regular commission via the Special Reserve. From his experience with the militiamen, he would be a degree more mature than the 'Gentleman Cadet' from Sandhurst. The oldest living member of the Officers' Club transferred from the Special Reserve in 1908.[2] He remembers playing cricket for the 2nd Battalion when it was at Glasgow, and recalls that after an away match another junior officer in the team remarked on the way home that he felt tired. At this one of his seniors, Major Bernie Sellar, who was to command 7th K.O.S.B. — later the 7th/8th — at Loos, on the Somme and at Arras, delivered himself of the following correction: 'In this Regiment an officer is never tired, he never feels the heat and he never feels the cold, and he never goes sick unless he is dying.'

In those days an officer's full dress uniform cost about £100, which can be imagined in modern terms. Officers did not expect to live on their pay; in Egypt and India most played polo, in Dublin

[1] It was also worn by the pipers of the 6th (Border) Battalion during the Second World War.

[2] Colonel C. S. Stirling Cookson, D.S.O., M.C., was commissioned into the 3rd Battalion in 1906.

they hunted with the Meath, and their style of living in general required the assistance of a private income.

In March 1914, in Dublin, the 2nd Battalion officers were rudely shaken. Domestic politics were dominated by Home Rule for Ireland. In Ulster a formidable partisan army, the Ulster Volunteers, was being raised and trained, and civil war seemed close. The dilemma in which the officers in the Irish Command were placed is well known under the name of the Curragh Incident. They were abruptly informed that in the event of operations against Ulster by the armed forces of the Crown, those officers whose homes were actually in Ulster would be allowed to apply for leave of absence, and that all other officers who objected to serving on the grounds of conscience would be dismissed the service. At the Curragh Camp near Dublin, Brigadier-General Hubert Gough, later commander of the Fifth Army in France, and most of his officers in the 3rd Cavalry Brigade, elected to be dismissed the service, and for a while it seemed likely that officers of all units at the camp would decide likewise.

At Royal Barracks, Dublin, Lieutenant-Colonel Stephenson, commanding 2nd K.O.S.B., assembled his officers on the morning of 20 March. The 2nd Battalion had had experience of aiding the Civil Power on the railway at Dundalk and in the Belfast shipyards when they were stationed at Holywood. In the shipyards, Protestants and Catholics had fought in the lunch breaks, but after a time a successful way of dealing with the fights was to turn on a piper to play. The crowds of workmen were well enough disposed towards the troops, and both sides would come and watch the piper.[3] However, in common with the other officers in the Irish Command, the ultimatum now fired at the K.O.S.B. officers aroused their bitter resentment. Their careers were in jeopardy. The blunt requirement put to them by the Commanding Officer, in duty bound, was that they state in the span of a few short hours whether they wished to resign their commissions.

At first, all except Colonel Stephenson himself, and the Second-in-Command and the Adjutant, chose to accept dismissal — which was what it amounted to, as they all knew. At the deadline that afternoon a majority complied with Colonel Stephenson's appeal to put the discipline of the Army above all else, but ten of their number still held out. The next evening, the G.O.C. 5th Division visited the barracks and by his sympathetic handling, and his reassurance that so far as he understood it the order to serve in Ulster had the King's sanction, he made a considerable impression. Indeed, it was the tact

---

[3] On 8 February 1912, in Belfast the 2nd Battalion was among 7,000 British troops who stood by when Winston Churchill came to the city to address Irish Nationalists in the Celtic Park Athletic Ground.

of the G.O.C. 5th Infantry Division, Major-General Sir Charles Fergusson, that largely prevented a state of mutiny.

The Curragh Incident was smoothed over, but the Army had been clumsily involved in politics, and the War Minister, and the C.I.G.S., Sir John French, and the Adjutant-General, all resigned.

The Irish Nationalists were, at the same time, forming their own volunteers, and a proclamation was issued forbidding the importation of arms into Ireland, although many thousands of rifles had already been taken into Ulster. The Nationalists began gun-running, and the 2nd Battalion diary records:

'On Sunday, 26 July 1914, when most officers were out of barracks, a telephone message arrived at about 3.30 p.m. to the effect that the National Volunteers were landing rifles near Howth and that 100 men of the battalion were to proceed by tram at once to the support of the Police, taking 100 rounds a man and using force if necessary.'

The party went out under command of an officer, and a scuffle with the Nationalists took place near Clontarf, 'in which two of the Borderers were hit by a revolver bullet and a few Volunteers were injured by bayonets'. A reinforcement of a further sixty men under one of the company commanders arrived, and at about 5.30 p.m. the whole party was ordered to return to Royal Barracks. 'The column was followed by a savage mob which pelted the soldiers with stones, inflicting severe injuries on many.'

In Sackville Street the Second-in-Command, 2nd K.O.S.B., arrived to take charge. The stone throwing continued and the crowd became still more threatening. The 2 i/c prepared to address the crowd and warn them that he would have to fire. 'If you don't disperse I shall have to order the troops to fire,' he called loudly. Unhappily:

'A shot was fired by one of our men, followed by several others. One woman[1] and two men were killed, and several were wounded. An inquest which lasted for several days was held in Dublin, and the battalion was defended by King's Counsel. The feeling against us in Dublin was very bitter and the battalion was strictly confined to their barracks.'

The verdict of the Court was that the circumstances did not warrant the use of fire . . . Then all was swept aside. The next entry in the diary of 2nd Btn. read: '*4th August 1914*. The order to *mobilize* was received.'

*   *   *   *   *

The outbreak of the Great War was recorded in the diary of the 1st

---

[1] Mrs Duffy, a name long remembered by the K.O.S.B.

Battalion, who were in Lucknow, without superfluous words. In the margin is the word 'War,' and the entry reads:

'War was declared in Europe between:

Austria and Serbia	28.7.14.
Russia and Austria	6.8.14.
Germany and Russia	1.8.14.
France and Germany	3.8.14.
United Kingdom and Germany	4.8.14.
Serbia and Germany	7.8.14.
Belgium and Germany	4.8.14.
United Kingdom and Austria	12.8.14.
Montenegro and Austria	8.8.14.'

The shattering impact of 1914, when none could foresee the ghastliness to come, when young men of spirit strove to reach the front before they missed out on the action, as they fondly supposed, was very different from the sombre mood in which the nation, already shrouded in a black-out and with conscription belatedly re-introduced, slid into war again in 1939. To those who lived through both, 1914 was when the old order changed, and it is to be marvelled at that the flower of the nation's manhood began its march to the trenches under an entirely voluntary system. Compulsory military service was not enacted by Parliament until the eve of the Somme.

The K.O.S.B. in the Great War tells a story of constant batches of men from Selkirk entering the recruiting office at Galashiels, not all to join the K.O.S.B., for many went off into Highland regiments, but all to enlist. Towards the end of August 1914, as yet another group arrived from Selkirk the recruiting sergeant was moved to say:

'I'm wonderin' if there's ony folk left in Selkirk at a'.'

'Aye, there are a few, but they're comin' on wi' the next train,' he was told.

And so, as the floodgates opened, the Regiment itself entered a new phase in its history, the world wars, when thousands who would not otherwise have had cause to do so became serving Borderers. The Regimental circle was immeasurably widened and the Regiment truly became a household name, upheld by many memories.

When 2nd K.O.S.B. in the 5th Infantry Division embarked for France with the B.E.F., the battalion had been brought up to war strength by its reservists and fully mobilized in Dublin in the space of four days as a result of the meticulous contingency planning — it was the first time in a hundred years, the Crimea apart, that a British army had taken the field against a Continental enemy. From barricaded positions and towpath entrenchments just across the Belgian frontier, at Lock 4 on the Mons-Condé Canal, a few miles west of Mons at the village of Les Herbières, on Sunday, 23 August

1914, the 2nd Battalion first sighted that enemy. At about 1 p.m. on that day of roasting sunshine, the enemy were seen in skirmishing order across the marshy meadows. As they opened fire at the K.O.S.B. positions, a soldier in one of B Company's platoons spontaneously said to his platoon officer, 'Don't worry. I'll look after you.' The officer was a strongly-built, good-looking young man who hardly looked as though he needed anyone to look after him, but a new fraternity had come into being in that momentous hour.

That evening, orders were issued for the first of those punishing marches that were the Retreat from Mons. Among those already missing when the first midnight march was made was Major Chandos Leigh, late Mounted Infantry, South Africa, whose company had defended the road bridge at Lock 4. Leigh died of wounds. At Le Cateau, three days later, shelling from the north clawed up the earth; a British battery close to the K.O.S.B. was blown to pieces, and masses of the enemy could be seen, coming on in column across the slopes. During the next stage of the withdrawal there was a good deal of confusion as many units had become intermixed. An unknown officer accosted the same K.O.S.B. subaltern of 'B' Company, whose platoon had lost contact with the company: 'What are you going back for? — it's all over — we'll get out of it somehow.' But the young Borderer kept on, undeterred, to regain contact with the rest of his company. His name was E. G. Miles, better known to Borderers as 'Tiger' Miles, who became Colonel of the Regiment just thirty years later.[5] Back they marched, and back, across the Somme, the Aisne, the Marne, to an area a day's march south-east of Paris. Within twenty-four hours they were ordered to turn round and advance again, for which the explanation is to be found in 'the miracle of the Marne'.

*   *   *   *   *

The battles of the First World War in which the Regiment fought are named in Appendix I, and cover all the great campaigns waged by British forces.

2nd K.O.S.B. fought on the Western Front throughout the war except for a period of four months, after the Italian disaster at

[5] Major-General E. G. Miles, C.B., D.S.O., M.C., commanded 126th Infantry Brigade in the retreat to Dunkirk, and commanded 56th Division, Eighth Army in Tunisia in 1943, where he was wounded. In two world wars he was six times Mentioned in Dispatches. He died in his 87th year, shortly before this book was completed.

Caporetto in November 1917, when their division, the 5th Division, was sent to the Piave front in Italy. The German offensive of March 1918 brought them back to France.

The 1st Battalion was brought home from India at the end of 1914. Turkey was now allied with the Central Powers, and the 1st Battalion joined the 29th Division, the last of the old pre-1914 army, secretly assembling in England for the forcing of the Dardanelles. They embarked for Alexandria even as the naval action to force the narrows was broken-off, and at 4.45 a.m. on 25 April 1915, ever since commemorated by the Regiment as Gallipoli Day, 1st K.O.S.B. landed from boats towed by trawlers on 'Y' Beach, on the Aegean coast at the tip of the Gallipoli peninsula: 'Twenty-eight officers and more than 900 other ranks, true to type and at unity among themselves, one of the few remaining specimens of a British Regular Infantry Battalion'.[6] They scaled cliffs, to find the peninsula a fortress, and after they had held an impossible position for some thirty hours at a cost of 300 casualties the order came to re-embark. They were landed again farther along, and later at Suvla Bay. The rate of human wastage in the 29th Division, including an appalling toll of sickness, was reckoned at 100 per cent every two months, and eventually, 1st K.O.S.B. were among the rearguard at the final evacuation of Cape Helles in January 1916. The battalion went to France in March 1916, and fought on the Western Front throughout the rest of the war.

The 4th (Border) and 5th (Dumfries and Galloway) Battalions were both mobilized in August 1914, in the Lowland Division, Territorial Force, which in May 1915 was given its famous number, the 52nd. This division also sailed for Gallipoli. Landing in June 1915, the remains of 4th and 5th K.O.S.B. were taken off Cape Helles seven months later, and thereafter fought in the Egyptian Expeditionary Force, in the campaign in Sinai and Palestine which led to the collapse of the Ottoman Empire. With the 52nd (Lowland) Division they played a great part in the operations that included the capture of Jerusalem. Finally, in April 1918, they were transferred to France.

The recruitment of the nation in the Great War was complicated in its details, but broadly the picture was as follows. The Territorial Force as created by Haldane was for home defence, there was no legal obligation to serve overseas, although when the time came the great majority volunteered to do so. Reserve Territorial battalions were formed under existing provisions for the expansion of the Territorial Force, and in the early months of the war the flood of

---

[6] *The K.O.S.B. in the Great War.*

recruits to the K.O.S.B. resulted in both the 4th and 5th Battalions triplicating themselves, and there were formed the 2/4th and 3/4th K.O.S.B., and the 2/5th and 3/5th K.O.S.B., at Galashiels and Dumfries. These four T.F. reserve battalions were amalgamated into two battalions in 1915. They were home battalions, sending drafts to the overseas battalions, and they also contained those who were unfit for active service.

Kitchener, however, had always been sceptical of the Territorial Force. That remarkable figure, whose great name was required at the War Office in 1914 when he became Secretary of State and the nation's war lord, directed the main recruiting impetus into channels of his own. Of the two and a half million recruits he brought forth, the greater part were not Territorials, but the New Armies which bore the hallmark 'K'. Among them were the 6th, 7th and 8th Battalions of the K.O.S.B., which were known as the service battalions.

To 6th K.O.S.B. fell the distinction of forming part of K(1), 'The First Hundred Thousand':

> 'And now today has come along.
> With rifle, haversack, and pack,
> We're off, a hundred thousand strong.
> And — some of us will not come back.'

7th K.O.S.B. and 8th K.O.S.B. quickly followed in K(2), and all three battalions, the 6th Battalion in the 9th (Scottish) Division, the 7th and 8th Battalions in the 15th (Scottish) Division, went over their parapets at Loos on 25 September 1915, at a cost in casualties which the Regiment had not known before.

The former militia battalions were not allowed overseas, and in consequence 3rd K.O.S.B. became a clearing-house of drafts for the 1st and 2nd Battalions.

With the forming of a 9th Battalion early in 1915 when 8th K.O.S.B. were complete, the Regiment had expanded to no less than thirteen battalions. 9th K.O.S.B. did not go overseas, but remained a reserve battalion, sending drafts particularly to the service battalions. Nevertheless, it was found impossible to maintain the 7th and 8th Battalions at their original strength, and shortly before the Somme they were amalgamated into 7th/8th K.O.S.B., and fought as such on the Western Front until the Armistice. As the Territorial reserve battalions had been amalgamated, the Regiment now totalled ten battalions.

Two awards of the Victoria Cross were made to men of the 1st Battalion for their exploits on the same day, 16 August 1917, at Third Ypres, that dreadful campaign known as 'Passchendaele'. One award was to Company Sergeant-Major J. Skinner, a

Glaswegian of extraordinary bravery who had won the D.C.M. at La Bassée with the 2nd Battalion in 1914. Collecting a party of six men he cleared three blockhouses, one of them single-handed, taking sixty prisoners, three machine-guns and two mortars. He survived, only to be killed by a sniper in March 1918. During his career he had been wounded eight times, and he was regarded as one of the most remarkable men in the British Army. Six V.C. pall-bearers attended his burial.

The other award was to Company Quartermaster-Sergeant W. Grimbaldeston, from Blackburn, Lancashire, who directed the fire of a party of rifle grenadiers at another blockhouse, stalked it, gained the entrance and with bombs compelled its surrender, taking thirty-six prisoners, six machine-guns and a mortar. Grimbaldeston survived the war.

A third V.C. was won by Sergeant McGuffie from Wigtown, of the 5th Battalion. On 29 September 1918, he took command of his platoon at 'Piccadilly Farm' near Ypres, in the attack on Wytschaete Ridge, stormed a number of dugouts, disarmed single-handed a German party escorting British prisoners from another regiment, and later in the day captured a blockhouse by firing rifle grenades through the loopholes. He was killed a few days later without knowing that a V.C. was his.

The fourth Borderer to win the V.C. during the Great War has become a legend: the Piper of Loos. He was Piper Daniel Laidlaw of 7th K.O.S.B., a reservist, in his thirty-ninth year, who came from Berwickshire. Rain, followed by a ground mist, an intense bombardment of high explosive, and forty minutes of gas and smoke, preceded the hour of 6.30 a.m. when the 7th Battalion with fixed bayonets, half-suffocated by their smoke helmets, which they tore off only to court death from gas, clambered over the parapet from the slippery, crowded fire trench on 25 September 1915. They squelched through the gaps in the wire and fanned out into no man's land. As they went heavily over the top their impetus nearly failed, but a thin, unmistakable sound rallied them as Piper Laidlaw coolly swaggered up and down the parapet playing *Blue Bonnets over the Border*. As Laidlaw said afterwards, the advance was sounded and he got over the parapet with Lieutenant Young and set the pipes going. In the course of the attack Laidlaw was wounded in the leg by shrapnel, but he hobbled along after the laddies and changed the tune to *The Standard on the Braes o' Mar*.

There was another piper at Loos, Pipe Major Robert MacKenzie of the 6th Battalion. Incredibly, at over sixty years of age, he played the 6th Battalion over the parapet in the same attack, until he was shot in both legs. 'He was the finest and grandest old man in the Regiment,' it was written of him. He died of his wounds, without a decoration.

*   *   *   *   *

On 13 December 1918, at the same hour, the 1st and 6th Battalions marched behind their pipe bands over the Hohenzollern Bridge and the Mulheim Boat Bridge respectively, across the Rhine at Cologne. They were part of the Army of Occupation.

'Hard, weather-beaten, somewhat dour-looking Borderers, with their waterproof shirts hanging dripping over their shoulders',[7] they tramped across in pouring rain.

There remains the poignant story of the Mons Tablecloth. At Lock 4 on the Mons-Condé Canal, on Saturday, 22 August 1914, the day before 2nd K.O.S.B. sighted the enemy approaching across the meadows and the battle began, the officer commanding B Company, Major E. S. D'Ewes Coke, was ordered to put a little house on the far bank of the canal into a state of defence. A strange thing to have to do, it seemed, on that peaceful day. Trees had to be cut down for barricades, loopholes made in the cottage walls, and its windows sandbagged. In the cottage were a Belgian couple and their daughter, but despite what was being done to their homes they insisted on being hospitable, providing omelettes and coffee for the K.O.S.B. officers and numerous French or Belgian liaison officers and attachés. Upon the table was a plain tablecloth, and the Belgian lady had the idea that everyone should sign it, as a souvenir. This they all did, as they left to go to their posts. Altogether more than sixty people signed the tablecloth. At dusk next day, one of the K.O.S.B. officers brought out the two ladies and the man; their cottage had already been hit by several shells.

At Le Cateau, Lieutenant-Colonel Stephenson and his Second-in-Command were casualties, and Coke took command of 2nd K.O.S.B. and commanded the battalion until 1916. In November 1918, five days after the Armistice on the Western Front, he found himself, now a Brigadier-General, near Mons again, and only seven miles from Lock 4. So he borrowed a motor car to revisit the scene, making his way with difficulty through much destruction. Alas, the little house was barely a shell, unrecognizable; but as he was wandering into the back garden, which he felt sure he remembered, he heard voices, and the two Belgian women of 1914 appeared from the cellar. In a moment he was having coffee with them over a stove, and they produced the very tablecloth. All the signatures had

---

[7] *The K.O.S.B. in the Great War.* In January 1919, the 5th Battalion also joined the Army of Occupation.

been embroidered. Then they asked Brigadier-General Coke to sign again; accordingly his name appears twice on the tablecloth, which eventually hung framed in the Officers' Mess of the 2nd Battalion.

Today it is an honoured relic in the Regimental Museum.

Chapter 10

THE REGIMENT: 1919-39

At Aldershot at the end of June 1919, a ceremony took place, symbolic of the passing of time. The 1st Battalion, having returned from Germany, paraded in farewell to its old Colours which had been consecrated more than sixty years before in 1856. One of the few sets of Colours carried in the Afghan War of 1878-80, they were among the last in the army to have been taken on active service.[1] Honourably tattered, and carried by two recipients of the Military Cross, Lieutenants Thursby-Pelham and Bullen-Smith, they were deposited in St Giles's Cathedral, Edinburgh, at a memorial service for the Regiment on 3 July. Almost at once, a 1st Battalion Colour party with new Colours left for Paris and, with a Colour party from 5th K.O.S.B., took part in the great 1919 Victory March. At the London Victory March which followed, Lieutenant-Colonel A. J. Welch, commanding 1st K.O.S.B., was in charge of the Colours of the British Army. Meanwhile, demobilization proceeded briskly. The service battalions passed away, and the Territorial Force battalions, likewise, were demobilized. The last K.O.S.B. unit to be withdrawn from the Continent was the 5th Battalion in October 1919. The 2nd Battalion left Belgium, and absorbed the 3rd Battalion at Dunfermline.

The active days of 3rd K.O.S.B. were now over, and although the battalion had its place on paper, and in 1922 the old title of Militia was restored, it was never to be re-embodied. For some years it was represented in the Army List by the solitary name of its Honorary Colonel, Colonel Archibald Hume. The 4th and 5th Battalions, on the other hand, were re-formed, 4th K.O.S.B. by Lieutenant-Colonel E. D. Jackson, D.S.O., and 5th K.O.S.B. by Lieutenant-Colonel W. J. Millar, D.S.O. Colonel Millar had served in every rank since he had joined the old Dumfries Volunteers as a bugler. In 1922, the Territorial Force was renamed the Territorial Army, and its members undertook to serve overseas if necessary.

The man who soldiered-on after the Great War, in a regular battalion, or who was a recruit from the 'land fit for heroes', was

[1] The last occasion when a British regiment carried its Colours in action was at Laing's Nek, South Africa, 28 January 1881. (*National Army Museum*)

tough. He was not conspicuous for his literacy, and basically if he could drill and shoot he fulfilled his function. Unless he was one of the nucleus who followed a family tradition of service in the army and in the Regiment, it could be said that he was, as likely as not, in the ranks for the square meals. Generally there were few men up for misdemeanours, for the N.C.O.s had their own way of settling matters, and it is fair to say that, as always, the Borderers made a tough regiment, and a good one. As the post-war years passed, The King's Own Scottish Borderers' Association[2] persevered at what was, alas, an uphill struggle to aid the Regiment's ex-soldiers who were in distress, finding jobs, assisting emigration, as well as providing financial relief from The King's Own Scottish Borderers War Memorial Fund. For through all those domestically black years, when men with war medals, many of them disabled, begged in the streets of our cities for coppers, the Regiment endeavoured to care for its discharged soldiers. They were not dispensed with. For 'Once a Borderer always a Borderer' did carry meaning. Proud of its war record, conscious of its past, the Regiment also did everything it could to foster its *esprit de corps*. The quality of its recreational and sports facilities was a point of honour, and within the framework of the conventions, every officer was expected to be the friend of every soldier.

In 1926, *The Borderers' Chronicle*, after two false starts — one in India in 1871, and one in 1893 — was brought forth again. This time it came to stay, and it provides a distinct social commentary on the soldier's life between the World Wars; albeit inserted into a great deal of reportage on sporting activities. The issue of June 1926, carried an article by the wife of the outgoing Commanding Officer of the 2nd Battalion, then in Cairo. This lady had calculated, on the basis of a speech in the House of Commons, that more than half the population of Scotland had never known what it was like to have a home of three rooms, or a hot water supply, or baths or lavatories, and she compared this with the comforts enjoyed by the married soldiers' families, the easy shopping provided by the N.A.A.F.I., the medical attention, the open-air lives of the soldiers' children, the diversions and the 'socials'.

The *Chronicle* gave space in its obituaries to the deaths of stalwart old Borderers of all ranks; it chronicled a social calendar punctuated by officers' weddings; and invariably it reflected the emphasis on sport. The sporting activity of the 2nd Battalion in particular was immense. The battalion notes from India in December 1931, reported pigeon racing, golf, hunting, horse racing — Regimental Cup and Subalterns' Cup — football and boxing. It

[2] Constituted in 1898.

even included an article on cheetah hunting, contributed by Lieutenant C. W. P. Richardson. As always in India, officers played polo and went pig-sticking. The 1st Battalion, on the other hand, had the K.O.S.B. Beagles, started and hunted by Captain H. P. Steed, at Fort George. Nor was the 1st Battalion outdone in the matter of other sports. It won the Scottish Command Athletics Cup three years in succession, cricket cup two years in succession, the Scottish Command boxing tournament, the Aldershot Command Athletics Cup and, in 1929, the Army Football Cup.

During the years of the depression, *The Borderers' Chronicle* reflected concern for the soldier's re-employment in civilian life after he had served his time with the Colours, and for his vocational training. The wretched state of the labour market was reiterated. There was an instance in 1930 of 450 applicants for the post of night-watchman. Soldiers, and married couples, were encouraged to enter domestic service, 'private service' as it was called, the one area of employment in which demand exceeded supply. An article in 1932 described the state of the labour market as 'deplorable' and urged on soldiers the merits of obtaining a 1st Class certificate of education. Re-employment was a constant theme, and as late as 1938 an ex-Borderer wrote to *The Chronicle* on the subject:

'I would like to end by requesting all men to consider very carefully before going on the Reserve, and at least make sure they have a job, as I was under that impression myself as a bus driver, but like so many of these jobs it was only casual employment.'

As the international scene darkened, a new note sounded in *The Borderers' Chronicle*. There was a drive for recruits, although at first this too, was uphill work. It has to be remembered that the Border country was not a populous region; the total population of the whole Regimental area was less than 250,000, and although, in the light of this, the support for the Territorial Army battalions was all the more remarkable, it was inevitable that there was a dependence on men enlisting on regular engagements from further afield. In 1938, it was felt that the Regiment should be able to raise 50 per cent of the numbers required from its own area, and in the winter of 1938-39 there was an appeal to all serving soldiers in the Regiment to try and secure at least one new recruit each.

*   *   *   *   *

The Regiment's movements in the years between the wars should here be recorded. From Aldershot, in 1919, the 1st Battalion returned to India to resume the tour which had been interrupted in

1914. It was stationed at Bombay during and after the industrial strikes that disturbed the city, then went to Agra. The 1st Battalion's new Colours, which had been prepared as long ago as 1911 and had been held in a kind of abeyance until the 1919 victory marches, were formally presented by H.R.H. The Duke of Connaught at Agra in 1921. Much work had fallen on the Colonel of the Regiment in arriving at the Regiment's many Battle Honours in the Great War, for the King's approval, taking into account all battalions, and the list was not finally decided with the War Office until 1924. By 1925, proposals for the design and wording of the Regimental bay in the Scottish National War Memorial were being discussed.

In 1922, the 1st Battalion had moved to Egypt, and in September of that year embarked for Canakkale (Chanak) in Asiatic Turkey, just across the Dardanelles from the scene of their former deeds at Gallipoli, on what was deemed to be active service. This arose from the involvement of Britain, France and Italy in the Graeco-Turkish war of 1920-22, which led to the establishment of modern Turkey under Ataturk. A peace treaty had not been concluded with Turkey by the Western Powers, but France and Italy withdrew, and Britain was left to support the Greek cause. The Greeks, however, were thrown into the sea at Smyrna (Izmir) in September 1922, the Sultanate was swept away, and the resumption of war between Britain and Turkey was narrowly averted.

The Turks accepted international control of the Straits, a peace conference opened in Switzerland, and in August 1923, the British forces in Turkey were stood down. The 1st Battalion came home to Redford Barracks, Edinburgh, and the Lord Provost and Magistrates entertained the officers to luncheon at the City Chambers. The next day, all ranks were entertained to a luncheon at the Forrest Road drill hall, which was followed by a march through the city with Colours flying and bayonets fixed. Apart from when the depot companies were stationed at the Castle ninety-odd years before, it was the first time the Regiment had been stationed in the city of its origin since Lord Lennox's day; to be precise, one hundred and forty-one years before.

The 1st Battalion moved to the Aldershot Command in 1925, then back to Scotland to Fort George. At that time, the battalion's transport was still horsed, but during the early 1930s, mechanization was slowly introduced. From Fort George the battalion went to Catterick Camp, where troops were held in readiness for the emergencies of the time, such as the Saar Plebiscite, and in 1935 1st K.O.S.B. were among three battalions sent to reinforce Malta, as a result of the tension with Italy when Mussolini invaded Abyssinia.

The battalion diary records that in 1929 'the Service Dress jackets of the Other Ranks of the Battalion were rounded at their own expense'. On 1 October 1931: 'Owing to the state of the National Finances certain reductions not exceeding 10% in the pay of all personnel who joined previous to 1925 were made.'

The soldier's round was diversified by Tattoos, Guards of Honour, Armistice Days, Gallipoli Days, and the occasional Royal event. Then, in 1936, the 1st Btn. was sent to Palestine, administered under the British Mandate, to assist in quelling an Arab uprising. Shortage of manpower was always a problem when the Home battalion had to be sent on active service abroad, a shortage that was felt keenly during the tour in Malta, and the battalion could not have operated in Palestine without the call-up of its Reservists. The battalion went to the Nazareth area, where its duties included the protection of the Iranian Petroleum Company's pipeline and a high-tension cable, escorts for civilian and military vehicles, the protection of Jewish settlements, and searches and punitive measures against Arab villages. On one occasion Bedouin tents were searched. 'A rifle was found and one arrest made.' Another time C Company played the Arab village of Sulam at football, drawing, two goals all. 'The strength of the opposition varied between eleven and twenty-two players throughout the game.'

*   *   *   *   *

The 2nd Battalion had moved from Dunfermline to Devonport in 1919, and in January 1921, was sent to Ireland, to Bantry Bay, County Cork, where it remained for the rest of that year. Those were the troublous days of what amounted to civil war in Ireland, days of the I.R.A. and the 'Black and Tans', that preceded the birth of the Irish Free State in 1922. On 14 June 1921, three private soldiers of the 2nd Battalion, on their way to the local post office to buy stamps, were 'murdered by rebels'. When the battalion left Ireland in February 1922, it was clear, however, from the tone of their Brigade Commandant's very high commendation of their flying columns, that the Borderers had not exactly turned the other cheek. His remarks included the comment: 'Your duties have been heavy and often monstrous.'

Returning to Devonport, the 2nd Battalion went to Egypt in 1923. At sport it won the 'Best all round Unit' Challenge Cup, and the Gordon Polo Cup for dismounted units. In 1926 the 2nd Battalion sailed for Hong Kong.

The days with the Regiment in Hong Kong would always be remembered by those who were out there during those four years, during which time the sociability of the Officers' Mess became a feature of the Colony's British community. The Regiment's old links with the sea were brought to mind by much close contact with the Royal Navy, and particularly by the visit to Hong Kong of the new County Class cruiser, *Berwick*. The Regiment was presented with a fine model of the ship, which reposes to this day in the Mess at R.H.Q., Berwick-upon-Tweed. In the Imperial rôle, an outstanding aspect of life was the piracy guards which had to be placed on all British ships plying in Chinese waters. Small detachments of 2nd K.O.S.B., an officer with an N.C.O. and fourteen men, sailed the seas on these guards from Shanghai to Singapore. Another commitment was to provide a detachment at Canton — a rifle company and a machine-gun platoon — to protect Shameen Island, a tiny Anglo-French outpost in the Pearl River. Across a narrow creek was Canton city, then in the grip of the civil war which occupied the Chinese for so many years.

In 1930 the 2nd Battalion embarked for India, where its prime task was the maintenance of internal security; the protection of the administrators who were scattered all over the country, the prevention of disorder and fighting between Hindu and Muslim, and the security of the roads and railways. The 2nd Battalion was stationed at Poona, and memorable were the Sholapur flag marches of 1931, through the district of that name, lying towards Hyderabad. In 1934, the battalion moved to Lucknow, and later to Calcutta.

The formal ending of the 3rd (Militia) Battalion in 1929 should also be recorded. Their former Colours, dating from the time when they were The Scottish Borderers Militia, which had been the gift of the ladies of the Border counties in 1877, were aptly handed over to the kirk session and congregation of Greyfriars Church, Dumfries, where the historian and chaplain of the Scottish Borderers Militia had been the incumbent for thirty-six years.[3] Indeed, the title had been The Dumfriesshire Militia until 1864, and the militia battalion received the Freedom of Dumfries after the South African War. The Colour party of 1929, wearing K.O.S.B. service dress, was an unusual one, the Colours being carried by two elderly retired officers. The King's Colour was carried by Lieutenant-Colonel John M'Kie, C.B.E., D.S.O., who had received the same Colour on bended knee when it was presented by the Countess of Dalkeith fifty-two years before. The battalion Colour was carried by Major Sir James Wilkie-Dalyell. Three warrant officers formed the escort.

*   *   *   *   *

'Animated by that vigorous esprit de corps which has always

[3] The Revd. R. W. Weir, D.D.

existed throughout the Regiment, all ranks will always be ready to seize every opportunity to add to the great record of the Regiment to which they have the honour to belong.'

Standing Orders of The King's Own Scottish Borderers (*1st Battalion*), issued in 1930, made crisp reading. Standing Orders were only formulated in regiments from time to time. They were the written constitution so to speak, and in the K.O.S.B. there have been none since those of 1930. They merit some attention, although they can be no more than selectively indicated here:

The authority of the Commanding Officer was paramount, whether on parade or elsewhere. His disposal of all questions was final.

The Adjutant would set an example to all ranks of smartness and strict attention to duty. He would treat all matters outside routine as strictly confidential until — somewhat ominously — 'it becomes his duty to make them known to those concerned.'

Under normal circumstances, no one except the Commanding Officer or the Adjutant would interfere with the Regimental Sergeant-Major in the course of his duty.

All officers would have in their possession the issued *Short History* of the Regiment and *The K.O.S.B. in the Great War.*

The senior officer on parade and at all other times and places was responsible that no impropriety or ungentlemanly behaviour on the part of any officer passed unnoticed by him, and that immediate steps were taken by him to check or correct any such conduct.

Officers would not permit discussion by themselves or others of their Commanding Officer's acts or policy. They were called upon by every high sense of duty to prevent matters of purely regimental concern becoming subject for general gossip. The interest of the Regiment should ever be first with an officer.

The Officers' Mess should approximate as nearly as circumstances permit to the home of a private family. It was also the repository of the fine traditions and history of the Regiment and the shrine of its Colours.

The Standing Orders laid down without verbiage all basic matters of routine and administration, and the duties of all ranks. It was every man's bounden duty to keep himself fit. Obscene and foul language was forbidden and if used in the presence of a senior was insubordinate.

The orders concerning marriage were in those days stringent. Soldiers before getting married would obtain the Commanding Officer's approval. This would normally be given provided the man was twenty-six years old and he and his intended wife were of good character. He was then placed on the married quarters roll. Married soldiers were literally i/c their families; the soldier was responsible for the conduct of his wife and children, for the cleanliness of their quarters, and for the cleanliness and tidy dress of his children. He was responsible for his children's school attendance. 'Married women' were forbidden to approach officers directly, except for the Quartermaster, but they could place any complaint or difficulty before the Commanding Officer when he inspected married quarters, and they were encouraged to ask for the help or advice of the officers' wives at all times.

Under the heading of *Soldiers in General* was the dictum: 'Obedience is the first duty of a soldier'.

'All Borderers will remember their oath of allegiance and feel it is their privilege to maintain the good name of the Regiment by their behaviour, courage and self-respect at all times, more especially when in the presence of outsiders, or of the enemy.'

Despite the uncompromising terms in which Standing Orders were set out, those whose memories of the Regiment go back to before the Second World War recall a very happy family Regiment. There was always the continuity of family traditions in its ranks, as there is today, and a happy relationship between Officers' and Sergeants' Messes. It was not the Regiment's policy to advertise itself so there was no particular interest in fostering a public image. Since the Great War, the Staff College had become the recognized gateway to high rank, but officers in the Regiment were not encouraged to take Staff appointments — indeed, in 1939 only three on the Regimental list had attended the Staff College. It was as though an officer joined the Regiment rather than the Army.[4] On the other hand, secondment to Colonial Forces was very much encouraged, and in the 1930s the Regiment had many officers on such secondments, particularly in Africa.

An officer was expected to conform with the Regiment's interests, socially and in the sporting sphere, and generally to 'toe the line'. Otherwise, the attitude would be: 'We're sorry you are not happy with the Regiment.' The Regiment was the home, in which, in those days, he spent anything up to twelve or fourteen years as a subaltern, and he was not entitled to a marriage allowance under the age of thirty. He was definitely discouraged from marrying below that age, and had he been so bold as to marry in his mid-twenties on his own resources, he would probably have been invited to leave.

It had always been normal for drafts, and postings of officers, to pass between the two regular battalions, but a former rivalry

---

[4] W. A. H. Maxwell, of that generation, who retired in 1950 as Lieutenant-Colonel, was awarded the Sword of Honour and the Sword for Drill at Sandhurst in 1921, the first and only time both swords were won by the same cadet.

between the two was almost dead by 1930, and had probably entirely disappeared by 1939. The 2nd Battalion in Hong Kong and India had the more boisterous *esprit de corps* and was considered the harder to command. The 1st Battalion is said to have been very 'correct'. Regimental Sergeant-Majors long remembered were R.S.M. MacLennan[5] of the 1st Battalion, known as 'The Duke', one of the select band of K.O.S.B. Warrant Officers who won the Military Cross during the Great War, and R.S.M. Parkinson of the 2nd Battalion, whose family had totalled one hundred years of service in the Regiment.

The 1st Battalion returned from Palestine to Catterick Camp at Christmas 1936, and in 1937 carried out a Border Recruiting March through the Regimental District, as a result of which the number of men in its ranks who came from Scotland increased to 90 per cent. At the end of 1937, the 1st Battalion went to Portsmouth, to form part of the 9th Infantry Brigade[6] commanded by Brigadier B. L. Montgomery, D.S.O. In 1938, the year of Munich, the Bren gun came into service with British infantry. In India, the 2nd Battalion moved to Jubbulpore, where the spectre of war again in Europe began to shape their training programmes. 1938 was also the year when the Regimental Council was instituted.

On Hitler's occupation of Prague in March 1939, British re-armament measures included the intention to double the Territorial Army. In the Regimental heartland the response was now great. Again, 6th and 7th Battalions were formed; but this time they were called 6th (Border) and 7th (Galloway) Battalions, T.A., born out of the 4th and 5th Battalions respectively. Their training and administration caused some very hectic weekends in that summer of 1939, particularly for the hard-worked company commanders who had to organize their training programmes and tactical exercises in their spare time while attending to their professions and businesses. The two Regular officers, seconded from the 1st Battalion, who, as adjutants, piloted the 4th and 5th Battalions through this period, were Captains Hankey and Batchelor, better known as Jack Hankey and 'Father' Batchelor. Annual camp that year was a memorable one, held at Dreghorn Camp, Edinburgh, and attended by all K.O.S.B. Territorials, to coincide with the Regiment's 250th anniversary celebrations. The 5th Battalion had already split into two. The 4th Battalion had not yet done so and attended the camp as one unit over 1,200 strong,

---

[5] He was Depot R.S.M. in 1939.

[6] 9th Brigade, in the 3rd Infantry Division, consisted of 1st Lincolns, 1st K.O.S.B. and 2nd Royal Ulster Rifles, and remained unchanged until 1946. It became known as 'The Three Kingdoms Brigade'.

but marched as two battalions in the 250th anniversary parade. The dress for this parade was service dress with trews, but a detachment of 1939 militiamen were present wearing the new battle dress, the first time battle dress was worn in the Regiment on a ceremonial parade. The salute was taken by the Colonel-in-Chief.

The Regiment had been signally honoured in 1937 when King George VI, on the occasion of his coronation, appointed H.R.H. The Duchess of Gloucester to be Colonel-in-Chief, The King's Own Scottish Borderers. In the Regiment's history there has been no more felicitous event than this. A Border woman, formerly Lady Alice Montagu-Douglas-Scott, she was a sister of the 8th Duke of Buccleuch, who had commanded the 4th (Border) Battalion and was now its Honorary Colonel. The Regiment presented her with a brooch, a replica, on a slightly smaller scale, of the silver Regimental badge, in jewels and precious metals. It was presented in a fine casket decorated with silverwork and made from the wood of the wild cherry from the Buccleuch estate.

Chapter 11

THE SECOND WORLD WAR AND THE AFTERMATH

Although, in the phrase of the time, the Second World War was 'a war of movement', four years passed between the ejection of the B.E.F. from the European mainland at Dunkirk and the day when British land forces with their American allies were able to return to the Continent in strength. The story of the Regiment in the war years largely reflects this, for as no K.O.S.B. battalion served in the Middle East or Mediterranean theatres, or was involved in the Far East disasters when Japan attacked, the Regiment had no battalion in action between the fall of France and the invasion of Normandy, with the exception of the 2nd Battalion, which fought its first action against the Japanese in the Arakan in October 1943. A total of 1,352 Borderers laid down their lives, a figure almost identical with the numbers killed serving with the 2nd Battalion in the trenches from 1914 to 1918.

The full story of the Regiment in the Second World War has been told in *Borderers in Battle*, and the reader is referred to the Battle Honours listed in Appendix I. At the outbreak of war on 3 September 1939, the 1st Battalion was at Portsmouth, and the 2nd Battalion was in distant Jubbulpore where its rôle remained Internal Security. All four T.A. battalions on the Scottish Border had been called up, and were up to strength. These battalions were in need of plenty of training, indeed, the 6th Battalion had only been embodied on 1 September. They were immediately, or very shortly, concentrated as battalions from their various detachments and began their wartime journeyings, and although their T.A. identity was cast aside in the general flood of conscripted manpower, in those early days there was crystallized a team spirit that was never lost and which made them great battalions. Mention should also be made of the 8th Battalion, which was formed of older soldiers for Home Defence. Familiar patches of colour, the medal ribbons of the First World War, were often seen on khaki breasts here, and this was a fine battalion. A 9th Battalion was also formed, in 1940, and was fully trained, but it was never earmarked for service overseas. The war machinery broke up both 8th K.O.S.B. and 9th K.O.S.B. in 1943.

In 1939, 1st K.O.S.B. like their fathers' generation before them, sailed for France with the B.E.F., in the 3rd Infantry Division commanded by Major-General Montgomery. In May 1940, they crossed the Belgian frontier to support the Belgian Army, but the *blitzkrieg* had started, and again there was a retreat, from water line to water line. Through Louvain, through Brussels, over the Escaut, and through Ypres they went, back to the sea, and on the night 31 May/1 June, the 1st Battalion's parties were evacuated from the sand dunes and the mole at Dunkirk by Britain's boats.

The 4th and 5th K.O.S.B. had always been part of the 52nd (Lowland) Division. At the time of Dunkirk, the 52nd Division and the 1st Canadian Division were the only two fully equipped divisions in the United Kingdom, and they were disembarked on the coast of Brittany in a forlorn attempt to establish a bridgehead there with the French. The 4th and 5th Battalions landed at St Malo on 13 June, but the fall of France caused the hasty evacuation of the second B.E.F. The 52nd Division fell back on Cherbourg. 5th K.O.S.B. acted as rearguard and had the melancholy distinction of being the last British infantry to leave France, on 18 June 1940.

Later, 4th and 5th K.O.S.B. underwent special training in the Highlands to become mountain troops, only to be assigned to the Allied Airborne Army as air-transportable troops when the 'Second Front' opened. It had been intended to fly-in the 52nd Division as a follow-up to the Arnhem operation; at first, the Borderers were scheduled to fly in Dakota aircraft. This was changed at the eleventh hour to gliders, and then their flight was cancelled. The 4th and 5th Battalions were eventually committed to battle at sea level, with their objective partly covered by sea water.

The 6th and 7th Battalions both served in the 15th (Scottish) Division, a division that was placed on lower establishment for a period, finding drafts for the Middle East and North Africa, but which rose again and played a part second to none among British formations in the final campaign in the West.[1] The 6th K.O.S.B. remained in the 15th Division; in 1943, 7th K.O.S.B. became glider-borne troops in the 1st Airborne Division.

There must be few Borderers who fought in the Allied Expeditionary Force in that final campaign, who have not reflected somewhat ruefully on the course of history since then. If the Allied forces in Italy just might have reached Vienna, had not divisions been drawn off for landings in the south of France in support of the Normandy invasion; and more pertinently, if General Eisenhower's forces had taken Prague, could have reached Berlin . . . Well may those who came ashore wonder.

---

[1] In 1942-43, 15th (Scottish) Division was commanded by Major-General D. C. Bullen Smith, M.C., late K.O.S.B.

Four years to the week after the evacuation from Dunkirk, 1st K.O.S.B. scrambled from landing-craft on to the Normandy beaches in the assault landings of D-Day, 6 June 1944. On 15 June, 6th K.O.S.B. came ashore. Both battalions fought in the slogging battles around Caen, which was entered by 1st K.O.S.B. on 9 July. Both 1st and 6th Battalions fought throughout the ensuing campaign to the end, when 1st K.O.S.B. took part in the capture of Bremen, and 6th K.O.S.B., having made assault crossings of the Rhine and the Elbe, were a little beyond Hamburg, close to the Baltic. On 17 September 1944, 7th K.O.S.B. came down in gliders for their only battle of the Second World War, but one which gave to the Colours the name of an epic: Arnhem. Forty officers and 700 other ranks went into action, after being rallied to their companies in the landing zone by pipers playing *Blue Bonnets over the Border*. Four officers and 72 other ranks answered the roll-call afterwards at Nijmegen. In October, 4th and 5th K.O.S.B. disembarked at Ostend and on 1 November made assault landings on Walcheren at the mouth of the Scheldt, in the vital operations to open the port of Antwerp; thenceforth, they fought throughout the campaign until they, too, took part in the capture of Bremen.

Little inkling of history to come entered the minds of a small party of the 6th Battalion who actually witnessed the Iron Curtain descend. The battalion had moved forward to the vicinity of Schwerin, near Wismar on the Baltic coast (today in East Germany), where it was stationed on the then inter-zone boundary with the Russians. There was little contact, and a platoon sergeant who crossed a canal bridge to the Russian side, on a friendly visit, found Russian troops manning slit trenches as though the war were still in progress. Soon the boundary was readjusted and moved farther to the west, to Lubeck. 'Displaced persons' from the east were trekking west in great numbers, while on the appointed day, 6th K.O.S.B. vacated their billets, and only the rear party assembled at the main boundary post on the east side of Schwerin, with other rear parties from their brigade. Schwerin, a sizeable German town, was like a town of the dead. A picture of Stalin had prudently appeared on one building. At the boundary post a barrier pole was lifted, and Lieutenant-Colonel C. W. P. Richardson, D.S.O. and Bar, and his fellow Commanding Officers in the 44th Brigade, saluted a large and bemedalled Russian general who walked forward through a makeshift archway surmounted by a red flag with Hammer and Sickle, flanked by a small Union Jack and the Stars and Stripes. Beyond the archway were a mass of lorries and uniforms. Then the lorries clattered forward, full of Russian soldiers impassively singing stirring songs. Detachments of Russians were allocated to the Scottish parties, to be guided to special guard duties, and a seemingly endless foot column approached, of Asiatic-looking men, wearing forage caps, marching four abreast. They carried no weapons, except a light automatic to every sub-unit, and their marching was accompanied by the same impressive, impassive singing.

In little more than six months from that day in July 1945, the 4th, 5th, 6th and 7th Battalions of the Regiment had gone into 'suspended animation', as it was called, which, in effect, meant their disbandment.

$$* \quad * \quad * \quad * \quad *$$

In the case of the 2nd Battalion, the war had at first been remote. In 1941, the battalion left Jubbulpore for Razmak, a fortified British outpost in tribal territory on the North-West Frontier, in the middle of Waziristan. Here, while Hong Kong, Malaya, Singapore and Burma fell to the Japanese, 2nd K.O.S.B. were maintaining the *Pax Britannica* in the old manner, at a greater distance from India's eastern frontier than London is from Moscow.

At the end of 1942, the battalion was withdrawn into India to form part of the 7th Indian Division, which was being assembled for operations in Burma. After training in the jungles of Central India and the Bengal paddy-fields, 2nd K.O.S.B. embarked at Madras in September 1943, for Chittagong, and now became part of the Fourteenth Army commanded by the then Lieutenant-General William Slim. Limited operations in the Arakan, initiated by Field Marshal Wavell, had failed of their object, and South-East Asia Command had been created, with Admiral Lord Louis Mountbatten as Supreme Commander. Taking part in a renewed British offensive, 2nd K.O.S.B. crossed into the Arakan, and were present at the critical fighting at the Ngakyedauk Pass and in the 'Admin Box', where two successive commanding officers were killed.[2] Later, 2nd K.O.S.B. were flown to the central front at Imphal, close to the country of the Chin Lushai Expedition of more than half a century earlier. The sickness rate was hardly less dire than in 1890, and even when every resource of medicine and hygiene had been brought to bear, it exceeded battle casualties by several times. Indeed, sickness almost broke the battalion. After Imphal, in August 1944, when the battalion was considerably below strength, a special team of doctors sent to examine the battalion found that about 80 per cent of those theoretically fit for duty were suffering from dysentry and malnutrition.

[2] Lieutenant-Colonel W. G. Mattingley and Lieutenant-Colonel J. D. A. MacLaren.

Fortunately, the 2nd Battalion was reinforced and revitalized. Supplied by air during a six-week approach march, 2nd K.O.S.B. played their part in the assault crossing which turned the Irrawaddy line, south of Pakokku, in February 1945, and encompassed the fall of Mandalay. At the end of May the battalion fought its last action, one hundred and fifty miles further south, near Prome, by which time Rangoon had been taken by a seaborne landing. The Japanese forces in Burma had been trapped and the race against the monsoon had been won.

Whatever the future might have held in store for the 2nd Battalion in the further prosecution of the war against Japan, almost immediately became irrelevant. The battalion was in transit across the Bay of Bengal from Rangoon to Calcutta, bound for the great base camp at Ranchi, when the two atomic bombs were dropped. The destination of the 2nd Battalion became the North-West Frontier Province, and the famous cantonment of Peshawar.

Here, in October 1945, at Roberts Barracks, there began for the 2nd Battalion a strange, paradoxical existence, in which the atmosphere of Kipling's India seemed changeless while the British Raj drew to its end. The routines, formalities and diversions of peacetime cantonment life took control. As a wit remarked in the Officers' Mess, as he surveyed the steady stream of officers and men leaving the battalion for repatriation: 'Now we can get back to some real soldiering.'

Internal Security was a major commitment. Muslim, Sikh and Hindu communities lived in Peshawar City, and the tensions of approaching independence increased. 'Frontier warfare' was the other commitment, the traditional peace-keeping on the North-West Frontier, and the battalion underwent training in the identical tactics that had been used at the storming of the Malakand Pass and in the Afghan War, as though time had stood still.

Nevertheless, a very different battalion had arrived at Peshawar in 1945 from the one that had left Razmak in 1942. Keeping the other battalions of the Regiment up to strength with K.O.S.B. enlisted men had been a difficult enough task, which in the end proved impossible, as battle casualties took their toll in North-West Europe, and some formations were broken up to provide replacements for others, and much of Anti-Aircraft Command was retrained as infantry. The growth of other arms, to say nothing of the R.A.F., had altered the whole recruitment picture from what it had been in the First World War, with its system of reserve battalions within regiments. In the East, the problems of replacement were accentuated by distance, and more than any other battalion of the Regiment, the 2nd Battalion had changed its identity. Precisely five members of the battalion had served continuously with it throughout the war years,[3] and *Borderers in Battle* relates that the replacements in Burma had come from some fifty different regiments. In Peshawar the eyes of most were fixed on repatriation, and demobilization, when in January 1946, a senior Borderer, Lieutenant-Colonel R. Payton-Reid, D.S.O., whose service went back to the First World War, was appointed Commanding Officer. He had served in the 2nd Battalion between the wars and had commanded 7th K.O.S.B. at Arnhem. Under his dispensation the 2nd Battalion gradually returned to a 'pre-war basis', but in February 1947, Colonel Payton-Reid received confidential and distressing information in a personal letter from the Commander-in-Chief in India. It had been decided that the British infantry was to be reduced. The line regiments of the British Army were to lose their second battalions.

Meanwhile, communal hatreds were sweeping the Punjab. Their repercussions reached Peshawar, and the last operational duty of 2nd K.O.S.B. was the occupation of Peshawar City in aid of the civil power. For ten days, based on the civil headquarters in the Gor Khattri, formerly a temple area, the Borderers patrolled the city by day and by night, and by their presence extinguished the wave of murders, enabled the police to enforce law and order, and restored confidence among the minority communities, without a single instance of resorting to force.

Towards sundown on 25 April 1947, the 2nd Battalion Trooped the Colour; and in a matter of weeks the 2nd Battalion, The King's Own Scottish Borderers, and the Indian Empire, were no more.

* * * * *

The 2nd Battalion's Colours were handed over to the care of the Depot by the Colonel-in-Chief, in the course of a day of great ceremony, on 7 August 1947, when the Regiment received the Freedom of Berwick-upon-Tweed.

The Depot, as such, had disappeared in 1939 when it became the Regimental Training Centre, which was later absorbed into the 10th (Lowland) Infantry Training Centre, the second largest I.T.C. in the United Kingdom. The barracks at Berwick were put to other wartime uses until, at the end of 1946, the K.O.S.B. depot party there was raised in status to the Regimental Depot again. It was affiliated to the 25th Primary Training Centre which was formed at Berwick at the same time, and staffed mainly by the Regiment, for the initial training of National Servicemen who were not exclusively

---

[3] Major F. A. W. Courtenay Hood, Lieutenant (Q.M.) J. F. Macdonald, M.B.E., R.S.M. W. H. Green, Sergeant T. McGahey, Private J. Sim.

destined for the K.O.S.B., but had been called up in the Regimental area. Naturally, though, they filled a good many of the 1st Battalion's ranks.

A hopeful note sounded in May 1947, when the 4th (Border) and 5th (Dumfries and Galloway) Battalions were taken out of suspended animation and re-formed, the 4th Battalion under Lieutenant-Colonel C. J. Ballantyne, T.D., and the 5th Battalion under Lieutenant-Colonel G. G. M. Batchelor. Recruiting went well for them as Borderers who had served in the war came back.

*   *   *   *   *

At the end of 1945, the 1st Battalion had moved from Germany to Egypt, in preparation for Internal Security duties in Palestine. Entraining for Palestine, the battalion went into camp in the Plain of Sharon, at Hadera. It then returned to Egypt, to the Canal Zone, and was in camp at Fayid on the Great Bitter Lake during the summer of 1946, before moving back to Palestine, into a camp at Jerusalem, where it formed part of the 1st Infantry Division.

For the 1st Battalion, as with the 2nd Battalion in Peshawar, the rapid turnover of all ranks and essential staff through demobilization, and the problems of changing to a peacetime administration, made this a difficult time. There was a particularly unsettled period when the eighteen-month tenure of command of Lieutenant-Colonel W. F. R. Turner, D.S.O. came to an end, shortly before the battalion went to Jerusalem. Colonel 'Willow' Turner, later Colonel of the Regiment, had commanded 5th K.O.S.B. from Walcheren to the Rhine, where he assumed command of the 1st Battalion; but when the battalion reached Jerusalem in October 1946, it underwent four more changes of Commanding Officer in as many months.[4] For many, there was the frustration at having to do the job at all now that the war was over.

The job was to see out the British Mandate, as soldiers of the Power which, in two world wars, had expelled the Turk and kept the German from the gate, and that had decided on a Jewish national home in Palestine without giving the Jews exclusive priority. The main difference between the circumstances of 1946-48 and the 1st Battalion's tour in 1936 was that the Jews were now better trained than the Arabs and had collected more sophisticated equipment. 1st K.O.S.B. remained at Jerusalem until February 1947, when the battalion moved to Camp 87 near the coast between

---

[4] Lieutenant-Colonel J. G. Shillington, D.S.O. had been appointed in the first place, but his health had not recovered from wounds received while commanding 6th K.O.S.B. in Normandy.

Tel-Aviv and Caesarea, where it came under command of the 3rd Division again. By this time, all British proposals for autonomous cantons and a trusteeship had been rejected by both Jew and Arab, and Britain had referred the Palestine question to the United Nations at Lake Success. Meanwhile, the Jewish underground organizations had begun their terrorist activities.

Throughout the whole trying period, broken wherever possible by company training camps and relaxation, preferably by the sea, and by one period of a month's training in Jordan, the morale of the battalion remained remarkably high. All ranks were aware of the historical context of the struggle that was threatening in the 'Holy Land', and were keen to see their task brought to a satisfactory conclusion. Where opportunity offered the Borderers got on amicably with both Jew and Arab, but inevitably this was not the happy norm and the battalion learnt to react swiftly and with considerable toughness to any threat from any quarter, and made it clear — to use another interpretation of the old motto — 'Dinna stamp on a Scotch thistle'.

Much of the mounting Jewish terrorism throughout Palestine was thought to be directed from Jerusalem. The Jews had started attacking British troops and motor convoys, which were constantly being mined, particularly on the Jerusalem—Tel-Aviv road, necessitating the rapid forming and manning of road blocks. The southern part of Jerusalem was the battalion's responsibility, and when a British sergeant was kidnapped and hanged by the Jews the battalion carried out an extensive cordon and search operation in the Jewish quarter. It was found to consist of a mass of hovels, honeycombed with passages and stairways, that presented an impossible task, and several hours' search produced nothing.

'Ceremonially we were kept busy with guards mounted on His Excellency the High Commissioner's residence,' writes Major A. J. Rennie. 'Both the company commander and guard commander were invited to dine with His Excellency once during the tour of duty. These occasions were not always animated, with a High Commissioner too preoccupied for social pleasantries.'

At Camp 87 the battalion rôle included action against those illegal Jewish immigrants from Europe who had escaped the Royal Navy patrols off-shore, and were attempting to land in small boats under cover of darkness. The main rôle, however, was continual pressure against the hard core Jewish underground organizations, the Haganah and the Irgun-Zwei-Leumi, by means of searches, patrols, road checks, identity checks, convoy escorts and curfew enforcement, and the battalion was constantly on the move from one area to another, for security reasons, its destinations veiled in as much secrecy as possible. Jewish hostility was aggravated by the frequent searches of their villages, almost always in the small hours of the morning, for daylight searches were usually nullified by their telephone warning systems. Daylight searches were made only for urgent reasons, a conspicuous one being the search for two Palestine policemen kidnapped by the Irgun, who were later found hanged. The Palestine Police, who were composed of both Jews and Arabs, were held in great respect by the battalion for their courageous devotion to duty.

On another occasion the Borderers carried out a highly successful daylight operation. Lieutenant-Colonel F. M. V. Tregear, who assumed command in March 1947, writes:

'The most successful [search] operation carried out by the battalion was in full daylight working on its own in conjunction with the Palestine Police, ending with the complete destruction of a terrorist school when all the instructors and pupils were either killed or arrested. Hoping to catch the suspects without bloodshed, the Police went forward to the house on their own, banged on the door and told them to come out quietly. The individual who answered the door, however, raised the alarm and the whole outfit, about one dozen, came out shooting and the Police were lucky to escape. Our action platoon opened fire, killing and wounding several of the terrorists, and caught the remainder.'

Situated in an area of banana and orange groves, the school, which had been carefully surrounded by the whole battalion, had, in fact, been training recruits for the Stern Gang. Success was due to complete secrecy during the planning stage and the final deceptive moves by several columns to the area, so that the chances of leakage through civilians were reduced to nil.

Later, the Stern Gang took their revenge on Arab labourers working in the banana plantation, accusing them of complicity. This was but one of many instances where Jews blamed Arabs for tip-offs to British forces, which fanned Arab resentment.

On one occasion, an escort from the battalion accidentally caught up with a Jewish convoy on the road to Jerusalem at the moment the convoy was ambushed by Arabs, and suffered casualties through the Arabs being under the misconception that the Borderers were escorting the Jews. The battalion was also engaged in keeping the peace between Tel-Aviv and Jaffa, a thankless task which involved shepherding the rival races into their respective areas at curfew time.

Jewish hatred could be a startling experience for young soldiers who were there to keep the peace, but who were at the same time learning the hard way how far they could trust the Arab. Except for vital military duties the battalion was behind British perimeter wire each night, and well did the 1st Battalion notes in *The Borderers' Chronicle* wryly remark, 'Every man's hand seems against us.' *Nemo me impune lacessit* governed, however, and no one wittingly chose the K.O.S.B. as a target.[5]

From Camp 87 the battalion moved to a camp farther north at Beit Lid, inland of Natanya, then returned to the Tel-Aviv area, to the R.A.F. camp at Lydda. Meanwhile, a special commission of the United Nations had visited the country and on 29 November 1947, the United Nations General Assembly voted in favour of partition, with an international zone at Jerusalem. This was accepted by the Jews, but rejected by the Arabs, and the situation rapidly deteriorated until both sides were making full-scale armed attacks on one another's villages. For British forces, peace-keeping between Jew and Arab now had equal priority with the combating of terrorism, and 1st K.O.S.B. was heavily involved in and around Jaffa, patrolling, arresting curfew breakers, mopping up snipers' posts, and supporting the police.

In February 1948, the battalion moved to Sarafand Camp, not far away, near Rehovot, and was employed on so many guards that the men had an average of two nights in bed each week. On 29 February, the Cairo-Haifa express train was blown up by the Stern Gang as it was approaching Sarafand. They had placed mines on the track, killing nearly thirty British soldiers and injuring many others. Lieutenant-Colonel Tregear, two of his officers and three other ranks of the battalion were on the train but, luckily for them, escaped injury. Most of those on the train were drafts for the Parachute Regiment and the R.A.F. The incident seemed likely to strain the forbearance of the British troops to breaking-point.

Refusing to implement a United Nations policy that was not acceptable to both sides, Britain declared that the Mandate would end on 15 May 1948. On 12 May, the High Commissioner warned the inhabitants of Palestine that a peaceful withdrawal was expected, and that British troops would take full retaliatory measures if the withdrawal were hampered in any way. In the exodus, 1st K.O.S.B. were advance guard to their brigade, which led the way out of Palestine. The orders were to go fast, to clear the way so that those following would not have to fight a rearguard action. On the same day, the Jewish Agency announced the existence of Israel.

Writes Major T. H. Perkins, who was Adjutant at this time:
'The last 48 hours in Palestine was a period of maximum activity by the battalion. There was an outbreak of fire in the Sarafand

---

[5] The battalion lost three soldiers killed in Palestine.

shopping centre and the K.O.S.B. fire standby section rushed to the scene, put out the fire and saved a number of Jewish shops, only to be destroyed later by a Jewish mortar attack!

At dawn on 15 May 1948, the first vehicle passed out of Sarafand Camp heading south towards Gaza. The K.O.S.B. Guardroom had already been occupied by a ragged bunch of Arab irregular troops wearing a motley selection of uniforms. The Arab Commander saluted the Scottish Borderers, the Jocks shouted back, "Watch it, they will be after you." The sound of heavy firing from the "battlefield" of Tel Aviv/Jaffa could be heard in the distance when, finally, the last vehicle trundled out.

The column was commanded by Lieutenant-Colonel "Trigger" Tregear and had Royal Navy and R.A.F. support. H.M.S. *Phoebe* was off-shore on call and we had an air contact team. A number of empty British Army camps en route had already been looted by local Arabs and Bedouin. A Jock said that he saw a long white bath running over the sand dunes with four pairs of legs.

Just before reaching Gaza we heard heavy bombing to the east, and shortly after this, we passed a small Jewish settlement on the edge of the desert. We stopped and chatted to the Jewish defenders, men, women and children well armed with Soviet weapons. The Jocks did not like the idea of leaving the children to face the armed onslaught of the Egyptian Army, at that moment cautiously advancing into the new State of Israel.

Not far from the Jewish village we met the advanced elements of the invading force. The first vehicle was a makeshift armoured vehicle with an obsolete anti-tank rifle. The Egyptian troops looked very worried indeed. Then a staff car appeared and a very nervous young Egyptian officer told our Commander that the bombing of the British N.A.A.F.I. to the west had been carried out by Jewish pilots using false Egyptian insignia on their aircraft. Later it became known that the bombing we had heard had been by Egyptian aircraft who had mistaken the location of the camp and a number of British soldiers had been killed.

Then we came to the main body of Egyptian troops who made way for our column. Some Jocks helped them to recover some vehicles bogged down in the soft sand, saying, "You are going the wrong way." Our R.S.M. inspected some of the Egyptian troops and noted that they had torn uniforms and broken boots, indeed some had bare feet. They were a motley bunch by any standard. We saw many cast-off British weapons and vehicles mixed with civilian lorries. A number of more enthusiastic Egyptians were already celebrating their victory — little did they know what was in store for them.

At last we reached the Sinai and our column left the road to form a wide square to bivouac "in peace" for the night. Officer and Jock had mixed feelings, a certain amount of relief perhaps, but a cloud of worry about the Jewish and Arab families we had left behind.

We had planned to start across the Sinai Desert at dawn, but that was not to be because of the dense mist across the desert. When the sun rose we were off, once again, towards our goal, the Suez Canal. Our first sight was smoke on the horizon and the funnels of a ship peacefully making its way apparently through the sand dunes on the Canal.

The various check points manned by the Egyptian Army and Police were swept aside as we pushed on, we were in no mood for any formalities, till we reached our staging point at Port Fuad.'[6]

The Pipes and Drums, who had been prominent in Palestine and had contributed much to the battalion's high spirit, beat 'Retreat' at Port Said the evening before sailing and, on 20 May, 1st K.O.S.B. embarked for the United Kingdom.

[6] Port Fuad — British base and industrial port at the entrance to the Suez Canal opposite Port Said.

Chapter 12

KOREA

The 1st Battalion was stationed at Redford Barracks, Edinburgh, for the year 1948-49. In 1948, the battalion provided the King's Guard at Balmoral. At this time, the battalion was on lower establishment, at a strength of twenty-seven officers and less than 400 other ranks.

In the summer of 1949 the battalion embarked for Hong Kong, where it disembarked on 21 August; and so it was that 1st K.O.S.B. were at hand when in 1950 war erupted in a strange land which most of the young men called up for their National Service had never heard of. 'Korea,' the N.C.O.s said.

Korea . . . there was always another hill, sometimes it was as if the higher command assumed that Scottish troops would feel more at home when given the highest hills to climb. It was a war fought for the possession of hilltops, with ceaseless digging and wiring of positions. Digging was a feature of the campaign, not only from a fighting point of view, but also as the means of obtaining shelter. From start to finish, whenever the troops halted they dug.

It was a war of much monotony, fought in extremes of climate. The first impression of the Korean winter to a man flown-in as a battle replacement was the impact of the breath-catching cold at the airfield. The winds were Siberian. There could be 30°—40°F of frost, a cold which could easily numb sentries at their posts, which made digging impossible without explosives, and which froze weapons. The adhesion to metal in extreme cold resulted in an order that leather gloves would not be removed, and one memory is of a man who had disobeyed this. His hands were stuck to the jerrycan he was carrying, and could only be freed by pulling the skin off.

The problem of frostbite led to a daily foot inspection, and the platoon commander came to recognize his men as easily by their feet as by their faces. Careful checks of automatic weapons were essential to ensure they would still work in the freezing conditions, and various brands of oil were experimented with, from army issued oil to sardine oil. A particularly dramatic effect of the cold was produced by a frozen stream on the battalion's front during the final, static phase of the war. If anyone put his boot through the ice there was a tremendous splintering noise, which at night sounded like the crack of doom, causing tension as to whether there was a friendly patrol out or if it was 'Johnny Chinaman,' or merely an animal, for deer, wild pig and white hares roamed the battle area.

With spring came the mud and slush of the thaw, which gradually turned into an all-enveloping, choking dust. As the summer came, the temperature and the humidity rose until temperatures exceeded 100°F. An unpleasant consequence of summer was a sticky, staining and smelly substance which had to be sprinkled over all clothing in order to combat a fever carried by rodents. Then in July and August came monsoon-like rains, followed by heavy flooding.

It was a war that British troops fought with weapons of the Second World War; the Lee Enfield rifle, the familiar mortars, the Bren gun, the grenades, the Browning and the ageless Vickers M.M.G. In support was the Second World War's 25-pounder field gun, while the heavier guns were American. Those British troops who formed the original United Kingdom contribution to the United Nations forces went through the first winter in Second World War battle dress and greatcoats, but this was before the Borderers arrived in Korea, and by the second winter the troops had their splendid windproof clothing and Parka anoraks.

There was an immense isolation. When operations became static, companies in the forward positions lived in a world of their own, usually at the end of a spur leading down to a valley, the greater part of a mile forward of the main defended locality. Lengthy periods would pass without the men in one company meeting those in other companies, and as the soldier knows, the necessity of keeping his head close to the ground on forward slopes under enemy observation limits the horizon. Positions were dug as deep and narrow as possible, with usually four firing bays to a section, each bay with room for two men. Each bay or pair of bays had its dug-out, roofed so as to be proof against anything but a direct hit from a heavy gun. Only at night did those in the forward positions come to a wary kind of life — patrol activity, administration and replenishment, and the inevitable wiring of the forward slopes. At night came the 'Gook Train', the Korean porters who, in common with their countrymen south of the 38th Parallel, were known as Gooks. The porters carried up stores to the companies and took away refuse, under the supervision of the Company 2 i/c. Men for rest and recuperation, or for leave in Japan, or in need of medical attention, went back with the Gook Train; also men due for their fortnightly bath, a process which involved staying away the whole day and returning to the company position the following night. On reverse slopes there could be a certain amount of daylight activity, exercise and rehearsals for night patrols, but even here, when in Brigade reserve, there was still a very great sense of isolation.

There was a natural problem of morale. It was not easy to maintain a sense of purpose. Confidence in their arms they certainly had, but the men were not fighting for their own country. When the seemingly endless cease-fire negotiations opened, the site of the parleys at Panmunjom was marked by a vertical searchlight beam, a physical reminder of the 'phoney war' it had become, a stalemate, in which both sides made aggressive gestures.

The hills varied from a scrub-covered bleakness to well wooded regions of fir and larch. They dropped steeply to the valleys and it was an exhausting business climbing them with weapons and equipment, even when there was no enemy opposition. There were no roads, only a few gravel tracks, and dry stream beds giving lines of access until they were turned into torrents by the rains. Villages of timber and mud were dotted about, whose inhabitants scratched a living from a primitive agriculture; and through the heart of the battle area the Imjin River, crossing the 38th Parallel, cut its way through crag and sandstone to the Yellow Sea.

For sixteen months the Borderers were on active service in Korea, living in the open, in trench, dugout or, during the earlier stages, in tents of poncho capes. The rough living and the labours of fighting and digging in mountainous country kept the battalion remarkably fit and hardy in a land where there was not much damage a war could do except to the combatants.

*   *   *   *   *

In 1945, Korea had been divided into Russian and American zones of occupation, north and south respectively of the 38th Parallel. When Russian and American troops were withdrawn they left behind them régimes reflecting the two ideologies. On 25 June 1950, North Korea invaded the South with the object of uniting the country under Communism. The first United States troops to land under the auspices of the United Nations for the defence of South Korea were swept back down the length of the country, together with the South Korean forces, to a perimeter around Pusan. There followed the landings of the U.S. Marines far behind the North Korean front, at Inchon, and the recapture of Seoul, the breakout from the Pusan perimeter, and the advance to the Yalu River on the Manchurian border which brought about the Chinese intervention.

In December 1950, at Hong Kong, 1st K.O.S.B. had been brought to a high state of readiness, and on 9 April 1951, received the order to relieve 1st Argyll and Sutherland Highlanders in

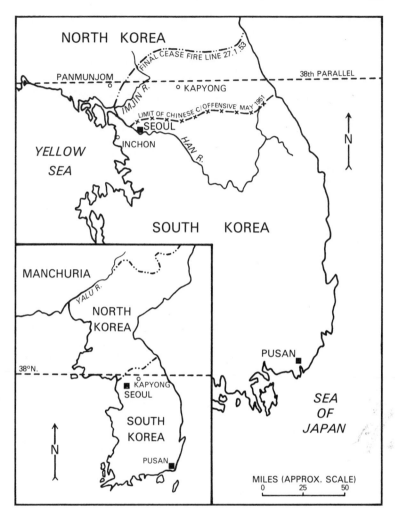

Korea.[1] This was just two days before General MacArthur was dismissed by President Truman on the dangerous issue of the strategic bombing of China.

The Borderers disembarked at Inchon on 23 April 1951, at an extremely fluid and critical time. The Communist counter-offensive at the end of 1950, in which Chinese 'volunteers' from several Army Groups had been identified, had driven the United Nations

[1] The Argylls and 1st Middlesex, joined by 3rd Royal Australian Regiment, had formed the original Commonwealth contingent in Korea.

forces back over the 38th Parallel and south of Seoul again. Regrouping, the mainly U.S. troops of the United Nations had forced the Communists back to the 38th Parallel. However, the disembarkation of 1st K.O.S.B. coincided with a renewed Communist spring offensive all along the front.

The battalion was at once sent into battle under conditions that could hardly have been more unfavourable. There was no time for any further training behind the front, but time in which to assemble the battalion, unload the heavy weapons, equipment and main ammunition supply from the ship's hold was a reasonable expectation. Even this was not granted. An unloading party remained behind at Inchon while the battalion, with twenty rounds of small arms ammunition per man, and issued with precisely two maps, moved through Seoul on the very evening of disembarkation and was guided in motor convoy straight to the forward area at Kapyong, just south of the 38th Parallel. This was the time when the Gloucesters were fighting a defensive action which became well known at home, but many a Borderer, after a flying hand-over by the departing Argylls, was still trying to adjust his thoughts to the question of what it was all 'in aid of'.

Fortunately the Borderers had a fighting leader in their Commanding Officer, Lieutenant-Colonel J. F. M. Macdonald, O.B.E., a man who thrived on the demands of action and the open spaces, and who had commanded 1st K.O.S.B. during the Second World War, in Normandy, Belgium and Holland. He has also written the operational narrative, *The Borderers in Korea*. It is not the aim of the present account to quote him, but to attempt to convey an impression of the general character and atmosphere of the campaign.

Fortunately, too, eighteen months of training and border patrolling in similar terrain in the New Territories, Hong Kong, had already brought the battalion to a high degree of physical fitness. The battalion was thus well-adapted to operating in Korea. The rest was acclimatization to battle conditions, and it has to be borne in mind that the situation, unlike the many set-piece operations of the Second World War, was too uncertain and fluid to have allowed of the kind of mental preparation and rehearsals associated with set-piece battles. The battalion had been brought up to strength by fresh drafts of National Servicemen and Reservists from other Scottish regiments who were transferred from the Argylls, and was simply pitchforked into a confused war in the name of the United Nations. There was no battle 'line', only localities of troops, of friend or foe. A 'line' never really crystallized until the winter of 1951-52. The battalion was minus its heavy weapons, its transport and its wireless equipment, and under the pressure of a major enemy offensive faced its baptism of fire. Not without the need for steady nerves, 1st K.O.S.B. learned from their early skirmishes and settled down into a fighting team in a manner that worthily upheld the traditions of the Regiment. With seasoned instinct, Colonel Macdonald had given orders before the battalion disembarked in Korea that the fine sleeping bags which had been issued were not to be used in the forward area, for he knew the penalty that was paid if troops were attacked at night and could not get out of them in time. He also gave orders that all ranks on duty in the forward area, normally 75 per cent of the battalion, would keep their boots on during the hours of darkness, and that except for badges of rank, all ranks would dress identically, including headdress.

In many aspects it was a company and platoon commander's war. It is especially remembered as a National Serviceman's war. Understandably, the Reservists who had been recalled were the least enthusiastic, but in 1st K.O.S.B. their numbers were few, and 60-70 per cent of the battalion were National Servicemen. They carried out their job in a manner indistinguishable from regular soldiers, although if a man's two years were completed while he was in Korea he was promptly repatriated, regardless of the exigencies of the campaign. Platoon commanders, themselves, were predominantly National Servicemen, and their high quality was a marked feature of the Korean War. Writes Colonel A. M. Thorburn, who commanded A Company during the later phase of the campaign:

'The strain on leaders was immense; they were on duty seven days a week and twenty-four hours a day; even more than normal, morale in these conditions depended very largely on their knowledge, forethought and example. The standard was very good and particularly, I think, did the National Service subalterns distinguish themselves.'

In the higher reaches of the battalion, the Second-in-Command, the company commanders, the Adjutant, were all experienced regular soldiers who had served in the Second World War and earlier. Warrant Officers and senior N.C.O.s, also, were regular soldiers, but the number of regular other ranks grew less through casualties or postings elsewhere as time went on. R.S.M. A. Lees, M.M., who had succeeded R.S.M. J. Walls, M.C. in Hong Kong, remained as Regimental Sergeant-Major throughout.

*   *   *   *   *

At the end of April 1951, the Chinese offensive lost momentum. They were believed to have suffered heavy casualties, nor could they compete with the United Nations forces in the matter of air support, of which they had none.

With the advantage of air cover, a tactic of the United Nations' withdrawal had been the American method of disengagement. This was a speedy procedure which went under the name of a 'bug-out'. It involved no rearguards in the British manner, but deep withdrawal from an unfavourable position and reassembly in new positions sufficiently far back to enable them to re-deploy without interference from the enemy's advanced troops. As is customary with U.S. troops, it was achieved in the grand manner, by a total reliance on mechanization. Areas of territory were disconcertingly abandoned as whole formations pulled back in huge motor convoys. The withdrawal was accompanied by the wholesale blowing-up of supply dumps to prevent them falling into enemy hands, in one of which conflagrations the Borderers, now part of the 28th Commonwealth Brigade, lost all personal property the moment it arrived at its due map reference from Inchon. Fortunately, the Q.M. staff had managed to get most of the war stores to the battalion, but the tracked vehicles — the Second World War-pattern 'Bren carriers' — suffered a dismal fate on their being handed over to the Q.M. staff by the officer of rear details who had brought them from Hong Kong. On higher orders they were at once destroyed.

The Communist advance, conducted on foot and liable to be left standing by the mechanized bug-out, had come to a halt some seven miles north of Seoul, on a general line running east and north-east across the country. There followed a period of offensive patrolling, as the United Nations forces prepared for a limited advance. Slowly the pendulum swung again. At the end of May 1951, the Communist outposts were attacked and the enemy was once more driven back to the approximate line of the 38th Parallel. The series of defended localities strung across the hills that the United Nations troops now strengthened and wired was known as the Kansas Line, and this stage was the beginning of static warfare in Korea, which was to lead to trench warfare reminiscent of the First World War in its immobility. Here, in the western sector, on the Imjin River, the newly-formed Commonwealth Division became operational in July 1951. With the forming of the Commonwealth Division the morale of its troops improved, and the Divisional Commander, Major-General Cassells, was held in great respect by all of them.

1st K.O.S.B. moved on to the Kansas Line on 30 May, into the area where in April the 29th Commonwealth Brigade, consisting of the Gloucesters, Royal Ulster Rifles and Royal Northumberland Fusiliers, had fought their defensive battle. Everywhere was the depressing sight of the dead still unburied, and of British tanks and equipment strewn about as battle débris. The battalion's positions were literally within yards of the 38th Parallel. Below was the river, broad and fast-flowing after heavy rain that had soaked our troops during the recent advance. Just ahead was the 'Ulster crossing' where in April the Communists came across. Beyond the river was a deep belt of no man's land and the Communist outposts. Patrols probed across the river, crossing in powered boats operated by Sappers, but it was obvious that the enemy's main positions were at a considerable distance.

The Kansas positions were heavily wired and covered by minefields, work which, together with the digging, could be carried out in daylight without enemy interference. An inquisitive Chinese reconnaissance aircraft formed the habit of circling over the battalion area, and became known as 'Bed-check Charlie'. From time to time, an American howitzer called a 'Persuader' went off with a shattering noise. Behind the forward positions, programmes of training and recreation were instituted, ranging from grenade throwing to football. The humid summer came on, and the violent downpours of the monsoon rains caused dramatic rises in the Imjin, flooding the tributary streams, undoing trenches, and turning the tracks into arteries of mud.

The battalion always operated as part of an American higher formation, at corps and, initially, at divisional level. The choice rations in the American 'C' Packs were devoured, including much corned-beef hash, until novelty became monotonous and everyone was surfeited with the one food. In the end, the Jock was thankful for British meals again, took the sweets, tin of fruit and cigarettes from the 'C' Packs and threw the rest away. On the other hand, British supplies conveniently included alcohol, whereas the Americans were 'dry'. This led to some extraordinary barters, and U.S. vehicles and equipment found their way into the hands of British troops, traded for liquor. When the Commonwealth Division was formed, a stop was put to the barter, but a bottle of gin or whisky was still good for an occasional American semi-automatic carbine. This weapon, although it had not the stopping power of the Lee Enfield, was fancied for its high rate of fire, and was also useful for shooting at the big pheasants with which Korea abounded.

Chapter 13

KOREA: THE GUY FAWKES BATTLE

The Chinese were a formidable enemy, tough, courageous, and well led. They were believed to receive regular ideological indoctrination, and probably it was the indoctrinated rigour of their lives that accounted for a certain mechanical, unimaginative character about their attacks, despite their native cunning. They employed various forms of rather crudely worded propaganda against our troops, using loudspeakers and leaflets, and at Christmas 1951 contrived to hang cards shaped as Christmas stockings on the K.O.S.B. wire, containing propaganda leaflets. Poorly equipped by the standards of the United Nations forces, they wore quilted jackets, rough trousers, rubber boots, and no gloves of any kind. The physical harshness of their conditions was immense. Most of those encountered by 1st K.O.S.B., mainly the dead, had frost-bitten hands and feet, and carried no form of identification. Chinese troops had little 'administrative tail', and in the oriental manner, water, and several days' supply of rice carried in a bag hung from the waist, supplied their main needs.

During the earlier phases not all of them were armed, but the unarmed would still surge forward, picking up the rifles of dead comrades. Small and stocky, it seemed that they followed leaders distinguished by white hats. If a white hat were shot they found another white hat to follow. Their favourite time for attack was when there was a full moon, or when the sun was setting, and the final onrush to their objective would be made with a flurry of bugle notes and whistles, and the hurling of their stick grenades or 'tatty mashers'. For our own troops it was a question of when the ammunition might give out against an enemy who attacked in great numbers and who held life cheap. They tended to fight on, however badly wounded, refusing to surrender, and despite their acceptance of any number of casualties were assiduous in carrying away their dead wherever possible. An enemy always enjoys an element of mystery, and it was reputed that some of the Chinese attacks were led by women dressed in black.

An extremely effective Chinese weapon was their mortar, the best weapon of its kind in Korea; and unmistakable was the sound of their 'burp guns', a type of Sten gun with a very high rate of fire. During the later phases, their machine-guns and artillery increased, and they used some tanks, but they never had air cover. Their troops were particularly audacious at crossing minefields, feeling their way through with twigs or strong pieces of straw, and they were highly skilled diggers. They dug their positions very quickly and to a considerable depth, and would even tunnel through the tops of hills to provide themselves with concealed observation posts and gun positions.

The North Koreans, although hardier soldiers than the South Koreans, lacked the martial skill of the Chinese. The R.O.K. (Republic of Korea) divisions of South Korea had a tendency to be absent from where they were thought to be; in a withdrawal they would evacuate their positions without waiting for the general movement to start.

*   *   *   *   *

Throughout the summer of 1951, 1st K.O.S.B. remained on the Kansas Line, brigaded with 1st King's Shropshire Light Infantry and 3rd Royal Australian Regiment. The Borderers went into reserve at the beginning of September, but after only a few days of rest were ordered forward again to take part in a general advance by the Commonwealth Division into the no man's land north of the Imjin. The advance, which had been prompted by the rapid fall in the river after the rains dwindled away, reducing its effectiveness as a defence, achieved a straightening of the line of 1st U.S. Corps, of which the Commonwealth Division formed part. It secured a position known as the Wyoming Line. There was still no contact with the enemy except by some long-range patrols; indeed, so far as the Borderers were concerned, all the fighting hitherto had consisted of small probing actions and patrol encounters. This was to change at the end of September 1951, when orders were issued for Operation Commando, a limited offensive to be undertaken by 1st U.S. Corps in which the Commonwealth Division was to drive the enemy from a dominating feature, Kowang-San, in metric terms Point 355, and its surrounding hills. Here were the main Chinese positions, held by the 65th Army,[1] some twelve to fifteen miles north of the Imjin. The object of Operation Commando was to forestall any enemy plans for an autumn offensive, and to exert pressure on his negotiators at Panmunjom.

An American division was to attack on the Commonwealth right. It will be seen from the map that at the 38th Parallel the Imjin makes a sharp bend, where its general direction changes from

---

[1] In strength the equivalent of an Army Corps. One division was forward, with two others in reserve.

south to west. The Commonwealth positions on the Kansas Line had been at the west leg of the bend, but with the northward advance into no man's land, a higher stretch of the river now lay behind the forward positions. The concentration for Operation Commando required 28th Commonwealth Brigade to move by motor transport to the east bank, and through the American area, re-crossing into assembly areas on the west bank by a ferry farther upstream. From there, on the Commonwealth right flank, they went into lying-up positions, facing westward, close to Canadian outposts.

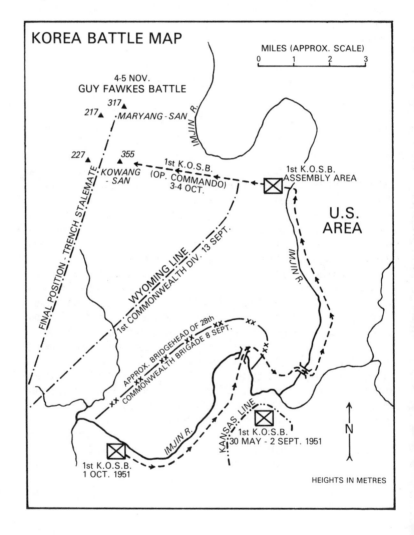

KOREA BATTLE MAP

MILES (APPROX. SCALE)
0   1   2   3

4-5 NOV.
GUY FAWKES BATTLE

317▲
217▲ ·MARYANG-SAN

227▲   355▲
·KOWANG   1st K.O.S.B.
- SAN   (OP. COMMANDO)
3-4 OCT.

IMJIN R.

1st K.O.S.B.
ASSEMBLY AREA

U.S.
AREA

FINAL POSITION - TRENCH STALEMATE

WYOMING LINE
1st COMMONWEALTH DIV. 13 SEPT.

IMJIN R.

APPROX. BRIDGEHEAD OF 28th
COMMONWEALTH BRIGADE 8 SEPT.

KANSAS LINE

IMJIN R.

1st K.O.S.B.
30 MAY - 2 SEPT. 1951

N

1st K.O.S.B.
1 OCT. 1951

HEIGHTS IN METRES

The attack on the Chinese positions began at dawn on 3 October and progressed doggedly to a roar of artillery, drifts of white smoke and bursts of phosphorous, flails of fire from Vickers machine-guns, the movements of Centurion tanks of the 8th Hussars, and a weight of reply from Chinese artillery, mortars and small arms. A little more than twenty-four hours later, after a battle that as an historical landmark in the Regiment's fighting history yields nothing to the storming of the Dargai Heights, the Borderers, supported by New Zealand field gunners, drove the enemy from their ultimate objective, the summit of Point 355 itself. The final assault was made by D Company, led by Major Robertson-Macleod, and the K.O.S.B. Battle Patrol.

The battalion's casualties had been remarkably light under the circumstances, but it was clear that the increased power of the Chinese artillery had been underestimated. On 9 October, 1st K.O.S.B. moved forward some 4,000 yards and relieved the 3rd Royal Australian Regiment in the area of Maryang-San, Point 317, where there had been heavy fighting. A number of the battalion's porters had already been sent to the area to help carry ammunition when the Australians' porter trains had been disorganized by shelling. A neighbouring ridge rising to Point 217 had been held by the enemy with particular tenacity, but after air strikes by South African Mustangs it was found to have been abandoned, and it was occupied by B Company, 1st K.O.S.B.

The K.O.S.B. positions were now on an arc of irregular ridges like a rough, inverted horseshoe, which protruded slightly forward of a general line, facing north-west, which had been gained by our troops. To quote from *The Borderers in Korea*:

'The front held by the battalion was some 3,000 yards and faced both west and north, from which directions it was overlooked by the enemy. Being a long and narrow ridge it was impracticable to get any depth within company localities. Except for the fact that the position provided some depth to the defence of Point 355 and the river, it had absolutely nothing to commend it as a defensive position.'[2]

The topographical prominences had been named, from left to right: 'United', 'Hinge', 'Knoll' and 'Peak'. On United, which included Point 217, the positions faced west. Hinge was the 'nose' of the whole position and the closest to the enemy, who were about 300 yards from it, and from here the battalion's front began to face north and ran, via Knoll, round to Peak on the right. Peak was Point 317 and its vicinity. On lower ground, in roughly the centre

---

[2] The author is grateful to Major-General J. F. M. Macdonald, C.B., O.B.E., D.S.O., for permission to quote from his account.

of the area within the horseshoe, was stationed the Battle Patrol, a permanent unit of the battalion, of platoon strength. In another area of low ground, behind Peak, were the reserve company and Battalion Headquarters. As was the normal practice, there was an artillery F.O.O. with each forward company.

An unpleasant period set in. The battalion was under constant harassment from mortaring, directed from the enemy's excellent observation posts, and shelling, from his tunnelled gun positions. Wiring was a dangerous business, and shallow trenches had to be dug among the wire itself, for there would be no time to get back to the proper trenches, thirty-odd yards away. Wiring, mostly at night, and mine-laying by Sappers, the improvement of positions and the construction of pits for ammunition, food and water, all with overhead cover, was the continuing work. On the Knoll position there was more cover from trees than on the other positions, and wiring and digging was possible there in daylight, but even on reverse slopes it was never a simple matter, for although hostile air interference was non-existent there was no respite from the enemy's mortars. On a forward slope the bomb could at least be heard leaving the barrel, but not on the reverse side, and men were posted on the crest to give the best warning they could. The Chinese also displayed an unerring instinct for the arrival of porter trains, which inevitably brought a minor bombardment. The porters were kept to dead ground wherever possible, and eventually their movements were confined to the hours of darkness. The chattering of these little Koreans was not easy to suppress, but their service to our forces deserves to be remembered.

Throughout these several weeks, air strikes with napalm bombs and concentrations from our own artillery and mortars were maintained against the enemy, but to little avail, and the battalion suffered a steady trickle of casualties.

On 25 October, Lieutenant-Colonel Macdonald was placed in command of 28th Commonwealth Brigade, and Major Tadman, his Second-in-Command, was promoted to the command of 1st K.O.S.B. Before long, the nightly noise of enemy vehicles in the distance began to be heard, but by day nothing stirred. Then suddenly, on 2 November, the observation post in the area of 7 Platoon on Knoll was destroyed by a single direct hit from an enemy gun.

*   *   *   *   *

There were two platoons on Knoll, 7 Platoon (C Company) and 11 Platoon (D Company). On 3 November, Second-Lieutenant

Purves from Kelso, commanding 7 Platoon, took a reconnaissance patrol down from the ridge into the country ahead, and although they found nothing, he had the sensation that they were being watched by hundreds of pairs of eyes. They came to a deserted village, and this sinister feeling persisted. A considerable shock awaited Purves, however, for at the largest house in the village he climbed up some steps and looked into a room, and beheld the most beautiful girl he had ever seen. She was Korean. She started up in terror from some straw, and an instinct warned him that if she was touched none of his patrol would get out of the place alive. He climbed down the steps and said nothing about her to his men, and they made their way back to Knoll. Chinese commanders were said to have 'comfort girls', and afterwards he was certain the girl in the village had been the comfort girl of a commander of some importance.

The Battle Patrol also went out and found much evidence of the enemy, mainly newly-dug crawl trenches, but made no contact. On the night of 3/4 November there was a distinct increase in enemy activity, the noise of tracked vehicles — undoubtedly self-propelled guns — starting and stopping, and a great many scraping noises that indicated digging. 1st K.O.S.B. Mortar Platoon fired continually as compass bearings were passed back.

First light on 4 November revealed a large white board on poles, stuck on a hill opposite which had been designated 'Baldy', and on the board was painted the legend, 'Go home Britishers or this hill will be your graveyard'. A stretch of trench which had not existed the previous day ran from behind Baldy for about 200 yards in the direction of our positions on Hinge. At 10.00 hours enemy were seen moving along the trench to a small copse; then came a report that many hundreds of the enemy were assembling behind Baldy. Aircraft panels were out, and cheers went up when Royal Naval Sea Furies, provoking an ineffectual storm of Chinese small arms fire directed skywards, smote the length and breadth of Baldy with napalm, rockets and machine-gun bullets.

For all that our own defensive fire could do, Chinese shelling and mortaring persisted intermittently throughout the day, and later in the afternoon intensified into a violent, sustained bombardment which lasted for some thirty minutes. The like of it had not been experienced in Korea before. Second-Lieutenant Henderson was commanding 11 Platoon on Knoll, and he later wrote:

'Our platoon position changed shape considerably. The precious trees which afforded so much cover were uprooted and lay strewn around each trench. Due to the dust visibility was nil. Tins, cardboard, webbing, paper and filth, were everywhere. Our Bazooka launcher had been twisted into a U-like object seen only in a school laboratory. The water cans, although well dug in, were punctured, torn and useless.'[3]

Then shortly after 16.00 hours, as the sun was setting and was in our men's eyes, the Chinese infantry came in, with a continuous hail of small arms fire.

The Borderers in Korea describes them: 'Appearing dazed, as if doped, they pressed on in their hundreds. Many fell, but others took their place and this flood of humanity surged relentlessly forward regardless of their own fire and ours.'

The attack was part of a determined attempt by the Chinese to regain the Kowang-San region, and afterwards it was apparent from Intelligence sources that 1st K.O.S.B. had been attacked by no less than an enemy division of 6,000 men. Intermingled with the sound of burp guns, the entire arc of ridge held by the Borderers crackled with Vickers fire, Brens and rifles, backed by the thundering cannonade of their supporting artillery. It is on record that the 3in mortar platoon discharged 5,000 rounds in the space of four hours. Much of the wire had been destroyed by the enemy's bombardment. Where it still stood in his path he came at it with pole charges and straw matting. All field telephone lines had been severed. Wireless communication partly broke down under a combination of shrapnel hits and the poor range of the sets among the hills. As darkness fell, the areas of the forward companies were time and again palely lit by parachute flares from their own 2in mortars, for the better aiming of the quantities of ammunition our men were pumping from their magazines. On Hinge, C Company (less one platoon on Knoll) received the first assault and was overborne by weight of numbers in close-quarter fighting. The survivors were withdrawn shortly after dark to the reserve company (A Company) in rear of Peak. On Peak, by 22.00 hours, D Company (less one platoon on Knoll) had been forced to abandon Point 317. On Knoll, enemy appeared 'from what must have been dugouts and bunkers dug the night before under our very noses.'[4] Early in the battle the two platoons here — between them they had twelve Bren guns — went off the air.

The nature of the battle is best understood when it is appreciated that a rifle company consisted of a company headquarters and three platoons, and that A Company, in reserve, was not engaged. In other words, this massed attack was made on a handful of platoon localities. Certainly ammunition supply was vital, for they blazed it off at a rate that cannot often have been required of

[3] With acknowledgments to Lieutenant-Colonel J. B. Henderson and the *British Army Journal*.

[4] Ibid, fn.3.

British infantry in the Second World War. It was 4 November when the sun was setting, but after this stark night in the Regiment's history it was 5 November as the new day dawned; and 'the Guy Fawkes battle' the Scottish Borderers called it.

On the left of the battalion's position, United was held by B Company. Chinese self-propelled guns and rocket-launchers had knocked out every B Company observation post and machine-gun position, simultaneously, before their infantry attacked. The Platoon holding Point 217 was soon overrun, and the survivors crawled back to the Battle Patrol which remained in its central

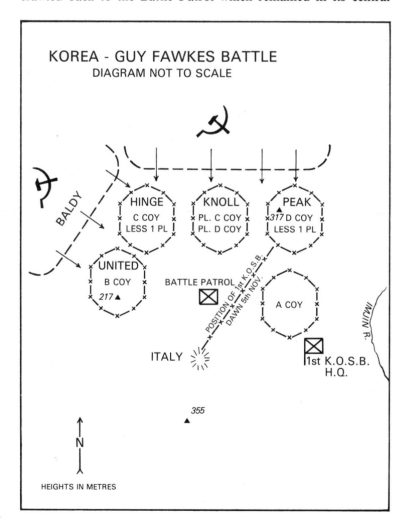

position, in reserve. The loss of Point 217 turned the United ridge, and the remainder of the company fell back to reserve slope positions previously prepared under the orders of Major Harrison, O.C. B Company. From these positions and by the light of parachute flares, B Company continued to wage a resolute fight. Parties of men with Bren guns and grenades were told-off to cover sections of the crest, and before they were finally withdrawn they wrought a terrible execution as the enemy came over the crest in silhouette, in swarms. It was at this stage that the man emerged who, when it came to the national publicity which in due course broke over him, may be termed a reluctant hero.

Private W. Speakman[5] was a gentle giant. He stood six-and-a-half feet and had a large personality to match, but he was not interested in telling other people what to do, and he was slow to rouse. He had been hand-picked as company runner by Major Harrison who felt, gallant officer though he was, that nature had not intended him to be a mountaineer. It was an important part of Speakman's function to ensure his company commander's ability to negotiate obstacles on steep hillsides. On this particular night of battle, his company commander told him to cover part of the crest of the hill, and it is a curious coincidence that, just as C.S.M. Skinner and C.Q.M.S. Grimbaldeston at Passchendaele before him had both been wounded by the time they began their exploits, so, too, Speakman had already received a painful snick in his leg. This had angered him, and must have lent him the utmost resources of human nature. An extract from the subsequent citation of his Victoria Cross in the *London Gazette* will suffice:

'Private Speakman decided on his own initiative to drive the enemy off the position and keep them off it. He collected quickly a large pile of grenades and led a party of six men in a series of grenade charges. The force and determination of his charges broke up each successive enemy onslaught and resulted in an ever-mounting pile of enemy dead. At the critical moment of the withdrawal, amidst an inferno of enemy machine-gun and mortar fire, as well as grenades, Private Speakman led a final charge to clear the crest of the hill and hold it while the remainder of his Company withdrew. Under the stress and strain of the battle, Private Speakman's outstanding powers of leadership were revealed and he so dominated the situation that he inspired his comrades to stand firm and fight the enemy to a standstill.'

At about midnight, B Company with the Battle Patrol under command withdrew some 1,400 yards south to a new position

---

[5] A Black Watch soldier serving in Europe, he had volunteered for Korea and joined 1st K.O.S.B. as a reinforcement. Later he transferred to the Regiment.

known as 'Italy'. On the right, D Company still held part of Peak. A Company was still in its original reserve position behind Peak, but as the battalion's front had been beaten back, pivoting on Peak, A Company was no longer in a reserve position. The remains of C Company, close to Battalion HQ became reserve company.

At the same time, a wireless message from D Company reported the two platoons on Knoll to be still holding out. Their withdrawal was ordered, but there was no further word of them. In the small hours, enemy shelling lifted on to A Company and the area of Battalion Headquarters, and the Chinese began firing tracer ammunition down the valley between Peak and Italy. The Borderers, depleted as they were, and with heavy loss of weapons and equipment, prepared to give an account of themselves again; but the Chinese appeared to have had enough, for a renewed attack did not materialize. Intelligence reports afterwards indicated that their attacking division had lost over 1,000 killed.

Finally, at dawn, a dishevelled and bloodstained figure appeared at Battalion Headquarters, to be greeted by an astonished Major Tadman: 'Where in the hell have you come from?'

It was Second-Lieutenant Purves, reporting 7 Platoon to be present and correct. His situation had been that after the Chinese had captured United, Hinge and Point 317 (Peak), 7 and 11 Platoons were still holding out on Knoll. His fellow platoon commander, Henderson, had been wounded in the arm and shoulder, so Purves took command of both platoons. In the course of the night he picked up a voice on the wireless from D Company suggesting he should withdraw, but as the Knoll position was intact he saw no reason to do so. 11 Platoon's ammunition trench had caught fire, the platoon sergeant had endeavoured to put it out with the last of their drinking water, the twelve Bren guns were down to their last ammunition cases, and the two platoons had fired some 200 parachute flares, when the same voice from D Company relayed an order from Battalion Headquarters to withdraw. So Purves, who was a methodical young man, collected together the fit, the walking wounded, the stretcher cases, and everything down to the last compass, and found a way back. The Korean porters with the stretcher cases took a wrong turning in the dark and proceeded towards the Chinese on Point 317, but he managed to retrieve them, dispatched 11 Platoon back to D Company, reported to his Commanding Officer with 7 Platoon, and with a shrapnel wound in his shoulder, collapsed in a state of exhaustion for thirty-six hours in a U.S. field hospital. Among the awards for gallantry made to officers and men of 1st K.O.S.B. for their conduct on the night 4/5 November 1951, was that of the D.S.O. to this National Service Second-Lieutenant, aged nineteen.

An immediate casualty check had revealed seven killed and a further forty-four missing, and eighty-seven wounded, almost all from B, C and D Companies.[6]

*   *   *   *   *

Congratulatory messages that reached the battalion from many quarters included the following from the Lord Provost of Edinburgh:

'The City of Edinburgh where your Regiment was raised nearly 300 years ago and whose arms and motto you bear is proud of your heroic stand in Korea. The traditions established at Killiecrankie are still maintained. At this time of remembrance our thoughts must necessarily be with those who mourn as a result of this action. We will remember Hills 217 and 317. Our best wishes to all ranks and our deepest sympathy with the wounded. *Nisi Dominus Frustra.*'   (*Signed*) JAMES MILLER.

After a few days of reorganization and re-equipping, 1st K.O.S.B. went back into the line, to confront their former positions which were now occupied by the Chinese, until relieved by American troops in somewhat alarming manner on Thanksgiving Day. The Chinese succeeded in recapturing Kowang-San (Point 355), but were driven off it again by an American counter-attack. Points 217 and 317 remained in enemy hands. The drawn-out trench stalemate had set in, and the Borderers spent the rest of their time in Korea holding another sector of the line, south-west of Kowang-San, with periods in brigade reserve. It was realized that there would probably be a withdrawal from the existing battle positions in the event of a cease-fire, when a retirement would doubtless be required of both sides, so in a sense the campaign had become a jostle for position with as little as possible given away. When the battalion was in reserve it worked on the defences of the Wyoming Line some 4,000-5,000 yards in rear, which had been selected as the position where the United Nations forces would ultimately halt.

The cease-fire was still to come,[7] but so far as the Borderers were concerned, Korean memories must here be laid aside — the dexterity of the U.S. negro medical orderlies in the hospitals, giving shots of penicillin like throwing darts; the enemy's attempt to attack A Company in April 1952, predicted from his wireless build-up and the pattern of his shelling, which brought down the

---

[6] 1st K.O.S.B. total battle casualties in Korea were: 62 killed, 228 wounded, 2 died of wounds.

[7] An armistice agreement was signed on 27 July 1953.

whole weight of the Commonwealth divisional artillery on the one company front; the high quality of the Australians, all volunteers, and of the U.S. Marine Corps with its rigid code of discipline; the menace of our own minefields, often unmapped and poorly marked, with fences obliterated by shelling; dug-out stoves, when the second winter hardened its grip, that varied in sophistication down to old ammunition boxes, filled with earth soaked with petrol, as dangerous as Chinese mortars; the lamps which shed light in command posts, but 'the men had mostly candles and lived much in the dark'; and the moving reminder of home which came with the death of King George VI. Men could be seen with tears in their eyes as the news went round the firing bays. Again the hot sticky summer came round, and the rains, leaving the abiding memory of the remorseless climate in its seasons which governed everyone's life.

On 12 August 1952, 1st K.O.S.B. sailed from Pusan for Hong Kong, on the first stage of their journey home. In due course, the honours *Kowang-San*, *Maryang-San*, and *Korea 1951-52* were awarded to the Regiment.

Chapter 14

THE TOUR IN MALAYA AND SINGAPORE, 1955-58

The 1st Battalion sailed from Hong Kong in November 1952, and was home for Christmas. The battalion reassembled from disembarkation leave in March 1953, and was stationed at Ballykinlar, Northern Ireland.

The Freedoms of three Border Burghs were conferred upon the Regiment in 1953 — those of Dumfries, Selkirk and Stranraer. In May 1954 at Ballykinlar, new Colours were presented to the 1st Battalion. Owing to the indisposition of the Colonel-in-Chief, they were presented by the Governor-General of Northern Ireland, Lord Wakehurst, but a new Quick March, *Her Royal Highness The Duchess of Gloucester*, composed for the occasion by Pipe Major McKinnon, was duly played for the first time. Later, the Colonel-in-Chief presented the 1st Battalion with a pipe banner displaying her coat of arms on one side and the Regimental crest on the other.

On 25 August 1955, the 1st Battalion sailed from Belfast for the Far East again, Lieutenant-Colonel D. W. McConnel, O.B.E. commanding,[1] and was to remain either in Singapore or on active service in the Federation of Malaya for three years, until after Malaya became independent. It is a strange reflection that Britain's contracting overseas commitments, and the whittling down of her armed forces, resulted in the Regiment's only regular battalion spending more than seventeen years outside the United Kingdom, mostly east of Suez, during the first twenty-five years that followed the Second World War.

*　　*　　*　　*　　*

The initial rôle of 1st K.O.S.B. was to act as Internal Security battalion in Singapore, and on disembarkation the battalion moved into Selarang Barracks on the east side of the island. This was an 'accompanied' tour and some fifty families came too, but remained in Singapore when the battalion subsequently went up-country, because of the 'Emergency' in progress in the Federation of Malaya at that time. This saw the slow strangling of the attempted

---

[1] He had also commanded the 2nd Battalion in Burma in 1944.

Communist insurrection that was born out of the Second World War, in particular the guerrilla activities of the Malayan Communist Party. The Emergency had existed since 1948, when emergency powers were adopted by the Government of the Federation, and the armed forces were called in.

It should be recalled that Malaya, when it formed part of the British Empire, consisted of a federation of nine protected states, of which Johore was one, and the two Straits Settlements of Penang and Malacca. About half the population were of Malaysian stock, the majority of the remainder being of Chinese origin, and it was the latter who composed the great majority of the armed terrorists of the Malayan Communist Party. Singapore was a separate Crown Colony, where those of Chinese origin greatly predominated.

The battalion's commitment to operations up-country began almost immediately, when three rifle companies were sent into South Johore to assist the police in gate checks at some of the new villages, searching the inhabitants for food and other clandestine supplies, medicine, ammunition, and checking identity documents, as they passed in and out. At the end of the year, the battalion carried out training by companies in jungle warfare, at the Far East Land Forces Training Centre in East Johore.[2]

Several K.O.S.B. companies returned to anti-terrorist operations in South Johore at the beginning of 1956, when their basic jungle training was completed, but in April the whole battalion was concentrated at Selarang Barracks in Singapore, preparatory to aiding the civil power. *Merdeka*[3] talks were currently taking place in London and disturbances on the island were threatened from several quarters — the People's Action Party, Trades Unions and students, all subject to Communist infiltration. In the event, the Borderers were not called upon, and as the battalion was eager for more active service, and more troops were required for anti-terrorist operation up-country, the battalion moved to the Batu Pahat area in West Johore in June 1956.

There followed nearly two years of anti-terrorist operations, but the battalion was still on call as Internal Security battalion in Singapore and in October 1956, was summoned to the island again, with other troops. On this occasion, student grievances had been fanned by the left wing, and the battalion became engaged in quelling serious rioting. The call for an immediate move by motor

[2] Later, Major R. G. R. Hill, 1st K.O.S.B., became Chief Instructor, Jungle Warfare Wing.

[3] Independence. The Federation became independent on 31 August 1957, and Singapore in 1959.

convoy had been received by Battalion Headquarters at Batu Pahat
on the evening of 25 October: the battalion was required in
Singapore by the next morning. There were some good roads in
Malaya, connecting the main towns, and a number of estate laterite
tracks could take vehicles, but unfortunately the call had been
received after the nightly wireless close-down, which was imposed
not only because noise carried, but also because of the atmospherics
at night. To extract the various companies from their operational
camps had been no easy matter, yet except for certain platoons
carrying out patrols and ambushes, and Headquarters elements left
at Batu Pahat, the battalion was in Singapore by breakfast time.

Three weeks later, 1st K.O.S.B. returned to Johore.[4]

The lasting memory of the Malayan jungle for one Borderer who
served there was a feeling of attachment towards it, rather than of
fear, and a certain amount of awe. In a sense the jungle was
protective. The Jocks, whose object was to reach their base camp
area in deep jungle as quickly and silently as possible, establish
their base and carry out a number of pre-planned anti-terrorist
patrols, were effectively screened from hostile eyes, even at a
distance of a very few feet.

To enter the jungle from the orderly lines of trees in the outlying
rubber plantations was to be enveloped by a tangled mass of vine
and putrefied branches, where the undergrowth struggling upwards
for light yielded only to the machete and the *parang*.[5] Occasionally,
clearings were reached where the sunlight penetrated, but these
would be hurried across, quickly and silently, until the soldiers
were hidden once more by the jungle screen. 'Quickly' and
'silently' are here but comparative terms, for the progress of man
was sufficiently clumsy and noisy to warn the natural denizens of
the jungle of his approach, and the more dramatic species of wild
life generally gave man a wide berth. But not the leeches, nor the
furtive jungle rats which were liable to invade the camp at night and
whose bite could be fatal.

The primary jungle was generally the easier to move through, as
the canopy of the tree-tops, of immense height, allowed of little
undergrowth in the gloom below. It was the secondary jungle,
where past clearances had grown wild again, that was the
wilderness. Bamboo was particularly thick and hard to cut, and
impossible to move through silently. Men could sink up to their
waists in the swamps. Writes Major J. B. A. Smyth:

---

[4] The battalion was given responsibility for the Internal Security of the Batu
Pahat Police Circle, but remained liable for recall to Singapore.

[5] Large Malayan sheath-knife.

'I once crossed a patch of *lallang* and swamp three hundred yards wide, which took me six hours to cross and ended with us all sitting exhausted and fully clothed in a stream to recover. *Lallang* was a kind of elephant grass that could be as much as ten feet high, where visibility was nil: 'It was like being baked in an oven, as you got the full sun on you and not a breath of air.'

'I should mention the ants,' writes Major A. J. Rennie:

'They varied in size from the common European-type ant to the large soldier ant, as big as one's thumb-nail. Passing through the jungle we occasionally saw the periodic mass movement of ant armies. Literally millions could be seen passing over the ground, into hollows, over and along fallen trees, and each and every one intent on a set purpose. The columns they formed were about a foot wide and were distinctly guarded on either side by the soldier ants, forming perfect flank guards with their greater speed, strength and height. I was always somewhat humbled at this sight and marvelled at the discipline and cohesion of these creatures and the silent, invisible influences guiding their dogged advance.'

Second-Lieutenant A. D. S. MacMillan wrote in B Company Notes for *The Borderers' Chronicle*:[6]

'Sound plays a large part in our jungle life. In surroundings which press close on all sides, the ears take over where the eyes fail. Birds and insects and monkeys all contribute to one grand never-ending jungle symphony. Monkeys, I find, can emit an eerie and nerve-racking wailing which sets the nerves tingling until one becomes accustomed to it. At nightfall, some species retire and others take over, but the noise continues. It is now that sound comes fully into its own.

The jungle night falls quickly, and trees and bushes assume menacing forms which move and threaten the longer one looks at them. You sit with your rifle across your knee and gradually the senses become taut as you strain into the darkness. The jungle floor is patterned with the luminosity of decaying leaves. You can lay a pattern of these to guide your hand to anything you may require during the dark hours. The brain becomes a sort of telephone exchange receiving and sorting out the myriad sounds into their respective origins.

Behind you, a comforting rustle and a deep breath tells you that you are not alone in this eerie world. It is good to know that a few yards away there are the others of your patrol . . . Crash-Thud! A long rolling thunder tears the jungle apart. One of our ambushes has fired. A whispered, but unnecessary, "Stand-to",

[6] August 1956.

brings the others from sleep to a tingling alertness, weapons ready to rip into anything out there that moves. We wait, slightly trembling, not with fear or with night chill, but with cold anticipating pleasure. Is this to be the reward for long grinding, smashing, exhausting marches through thorn and swamp? Will we claim another red star on our "kills" board? No, not yet. After a period of waiting we return to our blankets. We will find out in the morning the story of the shot in the night. Meanwhile, to move out to investigate would be to invite a hail of bullets from another of our own patrols.

Dawn comes slowly, filtering through the jungle roof. Gradually the jungle takes on shape and form, the luminous floor fades. The shadow you watched creeping nearer during the night becomes a bush once more. Another night is over . . . Presently the splutter of hexamine tablets in the small collapsible stoves announce that breakfast is under way and the start of another day.'

*   *   *   *   *

The battalion operated over a wide area to the north-east of Batu Pahat, shown on the accompanying sketch map; first, under command of the 63rd Gurkha Infantry Brigade in the 17th Gurkha Division, then for a period in 1957 under command of the 1st Federation Infantry Brigade, and finally, under the 26th Gurkha Infantry Brigade. On their shoulder flashes the Borderers wore the famous divisional emblem of the crossed kukris. The four rifle companies each operated over areas of about fifty square miles, and were each based on a wired-in hutted or tented camp up to forty miles distant from Batu Pahat where main Battalion Headquarters, Headquarters Company and Support Company were located.

From the operational camps the rifle platoons went out, one or more at a time, and set up their own base camps whence they operated small ambushes on likely C.T. (Communist Terrorist) courier routes, or sent out patrols, like spreading fingers, which moved through the jungle by map and compass and returned on back bearings. Despite the discomforts morale was always high, but tended to deteriorate after six or seven days in ambush positions; and a platoon normally returned to the 'Ops Camp' within that time.

'What goes on in an Ops Camp?' wrote Major F. H. Coutts in an article for *The Borderers' Chronicle.*[7] 'One's first impression

_____
[7] December 1957.

is of a band of men, stripped to the waist, magnificently sun-tanned, lean and superbly fit. It is with a shock that one later realizes that these warriors are not the members of the rifle platoons at all. They are the Base Wallahs, who carry out the many administrative duties in the Ops Camp, necessary to keep the troops in the jungle and to provide them with a comfortable base on return. No, your true jungle man is certainly not a sun-tanned hero — he is a pale, wan creature who blinks in the sunlight, for the sun seldom penetrates through the jungle canopy.'

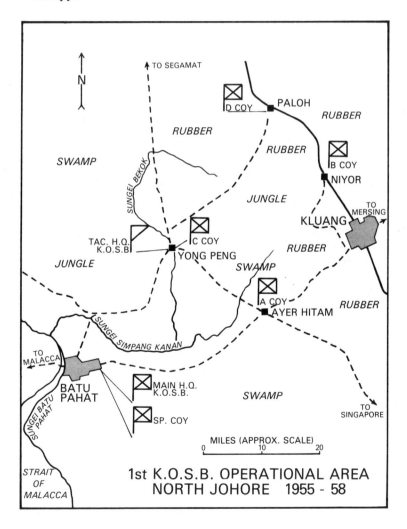

A platoon returns from the jungle, the men are given a rum ration and an enormous meal. As the sun sets a cool breeze rustles among the rubber trees, badminton is played, the Malayan national game which has spread to all Ops Camps.

'As darkness falls, the peace of the night is shattered by the roar of the electric generator leaping into life . . . The few comforts in an Ops Camp are completely at the whim of a machine of one kind or another: if any one of these fails life is a misery. In addition to the generator for the electric light, there is the water pump which miraculously produces drinking water from an evil-smelling swamp, the battery-charging engine which keeps the radios, official and otherwise, in working trim, and most precious of all, the paraffin refrigerators in cookhouse and canteen.'

Between sunset and lights-out there is probably a film show, provided by the Army Kinema Corporation, whose Malayan operators tour the camps with mobile vans.

'When the show finishes the audience disperse in little groups to their tents, the electric generator whines to a standstill and the stillness of the night is accentuated by the chirrup of the crickets. Nothing stirs apart from the flicker of the fireflies, the crackle of the 19 Set in the Signals Centre, and the shuffle of the prowler sentries as they patrol the camp perimeter in their unceasing watch for the enemy without.'

Doggedness was a quality that applied not only to the armies of ants. It applied to the putting down of the Communist insurrection in the Federation. The governing principle was to enforce the terrorists' total isolation from the rest of the community, denying them food or help of any kind. This entailed close control of the populated areas and the new villages established under the Briggs Plan,[8] by armed police, who were in full liaison with the security forces, while the main rôle of the army was to hunt and destroy the C.T.s in the jungle and on its fringes.

During the Second World War, the Malayan Communist Party had made common cause against the Japanese, but in 1945 the communist guerrilla fighters had left many of their weapons behind in secret dumps when they emerged from the jungle, to which they returned when the Emergency began. The C.T. leader, Chin Peng, had actually received an O.B.E. and had marched in the London Victory Parade. His followers were experienced fighters who

---

[8] Lieutenant-General Sir Harold Briggs, Director of Operations at Kuala Lumpur, 1950-51. The essence of the Briggs Plan was the long-term clearing of the whole country from south to north, establishing in its wake a strong police force and civil administration.

operated in groups under iron discipline, from well chosen bases deep in the jungle, but as the Briggs Plan took effect, they were increasingly unable to find isolated sprinklings of the population whom they could coerce into supplying their needs. They were compelled to come out into the open for supplies, information and propaganda purposes. During the Borderers' time in Malaya, the hard core was concentrated mainly on the Thailand border and in Johore, in small groups who pursued their aims as best they could. They were all extremely tough, with an instinct for danger gained over years of being hunted, and were as near to being jungle creatures as man can be.

Our troops were helped by Iban trackers imported from the Sarawak Rangers, and tracker dogs, and by the Australian 510 wireless-set, with sky-wave aerial, which gave easy communications over distances of fifty miles or more. The new Belgian 7.62mm self-loading rifle gave valuable service, substantially the same weapon that is used today. There was also the anti-malarial Paludrine tablet. It was compulsory to take a tablet a day, and to catch malaria was a chargeable offence. Yet for all the sweat, 1st K.O.S.B. in two-and-a-half years in the jungle, killed eight terrorists and wounded several others, in a total of twenty-two contacts made by the battalion.

Twenty-two contacts hardly sketches in the remorseless harrying which kept the terrorists on the run, the disappointments of contacts missed, or the weary hours in ambush positions when nothing happened. A 'contact' was where the security forces on encountering terrorists opened fire first, as opposed to an 'incident', which was when the terrorists were the first to open fire. The following was a typical incident:

Patrol Commander — Lance-Corporal Kernaghan. *Date/Time* — 1 January 1957, 21.25 hours. 'One ambush group lying next to track through swamp was observing in a southerly direction expected line of C.T. advance. Two C.T.s were seen about four yards away in opposite direction. Leading C.T. fired his carbine and dashed away into the swamp after his companion. Ambush party fired up the track for about two minutes after this. Small party returned to base for lights and dogs, and after ninety minutes follow-up was mounted. After about 1,500 yards lost track at approximate (map reference). Party was left overnight at this point in case C.T.s were in area. Follow-up mounted again at first light with three Ibans. Track finally petered out at (map reference) in dense swamp. Patrol then returned to base.'[9]

The following describes a contact which occurred at 09.10 hours,

---

[9] 1st K.O.S.B. War Diary.

19 December 1956. A small patrol of four Borderers and four Iban trackers, led by Second-Lieutenant Christie, was moving through 'dirty' — neglected — rubber. Also with them was an individual known as a Junior Chinese Liaison Officer, a Chinese Malayan recruited by the Police, and who was put to slightly covert uses. At the entrance to a track leading from a stream into tall fern 'some human excreta which was very fresh' was noticed.

'Bandits there,' said the J.C.L.O., pointing up the track. He tried a left flanking movement by himself, but the fern was too thick and noisy. Runs the patrol commander's report:

'I ordered "advance" with Private Dempi (Iban) on the left, Corporal Martin in the centre and myself on the right, all in a straight line. When we had gone about ten yards up the track Dempi fired one round. Immediately I saw a flash from within the fern about five yards to my left front and heard the explosion as a C.T. fired a shotgun at Private Dempi, who fell mortally wounded, but with his *parang* in his right hand determined to close with and kill the C.T. I fired six quick rounds with my carbine at the C.T. who had fired the shotgun. Corporal Martin (armed with an Owen 9mm automatic gun) stood in the centre and fired two single rounds followed by the remainder of his magazine in one burst at the movement within the ferns. Corporal Martin fired another magazine from his Owen at the same movement.'

There was a shout from the J.C.L.O., and Lance-Corporal Clelland, Private Munro and Private McCourt were sent round the right flank with him to cut off any C.T. escape route.

'By now, all three Ibans were weeping round the dying body of Private Dempi. Corporal Martin loaded a third magazine and continued to fire into the fern. I ordered "stop".'

They pulled back the fern and saw two bodies lying on the ground. Twice, one or the other moved. Twice more the corporal fired.[10]

C.T. bodies were brought back for identification wherever practicable, or if possible at least photographs and fingerprints, and were checked against lists and photographs of wanted people. If a local man was missing from his home, his name complete with duplicate identity card would be added to the list. The net was tight, and there were a number of special operations.

Earlier, for example, in September 1956, an increase in C.T. activity in the rubber smallholdings north of Yong Peng in 1st K.O.S.B. area caused a large part of the battalion to saturate the area with small ambushes. The Adjutant, Captain Lear, and

---

[10] 1st K.O.S.B. War Diary.

R.S.M. Downes, took the opportunity to mount a security deception at the Battalion Headquarters base area in Batu Pahat, by sending on shopping expeditions the few Headquarters personnel who had not been called out. They sauntered in uniform down the main street, and each time the ostensible shoppers reached the end of the town they strolled round a corner and were put into vehicles. They were then driven back to their starting-point by a devious route in order to repeat the process, thereby creating the impression that the normal number of Borderers were in the area.

Another special operation might be food denial, a 'blanket' operation throughout a Police Circle. 1st K.O.S.B. operational area covered two Police Circles, Batu Pahat and Kluang. Paradoxically, after the Union Jack had been lowered for the last time, there began a particularly arduous period. The towns and villages outside Batu Pahat had remained predominantly sympathetic to the C.T.s, and various large-scale jungle operations, ambushes and sweeps, were mounted around these villages, with the object of finding the C.T. living areas, including many deceptions and long night marches, and extensive searches of jungle swamps. During the battalion's last three months there were only three contacts; but the Borderers had played their part in the firm British action which, for a decade, maintained the stability and economy of the Federation that had now become an independent country within the Commonwealth.

On Merdeka Day, 31 August 1957, the Colonel-in-Chief had visited the battalion at Batu Pahat with her elder son, Prince William. At the end of the year, Lieutenant-Colonel J. D. Henson, M.B.E., M.C., was appointed Commanding Officer, and in March 1958, the battalion at length returned to Singapore. In October 1958, 1st K.O.S.B. sailed for the United Kingdom.

*   *   *   *   *

The last anti-terrorist operation undertaken by 1st K.O.S.B. in Malaya concerned a female terrorist known as 'the Pineapple Pin-up', and best concludes the chapter.

Female terrorists fought as men and were equally hardy, and as the War Diary shows, they had certainly been included among the battalion's 'kills'. The Pineapple Pin-up, herself, was a prominent Johore Communist leader. She was a remarkable woman who had taken to the jungle in 1949, and on various occasions had been seemingly trapped by the security forces' cordons, but had always escaped. Once she had been wounded, and for nine years she had defied all attempts to eliminate her. Her real name was Ah Chiau.

In May 1958, after the battalion had returned to Singapore, it happened that B and D Companies were required for another anti-terrorist operation in South Johore, and were based on an operational camp across the strait, outside Johore Bahru. While they were there, the preoccupation of the Police Special Branch with the movements of Ah Chiau by chance bore fruit, and a long-standing plan to ambush her could be put into effect. Its execution, on 15 June 1958, fell to the K.O.S.B. There was need for haste, and a combined ambush party of twelve men was assembled from the two companies: a subaltern, nine N.C.O.s and two private soldiers, under Captain Oatts as ambush commander.

'Remember now — this must not fail,' said the Brigade Commander over the telephone.

Captain Oatts and his group commanders went to the house of the Senior Special Branch Officer for a lengthy briefing that evening, where they also met the police informer, a rubber tapper, as it was important that they should be able to recognize him later. Ah Chiau was about to meet him to obtain some supplies between 06.30 and 07.30 hours the next morning. She would, the informer told them, be wearing a Sam-Fu, the conventional working dress of Chinese women, gym shoes and puttees, and would be bare-headed or wearing a scarf. She would be armed with a British S.M.L.E. No 5 rifle,[11] and was described as having a gold tooth and scars on her forehead and left buttock.

The Special Branch officer stressed that no matter how many C.T.s entered the ambush area, the ambush party were to make certain that they killed Ah Chiau first. No one was to open fire unless she alone was in his sights, or unless the ambush was compromised.

In the small hours of the morning, the ambush party armed with Bren guns and 7.62mm rifles were taken in transport some twenty miles to a point where a Police Inspector led them in intense darkness to the ambush position, at a junction of tracks in an area where thick undergrowth bordered 'clean' rubber.

By 05.45 hours, the ambush party were in position in three groups, posted at intervals along some 450 yards of a track, with dawn fast approaching. Shortly before 06.30 hours, the informer bicycled past, laid his bicycle down near Group 2, and began tapping for rubber down another track that led off. Ten minutes later a figure walked past Sergeant Thackray, who was behind a Bren gun two feet from the ambush track, in command of Group 2. It was a C.T. aged about thirty-five, wearing a grey shirt, dark blue trousers, and a white trilby hat with a black band, with a No 5 rifle

---

[11] A shortened version of the conventional Mark IV of the Second World War.

slung over his shoulder. He was walking in the same direction as the informer. The men a little farther along in Group 3 suddenly heard the informer's bicycle bell ringing furiously for about thirty seconds, and could see through the foliage a blue shirt and white hat. The informer had now returned to the main track and talked with the C.T. for about ten minutes. The C.T. then retraced his steps past Group 2 and Sergeant Thackray's Bren gun, and vanished, while the informer moved off the other way past Group 3.

Captain Oatts, 300 yards ahead up the track with Group 1, had so far seen nothing except the informer bicycling past, and he now faced a trying wait. A Communist sympathizer, who had previously been contacted on Ah Chiau's behalf by the informer, was expected to meet her just in front of Group 1 at 09.00. At 08.30 hours, a second tapper appeared who was assumed to be the sympathizer. Group 1 were watching for developments when at 09.00 hours the soldier who was facing to the rear of the ambush saw two C.T.s approaching through the undergrowth. The nearer one was carrying a No 5 rifle and moving warily. The other was some way behind and there was only a glimpse of dark blue trousers.

The leading C.T. came on, reached the ambush position, and began to peer through the bushes, and saw the ambush. Captain Oatts fired one shot, killing him at a range of six feet. There was a scurry in the undergrowth behind. Group 1 immediately searched the vicinity, firing their Bren gun into every likely bush, but no one else was found. About twenty minutes later, on the other flank, the informer materialized from the thickets in some agitation and leapt into the midst of Group 3, with whom he stayed. Called by wireless, a follow-up party arrived with dogs, who led off on a strong scent which unfortunately, was to be washed out by a thunderstorm.

From the debriefing of the ambush groups and the informer it transpired that the apparent 'man' who had twice passed the muzzle of Sergeant Thackray's Bren gun was certainly the wanted woman, vexatious as it was to Group 2 who had implicitly obeyed the orders they had been given. Meanwhile all available troops cordoned the area and swept it. Fresh ambushes were laid. Reconnaissance aircraft flew overhead. But to no avail. The Pineapple Pin-up had got away again.

Chapter 15

A NEW ERA

At midnight, 20/21 September 1958, Nee Soon transit camp, Singapore, was disturbed by the sound of the soldiers of the 1st Battalion, The King's Own Scottish Borderers, marching through the camp in various forms of night attire behind the Pipes and Drums. It was their last night in Singapore. Reaching the parade ground they formed a large impromptu circle, with the Pipe Band playing reels in the middle, and then dispersed quietly to their beds. Looked at from today, that night's proceedings marked the passing of an age. Within two years the Regimental Depot was to receive its last intake of National Servicemen, and the next time the 1st Battalion was stationed in Eastern climates, in 1962, its last National Serviceman were released. On 8 November 1963, the last passing-out parade at Berwick took place; in fact, although from 1960 the Depot had been shared with The Royal Scots while a new amalgam, The Lowland Brigade Depot, was being prepared at Glencorse, Edinburgh. This opened in May 1964. At Berwick, the last cricket match against the Eton Ramblers had been played, and only 'R.H.Q.' remained in the former officers' quarters beside the deserted barracks square, surrounded by Vanbrugh's grey, empty buildings which are reanimated periodically by the voices of boy cadets, among the mists and the winds and the ramparts, and the memories of eight decades, at Berwick-upon-Tweed.

The past twenty years have seen great changes. Successive defence cuts have been represented as a pruning of the 'tail' and a greater efficiency of 'teeth', and between the years 1958 and 1970 alone, the Borderers eight times survived amalgamations of the line regiments. The image of a highly professional, small standing army has been established, but the new professionalism largely derives from an attitude, a greater career-consciousness than in the past, for it is to be doubted whether the basic qualities needed in a soldier have changed. It is many years since General Wavell defined the ideal infantryman as a combination of cat-burglar, gunman, poacher. Today the army travels less on its feet than formerly, but a long time ago a senior officer at the conclusion of the Afghan War declared 'the patient endurance of hardship' to be the highest attribute of a soldier; and so, in the last resort, it is likely to remain.

The combat suit and the chunky jersey convey the new image, the modern equivalent of the thin red line. The old scarlet, which disappeared in 1914, nevertheless existed officially as full dress until the Second World War, and officers preserved it where possible for such occasions as levées and weddings. The full dress survives today in the familiar 'No 1 Dress' which was approved in 1950, with dark blue doublet[1] in place of the scarlet. White spats give a distinctive finish to Leslie tartan trews, and make a trim unison on marching feet when on parade. In place of the pre-1914 Kilmarnock, the Lowland bonnet of the Balmoral type was worn with blackcock feathers, but this was replaced by the Glengarry in 1961. The first time anyone in the Regiment, except for the Bands, wore the new No 1 Dress was at the Coronation of Queen Elizabeth II.

From 1959 until 1969, the infantry was reorganized on a brigade basis, and a Lowland Brigade badge was worn on bonnets. In 1969, the Regimental badge came back into its own, and today all surviving Scottish regiments maintain their separate identities within a divisional administrative framework — the Scottish Division, which has the one training depot at Glencorse, and another for junior soldiers at Bridge of Don, and its headquarters at Edinburgh Castle.

Meanwhile, a run-down of the Territorial Army was proceeding, and with questionable wisdom it was eventually demolished in its old form. Deep wells of loyalty and a great structure of service to country went for nought.

The 4th (Border) and 5th (Dumfries and Galloway) Battalions had both sent detachments to the memorable review of the Territorial Army by King George VI in the autumn of 1948, in London. The 4th Battalion, for a time, became a motor battalion. In 1957, National Servicemen were released from the obligation to serve their term with the Territorials, and were merely held on the books in case of emergency, but a full return to the volunteer spirit was a not unwelcome challenge. Both battalions were well up to strength in senior ranks when, in 1961, amid some uproar on the Border, the two battalions were amalgamated into the 4th/5th. The combined area was an unwieldy one, all six Border counties, containing twenty-three Drill Halls scattered from Duns in the east to Stranraer in the west, the largest area of any T.A. infantry battalion in the United Kingdom.

'It is hoped that all Borderers will join together to fight this stupid illogical plan,' declared *The Berwickshire News* and other Border newspapers. 'We do not consider it is too late to stop these

---

[1] Due to be replaced by dark green.

units from being messed up.'

Nevertheless, there it was. New Colours were presented to the 4th/5th K.O.S.B. by the Colonel-in-Chief at Galashiels on 25 May 1963.

Eventually, in 1966, plans were announced to re-model the Territorial Army and to create also a new Army Volunteer Reserve. There resulted the T.&A.V.R., an administrative title under which the 4th/5th K.O.S.B. dwindled away and subsequently provided the basis for two volunteer companies. These bear the involved designations of C Company (K.O.S.B.), 1st/52nd Lowland Volunteer Battalion, and No 3 (K.O.S.B.) Company, 2nd/52nd Lowland Volunteer Battalion. C Company (K.O.S.B.) has its headquarters at Dumfries. No 3 (K.O.S.B.) Company has its head-quarters at Galashiels, and initially the members of the former 4th (Border) Battalion Pipe Band supplied the Pipes and Drums of the 2nd/52nd Volunteers; but gone was the Buccleuch tartan. Mess silver and certain funds, and Colours laid up, are the only tangible reminders of the Regiment's two distinctive Territorial Army battalions.

*   *   *   *   *

The post-war years cannot pass from these pages without certain more personal events of Regimental interest being recorded. There was the retirement of one of the most colourful of Borderers, R.S.M. 'Fister' Walls, M.C., who was R.S.M. of the 6th Battalion during the Second World War, and thereafter R.S.M. of the 1st Battalion, and finally Depot R.S.M. He was discharged in 1954 after thirty-two years of soldiering, but he remained in civilian employment at the Depot, and later was custodian of the Regimental Museum, until 1970, completing forty-eight years service with the Regiment. R.S.M. Walls was the son of 'Joker' Walls, who had put forward his age and enlisted in the 3rd (Militia) Battalion when a boy of twelve, and who in his mid-'teens had served throughout the South African War as Commanding Officer's bugler and groom.

At length, by 1957, the Battle Honours of the Second World War were approved. Then older history was recalled, when on 27 July 1959, at the Guildhall, City of London, the splendid Minden Dinner was held to celebrate the bicentenary of the Battle of Minden. Her Majesty the Queen was in Canada at the time, but the Dinner was held in the presence of three other Colonels-in-Chief, Queen Elizabeth the Queen Mother, Princess Margaret and the Duchess of Gloucester, and was attended by the Master Gunner and the Colonels and past and serving officers of the six Minden regiments and the Minden batteries, Royal Artillery.[2]

For Borderers, mention of the Queen Mother inevitably brings to mind Pipe Major L. V. de Laspee, who was her personal piper for many years. He had joined the Regiment as a Boy Piper in 1926, was a champion Highland Dancer, and was Pipe Major of the 1st Battalion in Palestine after the Second World War. When the 1st Battalion provided the Royal Guard at Balmoral in 1948, Pipe Major de Laspee played the pipes and danced for the Royal Family. In 1952 his time as a regular soldier ended and he joined The London Scottish (T.A.) as a piper. During a visit to that regiment by the Queen Mother, as she now was, he was at once recognized by her, and at her request was appointed her personal piper at Clarence House. This appointment he held for twenty-two years, and was Pipe Major of the London Scottish for over twenty of them. He retired in 1975 after nearly fifty years service with the K.O.S.B. and The London Scottish.

In 1957, Lieutenant-Colonel P. St. C. Harrison, D.S.O., O.B.E., was appointed Regimental Secretary, and the fine Regimental Museum which can be visited by the public at the Barracks, Berwick-upon-Tweed, was his creation. In 1973, after sixteen years in the appointment that links the Regiment he was appropriately 'dined out' by the Colonel of the Regiment and others at R.H.Q.[3]

The 1st Battalion had returned from Malaya to Milton Bridge, Edinburgh, at the end of 1958. On 31 January 1959, the battalion, preceded by the Military Band and the massed Pipe Bands of the 1st, 4th and 5th Battalions, and followed by detachments from both the T.A. battalions, marched down Princes Street with bayonets fixed and Colours flying. The salute was taken by the Lord Provost, who was accompanied by the Colonel of the Regiment and the Duke of Buccleuch, and by Major-General J. F. M. Macdonald, D.S.O., O.B.E., who had commanded the 1st Battalion in Korea, and was now G.O.C. 52nd (Lowland) Division (T.A.). After only five months at Edinburgh the 1st Battalion went to Berlin, as part of the Garrison with its special rôle within N.A.T.O.

In 1961, the 1st Battalion returned from Berlin to Edinburgh, to Redford Barracks, and in June of that year an unusual family

---

[2] 12th Field Battery R.A., 32nd Light Anti-Aircraft Battery R.A., The Suffolk Regiment, The Lancashire Fusiliers, The Royal Welsh Fusiliers, The King's Own Scottish Borderers, The Royal Hampshire Regiment, The King's Own Yorkshire Light Infantry.

[3] He remained actively associated with the Regiment's affairs, and his recent death at Berwick-upon-Tweed was a sad loss to the Regiment. The Museum goes from strength to strength and is being considerably expanded.

ceremony took place when the battalion provided the guards at the installation of Lieutenant-General W. F. R. Turner, C.B., D.S.O., as 88th Governor of Edinburgh Castle and G.O.C. in C., Scotland. General Turner, who succeeded to the Colonelcy later that year, and was created K.B.E.,[4] was presented with the keys of the Castle by his son, Second-Lieutenant W. S. Turner, 1st K.O.S.B.

A few days earlier, at the end of May, a different kind of ceremony had taken place at Belfast, when representatives of the Regiment attended the commissioning of a new H.M.S. *Berwick*. Built by Harland & Wolff, she was a frigate of 2,144 tons. The Colonel of the Regiment, Major-General J. Scott Elliot, C.B., C.B.E., D.S.O., (retired), presented her captain with a silver comemorative plaque. General Scott Elliot was G.O.C. 51st (Highland) Division, 1952-56.

In April 1962, the 1st Battalion embarked for Aden, replete with the triumph of having won the Army Rugby Cup for the previous two years. A substantial family occasion was witnessed on the quayside as R.S.M. W. Murdoch of the 4th/5th Battalion came to say farewell to his brother, R.S.M. J. Murdoch, M.B.E., D.C.M., the only two brothers to have both served as R.S.M. in the Regiment at the same time.

*   *   *   *   *

The main rôle of the 1st Battalion in Aden was Internal Security, with subsidiary guard and ceremonial duties. From time to time there were platoon or company training exercises in the rocky hills up-country, and one company was flown to Kenya for an exercise.

Aden, originally occupied by the East India Company in 1839, for coaling their ships, was now a major oil bunkering port. The battalion was quartered in air-conditioned barracks of Swedish wood, at Khormaksar, on the flat sandy land near the race course; but the cookhouse was not air-conditioned and startling temperatures could be read on the thermometer there. The intense heat was very humid; only for about four winter months was the warmth pleasant with cool nights. A wide variety of sporting activities was pursued throughout the year, including some shark fishing. Second-Lieutenant D. M. W. Griffiths, a half-miler of note, represented Aden at the 1962 Commonwealth Games.

The tour, accompanied by families, lasted until 1964, during which time the colony acceded to the Federation of South Arabia. The Federation had been created in 1959 and consisted of a number

---

[4] He is today Lord Lieutenant of Dumfries.

of small Sultanates, Amirates and Sheikhdoms, all British pro-
tectorates. The battalion stood-by for Internal Security duties on
several occasions, and in September 1962, was called out to deal
with riots in the Arab township of Crater. Major P. H.
Middlemiss, a retired officer serving in the Education Branch at
G.H.Q. Middle East Command, which was then in Aden, was much
impressed by the battalion. He had no previous connection with the
Regiment, but in due course both his sons entered the K.O.S.B.

'The Regiment had to provide soldiers for some extra-Regimental
duties,' he writes, 'and among these was one private soldier for
us in Education. He also drove the R.A.E.C. officers in the
Education Land Rover. He was always called 'Jock' and I never
knew his real name. He came, I remember, from Dumfries and
he was with Education for the Regiment's entire tour in Aden.
He was a fine young chap, always beautifully turned out, with
his smart Leslie tartan hosetops and his Glengarry so gay and
attractive.'

Major Middlemiss also edited the local Forces newspaper, *The
Dhow*, and he obtained as his public relations man Sergeant
Speakman, V.C. 'Speakman was a huge success; his large frame,
coupled with his notoriety and happy manner made him very
welcome everywhere, he seemed to know everyone and he could
arrange anything.' When the first B.O.A.C. VC10 landed at
Khormaksar, Sergeant Speakman was on the airfield to meet it,
and *The Dhow* carried a headline: 'VC greets VC10.'

'The Regiment was very kind to me. I attended a Ceilidh, and
the Minden Day parade. This latter event was somewhat
dramatic, the G.O.C. forgot to wear his insignia of rank on his
khaki drill and the Sergeants' Mess were horrified when he went
to them for an after parade drink. There was also the last ever
Regimental Footlights show to be put on in Aden, in Waterloo
Barracks, Khormaksar. Allan Alstead[5] was A.D.C. to the High
Commissioner, the Jocks were to be seen in the bazaars, and
altogether it was a happy time. Alas, I can remember seeing the
Commanding Officer tumbling out of the aircraft when they had
to return so suddenly from the United Kingdom, to help out
in the Radfan.'

The Radfan emergency has passed into Regimental lore. In
February 1964, the battalion had returned home to form part of the
United Kingdom Strategic Reserve, and was stationed at
Shorncliffe. There, on Friday, 1 May, less than three months after
the battalion had left Aden, and not twenty-four hours after it took
over the rôle of spearhead battalion, 1st K.O.S.B. were ordered to

[5] Commanding Officer, 1974-76.

return immediately to Aden. The airlift remained a textbook example of a spearhead battalion move for years afterwards.

'It is not when we go,' Lieutenant-Colonel Alastair Thorburn had announced to his company commanders at 5 o'clock in the afternoon of that Friday, 'it is how quickly we can go tonight.'

The battalion was in Aden within forty-eight hours of the warning order. For nearly three months it operated in the desert hinterland in aid of the Federal troops, putting down harassment from Yemeni tribesmen, among the boulder-strewn valleys and dust storms and volcanic rock formations of the Radfan Mountains. Under the burning sun of the hot season the Borderers operated mainly in the two fertile plains among these mountains, in company localities, supplied from an advanced base and airstrip. The forward supply journey took three hours by Land Rover up the parched wadis, or five minutes by helicopter, the main supply problem being water. The medical authorities estimated water requirement at four gallons per man per day.

It was no easy task to locate the rebel tribesmen, as they kept on the move and their numbers were comparatively small. Sangars and fortified houses and villages, reminiscent of the North-West Frontier of India, afforded good positions for the battalion. Numerous patrols, ambushes, sorties and searches were undertaken, but the grim terrain was a haven for the Yemeni guerrillas, who hid when the sun was up, observing from crevice or cave, ready to harass at night. In the matter of tactics, however, the similarity with the North-West Frontier of India ended; for the Borderers, themselves, turned to night tactics, and while guns and mortars fired on likely Yemeni hideouts by day, the companies lay up, and sent out their patrols when the sun was setting behind the harsh mountain crests. These patrols became very proficient, and control of a 95 square-mile zone of operations was soon achieved. At the end of July 1964, the 1st Battalion returned to Shorncliffe, its casualties having been six men wounded.

The Yemeni Arabs underwent a period of internal strife involving both Britain and Egypt, in which the National Liberation front ultimately gained control, and in 1967 Britain ceded Aden and all the protected territories.

*   *   *   *   *

The gist of the Staff College definition of 'Counter-Revolutionary Operations' is that these are operations which British forces may have to undertake in support of an established legal government, whether its overthrow is threatened by the more serious kind of Internal Security situation or by open insurrection, and whether inspired from within or from outside the territory concerned. Counter-revolutionary operations have been the substance of the Regiment's active service ever since the Korean War.

The 1st Battalion was part of the United Kingdom Strategic Reserve from 1964 to 1967, and left Shorncliffe for a second time, in the spring of 1965, for an emergency tour of one year in the Far East, Lieutenant-Colonel C. G. Stonor, M.C. commanding. The battalion embarked for Hong Kong in April, and was stationed in the New Territories to strengthen the Security Forces, before sailing for Singapore at the end of July. After two months training at the Jungle Warfare School in Johore, near Kota Tinggi, the Borderers on 30 September 1965, embarked for Borneo.

From the time Sarawak and Sabah — formerly British North Borneo — had joined the Federation of Malaya, which changed its name to Malaysia, two years previously, President Sukarno of Indonesia had pursued a policy of confrontation. There had been Indonesian border incursions, and it became necessary to send Commonwealth forces to assist Malaysian resistance. Accordingly, 1st K.O.S.B., at that time organized into a Headquarters Company and three rifle companies, became responsible for the security of a wide area in the centre of Sarawak, taking over from the 3rd Battalion The Royal Malaya Regiment, in the Third (Civil) Division of the country. Battalion Headquarters disembarked at Sibu, the second largest town, forty miles up the Rajang River. From Sibu the rifle companies were taken a further sixty miles upstream by the same ship, specially designed for river navigation, in which they had sailed from Singapore. Reaching Song, an important transit post, the companies disembarked and dispersed to their respective bases by a combination of longboat, speedboat and helicopter. Remarkable was the river procession of A Company to their base up the tributary Katibas River, a distance of twenty miles, which the company accomplished in Norse-like splendour in seventeen longboats. B Company was located at Nanga Gaat, seventy miles from Song, up another tributary of the Rajang. Across the hills from B Company, and accessible only by the navigation of formidable rapids up a further tributary of the Rajang, or by helicopter, was C Company at a place called Long Jawi. C Company was 180 miles from Battalion Headquarters at Sibu.

From these company bases the Borderers kept watch and patrolled the frontier with Indonesia for a period of six months, the scene of their operations being the Iran Mountains, the watershed which divides Sarawak from the main land mass of Borneo. Here they lived through the same monsoon rain, the corrosive humidity and jungle decay that had been the conditions in Malaya, but life in Sarawak was more picturesque. In this country without railways or roads, all transport was by river, and the river traffic and the floating timber, and the native longhouses built on 'stilts' over the water and, above all, the friendliness and hospitality of the native Iban people, first met in Malaya as trackers for the Security Forces, afforded unending fascination. No less fascinating was the great variety of wild life, ranging from the Orang-outang to a variety of pets which the soldiers attracted to themselves, such as birds, tortoises, and even a B Company honey bear, a bear that indeed had a passion for honey.

Armed with a lightweight American rifle of small calibre, the AR 15, companies sent out patrols by helicopter or boat for periods of up to two weeks. Patrols were generally at platoon strength, and would often bivouac at comparatively high altitudes in the mountains, where night temperatures in the monsoon months of January and February contrasted sharply with the daytime heat. Local game frequently supplemented the rations. Supplies were maintained laboriously by river transport or helicopter. On the rivers the Army used speedboats, and assault-boats or longboats with outboard engines, the latter being used mainly upstream, requiring Iban drivers and look-out men for the perilous navigation. Uncertain in reliability, the outboard engines at least scared away a vicious breed of crocodile which normally infested these reaches.

Closest to the Indonesian border was A Company — later changed over with B Company — on the Katibas River at Bankit. One platoon was in a forward base at Katibas village, only eight miles from the frontier. At first there were some incidents in this area, intruders were several times seen and there was an attempt to attack a platoon camp, but after the first fortnight there were no further encounters in any part of 1st K.O.S.B. area.[6]

In January 1966, the Colonel-in-Chief visited the battalion at Sibu.

*   *   *   *   *

By the end of April 1966, the 1st Battalion had been flown home, reassembling at Shorncliffe from disembarkation leave in June of that year. The specialists of Support Company were reformed after

---

[6] The Regiment's tour in Sarawak coincided with disturbances in Indonesia which led to the banning of the Communist Party and President Sukarno's fall from effective power. In August 1966, the confrontation with Malaysia ended and Indonesia resumed membership of the United Nations.

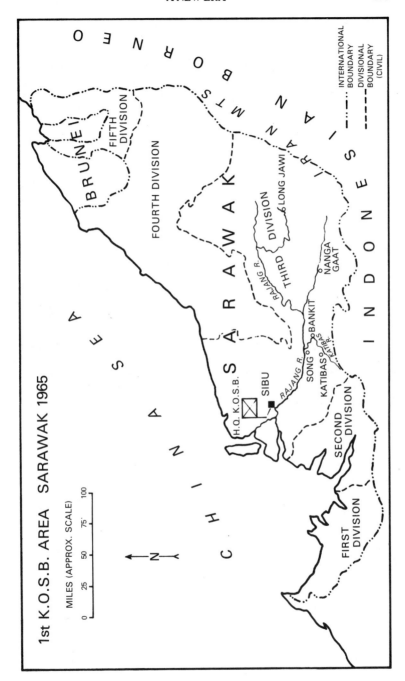

1st K.O.S.B. AREA   SARAWAK 1965

their period with the rifle companies, and much new equipment arrived. Troops invariably enjoy being on detachment and the Sarawak tour was a highlight in the soldiers' experience, despite an unhealthy climate and a high risk of disease. Nor should it be forgotten that more than two hundred families were left at Shorncliffe for a year's separation, whose welfare was the concern of Major Warman, the Families Officer. That there was a minimum of compassionate and welfare cases throughout this time was due to the great backing given to the soldiers by their families, and this was a considerable factor in maintaining the battalion's high morale.

A Company Notes in *The Borderers' Chronicle*, December 1966, spoke for many:

'The fascinations of Sarawak seem but a dream as the winds blow and the seas rage around the Folkestone shores. The charm and simplicity of the Ibans, the vagaries of the Rajang River and its adjoining tributaries, the chatter and noise of the jungle which so often changed to an eerie and haunting stillness only broken by the heavy breathing and whispered commands of our patrols, were experiences never to be forgotten.'

In February 1967, the battalion completed what had been an active and rewarding three years in United Kingdom Strategic Reserve, and there followed the first stages of conversion to a mechanized battalion, equipped with Armoured Personnel Carriers. In June 1967, 1st K.O.S.B. moved to Osnabruck, Germany, into the British Army of the Rhine, for what is always the first commitment of the British Army: the defence of the United Kingdom within the N.A.T.O. concept of the defence of Western Europe.

Life in B.A.O.R. was a full one, dominated by battle groups and combat teams, fitness for Rôle inspections, specialist training courses, and many exercises. Vehicles crossed water by 'flotation', army helicopters became familiar as combat vehicles or as a tactical means of deploying troops, and there could be Centurion tanks under command of K.O.S.B. company commanders. Exercises ranged in their setting from Jutland to the Moselle, and in the summer of 1969 the whole battalion was flown to Libya for one month's training in the Western Desert near Tobruk. Infantry must still ultimately fight on their feet, but while 1st K.O.S.B. had always to retain their basic infantry skills to this end, they also had to acquire, as a mechanized battalion, the driving and maintenance skills of an armoured regiment and a detailed knowledge of All Arms tactics, capabilities and co-operation. The versatility required of the modern infantryman was reflected by activities that were not in the routine of Borderers of the past, such as Outward Bound courses in Norway, adventure training in the Black Forest or the Bavarian Alps, ski-ing — which quickly attracted its enthusiasts, and free-fall parachuting. Four teams were entered for the B.A.O.R. free-fall parachuting and tactical competition, held in the autumn of 1968, at which the battalion's A team gained second place.

All these activities came to an end in March 1970, when after a return to Osnabruck from training in Westphalia, the battalion underwent a month's intensive rehearsal of Internal Security duties in preparation for a new spearhead rôle. The Commanding Officer's reconnaissance party disappeared to the island which the Regiment had garrisoned in the past for periods totalling some fifty years; and returned with strange tidings. An accelerated flurry of preparations included the fashioning of shields, and 1st K.O.S.B. in the first week of May 1970, found themselves, unbelievably, in the streets of Belfast.

Chapter 16

TO SECURE THE PEACE

'We believe that we have made a successful contribution to saving bloodshed in a country, most of whose people want peace, and most of whose countryside is too beautiful to spoil.'

This passage was written for *The Borderers' Chronicle* when the first emergency tour of 1st K.O.S.B. in Belfast ended, more than seven years before this concluding chapter is filed, and the time has not come for a conclusive account of the Regiment's peace-keeping efforts. The tragedy of Ulster is still with us.

That the Queen's protection, within the bounds of the United Kingdom, needs be enforced by troops — many of whom are on a paper order of battle in B.A.O.R., and that British soil has produced the urban guerrilla, has added a nightmare dimension to counter-revolutionary operations. In former times, in India and elsewhere, and in Dublin itself when 2nd K.O.S.B. were there in 1914, the civil magistrates moved or lived with the troops, and through them Internal Security action emanated from the Civil Power in a very visible way. Today in Northern Ireland the soldier's yellow card obviates the necessity of the physical presence of the civil authority in whose name he acts. The yellow card will tell the soldier what to do within the framework of the law of the land. If he causes the death of a civilian there will be a Coroner's inquest, and the Coroner will decide if death was due to terrorist activity or if there is a case to answer. In the latter event the soldier will be charged, and will need the services of Counsel in a Civil court. The story of the handling of the troubles in Northern Ireland is that of a legalistic treading of a quagmire of history.

The T.V. viewer, who has watched the violence over the years, can have little conception of the forethought, the painstaking amassing of Intelligence, the analysis, the scrupulousness, that lies behind the operations of the Security Forces, and results in their comprehensive instructions. 1st K.O.S.B. Policy Notes of June 1970, contained among their many paragraphs a section dealing with the correct phases of crowd control tactics, in which it was laid down that the various phases began once a citizen had thrown a stone and 'Jaw-Jaw' had ended; there was a telling marginal note in Lieutenant-Colonel Myrtle's hand: 'We may have to take more than one stone to allow others to Jaw-Jaw.'

Three unaccompanied emergency tours, all in Belfast, and a fourth tour as the Belfast resident battalion, have marked the 1970s for the K.O.S.B., as follows:[1]

First Tour: Belfast, May to September 1970
Lieutenant-Colonel A. D. Myrtle, M.B.E., commanding.[2] 1st K.O.S.B. then returned to B.A.O.R. until April 1971, when the battalion came home to Redford Barracks, Edinburgh. On 15 May 1971, the battalion exercised the ancient right to march through the city, the Recce Platoon being conspicuous in their Land Rovers 'with guns mounted, camouflage nets flapping and engines throbbing.' In July there was a brief return to Ulster —
The Orange Parades, July 1971
The battalion spent four days in Belfast to cover the Orangemen's marches.
Second Tour: Belfast, December 1971 to April 1972
Lieutenant-Colonel R. W. Riddle commanding. At the end of this tour, 1st K.O.S.B. returned to Edinburgh.
Third Tour: November 1972 to February 1973
Lieutenant-Colonel Riddle was again commanding, and 1st K.O.S.B. again returned to Edinburgh. In May 1973, the battalion went to Berlin for two years.
Fourth Tour: Belfast, May 1975 to November 1976
An accompanied tour of eighteen months as the Belfast resident battalion, at Palace Barracks, Holywood. Lieutenant-Colonel F. A. L. Alstead commanding, who was succeeded in September 1976, by Lieutenant-Colonel M. Thomson, M.B.E.

For service in Northern Ireland, members of the Regiment have been awarded one O.B.E., one M.B.E., two M.C.s, two M.M.s, one B.E.M., eleven Mentions in Dispatches, one Queen's Commendation for Bravery, and thirteen Commendations from the General Officer Commanding. Four N.C.O.s have lost their lives, and a memorial window in St George's Church at Palace Barracks was unveiled by the Colonel of the Regiment at the end of the fourth tour. A number of men were wounded, two of them severely.

The initial tour took the battalion to the New Lodge and Shankill areas of the city, where it took over from 2nd Queen's Regiment. Tactical B.H.Q. and one rifle company were located at Girdwood Park, and another rifle company was at the Brown's Square

---

[1] There is to be a fifth tour, unaccompanied, in 1979.

[2] The son of a Borderer, his father was Lieutenant-Colonel J. Y. E. Myrtle, D.S.O., who was killed in action in the Second World War. Both father and son won the Sword of Honour at Sandhurst.

police station, with a platoon on detachment in a butcher's shop beneath the Catholic dwellers in Unity Flats. As part of an appeal to 'hearts and minds', as the army had hitherto called it, renamed 'community relations' in Northern Ireland, sanction was given to A Company to open a community centre for young people at Unity Flats, which remained open for the rest of the tour. A third rifle company operated as battalion and brigade reserve, based at Palace Barracks, Holywood. This company later moved to Unity Flats, and Support Company operated as rifle platoons at various locations.

The first stones were cast at Borderers, and the battalion's first riot squad appeared on the scene, on 9 May 1970, at Catholic and Protestant junctions with North Queen Street. Riots that night resulted in injuries to thirty-five soldiers, eight of whom were K.O.S.B. A week later, another night of violence brought out the Fire Brigade and caused £100,000 of damage. A new tactic was introduced, of moving Saracen armoured cars into the rioters from behind, in an attempt to execute more arrests. The next month was a period of much tension in the Crumlin Road neighbourhood, and of Orange Lodge marches, and included a particularly bad night of fires, shooting and rioting throughout the flashpoints of Belfast in which more than £1 million of damage was done. Borderers again faced the crowd and, assisted by a platoon of The Queen's Lancashire Regiment, arrested fifteen citizens.

1st K.O.S.B. Log Sheets present a bizarre picture of events, day by day, week in, week out, all round the clock. Under no circumstance were the troops to open fire unless under persistent petrol bomb attack, and then only by marksmen at specific targets after many warnings . . . C Company snatch squad has gone in . . . A priest states he cannot talk reason to hooligans in the Flax Street area . . . We are being stoned, most of the street lights are out, but the Electrolux is working wonders . . . A very drunken woman is being restrained at the butcher's shop: request for an ambulance and a policewoman . . . An explosion at a house in Donegal Park Avenue, front door blown in . . . Civilian vehicle standing outside docks, two girls aged nineteen years found in the boot . . . A nightmare indeed.

In the first week of July, Support Company was moved in armoured vehicles into the Lower Falls under command of 2nd Queens, after successful searches for hidden arms by The Royal Scots had attracted rioters. C.S. gas was used, and Support Company when clearing Leeson Street captured two gunmen. The big Orange marches of 12 July passed off without untoward incident, but at the end of that month further trouble broke out in the New Lodge area, and men of the battalion became targets for stones, bottles and petrol bombs. As a result, a petrol bomber was shot and killed. 1st K.O.S.B. report to Brigade Headquarters on this incident ran to seven closely-typed pages of foolscap, and a diary of events. The next night was conspicuous for thirty-one arrests, but trouble around the New Lodge Road persisted for a week. It had been some Minden Day. Later, there was an unpleasant scene at the gates to the camp at Girdwood Park, when a procession of nearly 200 women scratched and spat at a platoon of B Company who were passing into the camp.

The Orange Parades of 12 July 1971, were monitored by a massive presence of troops. 1st K.O.S.B. moved from Edinburgh on 9 July and became operational on 10 July for four days, based on the Dunlambert boys' school in North Belfast, responsible with other troops for preventing inter-sectarian clashes in the area of the Ardoyne and the Crumlin Road.

The second and third tours coincided with the beginning and close of 1972, the worst year of violence during the present troubles, and the fine and patient conduct of the battalion resulted from the meticulous training it received before each return to Northern Ireland, and its high discipline. The second tour, December 1971 to April 1972, followed the reintroduction of internment the previous August, and covered the period of 'Bloody Sunday' and the Catholic reaction, and the eventual suspension of Stormont and the announcement of Direct Rule from Westminster, after which the army was ordered to adopt a 'low profile'.[3] The battalion was responsible for a large and predominantly Catholic area in West Belfast, where some 40 per cent of the population were unemployed and the desolation of some of the housing estates had to be seen to be believed. It included Beechmount, Ballymurphy, Turf Lodge, the interface between Ballymurphy and Protestant Woodvale, and part of the Falls Road. Tactical B.H.Q. was at the Springfield Road police station, with companies based at the Blackmountain School, the Vere Foster School, Paisley Park, and in the former annex to the Royal Victoria Hospital. Support Company, administrative personnel, even the Pipes and Drums, operated as riflemen, and house searches and arrests. usually late at night or in the small hours, and many foot and vehicle patrols, were the uncongenial routine. Civilians arrested could be held for a period of up to four hours, for obtaining immediate information, before being handed over to the police who brought any necessary charges. The battalion unearthed 22,600 rounds of concealed ammunition, 180lb of explosive, 64 assorted weapons, and arrested 125 I.R.A. suspects. An extraordinary situation arose on Easter

[3] Reversed by Operation Motorman on 31 July 1972.

Sunday 1972, when the battalion stood by in case of a clash between Provisional and Official I.R.A., who were holding separate parades at the Milltown Cemetery.

The third tour, November 1972 to February 1973, again saw the battalion in West Belfast, in the strongly republican district of Andersonstown. Unpredictable 'cowboy' shootings at units of the battalion occurred almost daily, and bombings, stoning and abuse. Refinements encountered were the nail bomb, and an anti-personnel directional mine known as a claymore mine. B.H.Q. during this tour was at Monagh Camp, which became 'Fort' Monagh, and companies were at the fort, and in Roger Casement Park, and at a new camp at Glassmullin. In addition to patrols and searches there were guard commitments all over the city, including the city centre, to protect the main shopping area. A highlight of the tour was the arrest by Support Company of an entire 'company' of I.R.A., with all their weapons. Another action occurred at midnight on the anniversary of 'Bloody Sunday', when a C Company patrol was fired on at Turf Lodge. This led to a running gun-battle between several C Company patrols and a group of I.R.A. gunmen, in which the Borderers fired some 1,000 rounds of ammunition and claimed three hits. Two hits were subsequently confirmed.

*   *   *   *   *

Other events have taken place. 1971 was the year of the 'Big Blaw', when the 1st Battalion's Pipes and Drums took part in the beating of the Queen's Birthday Retreat by the Massed Pipes and Drums of the Scottish Regiments at the Horse Guards. None who watched it is likely to forget the tremendous Drummers' Call which preceded the marching and counter-marching of twelve bands before Her Majesty Queen Elizabeth II and the Duke of Edinburgh.

On 22 October 1971, the Colonel of the Regiment and the officers gave a lavish Ball in the Assembly Rooms, Edinburgh. Brigadier Frank Coutts, C.B.E., at that time Commander, Highland Area at Perth, had been appointed to the Colonelcy in June 1970. A son of the manse and a man of wide interests, his career began in the Metropolitan Police in the 1930s and included war service in the 4th (Border) Battalion. He is today General Secretary, Royal British Legion Scotland. A former Scottish rugby football international, he recently served as President of the Scottish Rugby Union.[4]

[4] 1977.

As Public Duties Battalion in Edinburgh, 1971-73, 1st K.O.S.B. provided the various ceremonial guards, and hence provided the Royal Guard for two consecutive years when the Queen was at Balmoral; but today's Borderer takes ceremony in his stride, and in Edinburgh the battalion was in fact spearhead battalion on stand-by for any part of the world.

Recent years have also been memorable for the many Border Freedoms conferred upon the Regiment. At appropriate ceremonies, the Freedom of Duns was granted in 1972, Kelso in 1973, followed by Melrose, Wigtown, Newton Stewart, Kirkcudbright, Hawick and Coldstream in 1974, and Jedburgh and Sanquhar in 1975. Together with those of Berwick, Dumfries, Selkirk and Stranraer, previously granted, the Regiment has received fourteen Freedoms of the Scottish Border. These carry the right to march, with bayonets fixed and Colours flying, through those ancient burghs,[5] but as a matter of historical accuracy it should not be inferred that the very much older privilege of exercising the same right in Edinburgh derives from an actual grant of the Freedom of Edinburgh to the Regiment, although the Earl of Leven, himself, in March 1689, was granted honorary burgess-ship. Rather does the Regiment's privilege in Edinburgh signify the close relationship between the City and the Regiment, raised 'to secure the peace of the toune'. This was well recalled on 19 March 1973 (see Appendix III), before the 1st Battalion left for Berlin, when the bronze commemorative plaque on the Castle Esplanade was unveiled by the Fourteenth Earl of Leven, the direct descendant of the Regiment's founder, in the presence of the Lord Provost, the Governor of the Castle, the Colonel of the Regiment and the assembled ranks. It was typical of the Regiment's intimate connection with the capital of Scotland that the Castle Superintendent who had supervised the preparation of the stonework was the son of a Borderer killed at Gallipoli.

Probably the Regiment's bearing on parade has achieved no finer performance than in Berlin on 28 February 1975, when the old Colours of the 1st Battalion were marched off and new Colours were consecrated, and presented by the Colonel-in-Chief. The parade, held in the Deutschlandhalle in front of many guests, attracted an audience of 6,000 Berliners and had been codenamed *Auf Wiedersehen Jock*. It was part of a Colours Weekend of ceremonies and celebration, notable even in that city of many diversions.

*   *   *   *   *

[5] Now no more, because of reorganization of Local Government.

There followed five weeks on the urban training ranges at the Infantry Training Area at Sennelager, West Germany, to practice the battalion in the tactics, equipment and procedures required in Northern Ireland, which change with the changing political scene. On 15 May 1975, the battalion again became operational in Belfast, for the long fourth tour, eighteen months as resident battalion, at Palace Barracks, Holywood, accompanied by families. The battalion was liable to be committed anywhere in Belfast as Brigade Reserve, and had wider commitments extending to the rural areas as Province Reserve. In rotation of companies there was a detachment at Ballymacarrett, a small Catholic enclave in East Belfast, during the earlier part of the tour; for the later phase of the tour, the detachment was at Fort Monagh.

At Fort Monagh, in Republican West Belfast, where the Andersonstown and Turf Lodge districts meet, a concrete sangar with steel shutters gave a domestic view, every afternoon, of schoolchildren going home up Monagh Road; but solders could only go up that road armed and in flak jackets. It was a strange paradox, and it was a strange fort. The K.O.S.B. company lived here under command of another regiment. High wire, and corrugated tin, which was spy-proof if nothing else, surrounded a collection of substantial huts. One of them was a formal Officers' Mess. In others, men in combat suits were here and there asleep on the bunks. One sleeping quarter was entirely wallpapered with the posed female form, the photography of choice magazines, in a masterpiece of variety. Wire mesh protected the roofs of the huts from possible mortar bombs. Maps of Belfast, with much green, orange and yellow overprint, covered a wall in the Operations Room where there was the crackle of wireless messages. Entrances were protected from blast, as were the police stations and the public houses all over the city.

At Palace Barracks, armoured vehicles known as 'Pigs' were parked, ready for alarms. Each could carry ten men, and upon each was neatly painted in white: 'Rent-a-Jock'. The soft vehicles, the lorries and Land Rovers, were covered with Macarolon, proof against stones, shrapnel and low-velocity shots. Stored were the riot shields and helmets. In the B.H.Q. Operations Room, the same spread of coloured maps gave a complete and chequered lay-out of Belfast: green for the Catholic areas, orange for the Protestant, yellow for the mixed areas. They bore a printed deletion, the words 'United Kingdom Town Plans' being struck out and 'Belfast Religious Areas' substituted.

The city looked as if it had suffered from air raids, except that metal grilles covered the lower windows of public buildings. At strategic points, ramps in the road lay in wait for get-away cars.

The graffiti gave out its messages on walls — daubed green flags above 'I.R.A.' . . . a girl's name, followed by *six months is a long time* . . . a four-letter word . . . *Kill Sectarianism* . . . and big printed slogans on hoardings, reminiscent of the Second World War, but the words were different. Several urged the citizens not to let their children play with toy guns. At a blind, bricked-up interface between the green and orange, on the Catholic side of the street, one of these hoardings proclaimed that Christ had died at Calvary, and on the third day had risen again — and asked: Why? And following their own safety precautions, the Jocks, whenever they passed into or out of their posts, and at the gates of Palace Barracks, made a 'click-click-click-click' with their bolt actions, clearing their weapons, unloading or loading as the case may be, in front of special beds of sand.

Palace Barracks is not far from the cranes of Harland & Wolff, on the shore of Belfast Lough. At the end of eighteen months there, the 1st Battalion, The King's Own Scottish Borderers, maintained an impressive character. Speech sometimes indicated regions nearer Glasgow than the Tweed, for the Regiment has been given a wider recruiting area since the disbandment of the Cameronians, and it was difficult to understand what a tired young soldier from Motherwell was saying in the city centre. His platoon was sprawled about, resting between patrols, in the bowels of the glum building known as the 'G.C.H.' There was no daylight. Their faces looked sallow and tired under the naked light bulbs. The G.C.H. was — or used to be — the Grand Central Hotel; everything is initials in Northern Ireland.

They all spoke of the mental strain, and officers and men certainly tended to look tired. They were never really off duty. One day in three, those in the barracks were on guard duties. Another day in three, a man was at forty minutes' notice to turn out, or was on patrol in the city centre. Even on his so-called day off he was at four hours' notice, which would shorten to two hours if the forty-minute company were called out. The barracks was like a cantonment, entirely self-sufficient. It even had a sauna, and three squash courts, and was surrounded by high wire patrolled at night by dogs. If a stranger entered the Dog Section, the search and tracker dogs, the Labradors, remained calm in their kennels; but the patrol dogs, Alsatians of savage appearance, leapt at the wire mesh with a frenzied baying and bared fangs. Did they go for the arm?

'Anywhere,' the Dog Sergeant answered laconically with a grin, leaning back in an old armchair in his office. 'Anything that's loose.'

The battalion functioned with a practised co-operation. As

soldiers they pulled together; for whatever the reasons which led them to join, they had in mind the common good. Nowadays, the lure of seeing the world is wearing thin, but with remarkable consistency they declared that they enjoy the life. That they had nevertheless joined for a kind of adventure seems not so wide of the mark; perhaps a release from conventional restraints. Or it may be that a soldier is a special breed.

Possibly there was a hint of mixed feelings among N.C.O.s at the passing of older methods of imposing discipline. Today these have been broadly replaced by the encouragement of self-discipline; but trouble in Belfast when it came, came quickly, and when two men chunky and heavier by nearly a stone in their flak jackets, had to go in with truncheons to extract a ringleader, it was a matter of *You — and you — get him.* The end-product was the same. There was no time for a debate. Obedience is still the soldier's first duty.

*   *   *   *   *

The battalion lives through its recreational focal-points and its Messes and the large adjunct of the Married Quarters. Certain differentials, as everywhere, have narrowed, and their social life and off-duty style reflects civilian trends; but the Officers' Mess is still 'the Shrine of the Colours'. Against a wall they hang, and are duly taken down each night by the junior subaltern. The Pipe Banners presented by the Border burghs hang displayed; the paintings, the prints, the silver, tell of the past; the shining banqueting table preserves its mystique.

The battalion adapts to its environment and to that extent changes. It was less 'Regimental' in Belfast, where the Jock regarded his rôle as primarily a civil one, than, say, in Berlin. Then, every two years or so, there will be a fresh influence upon the tone, a new style, a new broom: a new Commanding Officer. His soldiers are products of post-war welfare Britain. They are more independent than formerly, on the Military Salary. Nevertheless, great obedience, loyalty and support centres upon him, and with his former authority over his soldiers' matrimonial aspirations swept away he will have something like three hundred families on his books, and as many children as soldiers. He is the apex of a community about the size of a small market town.

They are like some migratory host . . . From Palace Barracks, they would all depart again, would thankfully leave Belfast behind and move to wherever the Service requires, following the Colours, each married family with its so many cubic feet of baggage space, the deep freezers, refrigerators, and the rest of it. To Scotland, to Fort George, they would go, and to Public Duties in London, and Exercise 'Long Stride' in Kenya . . . to British Honduras and the mangrove swamps of Belize; and to Northern Ireland once more, and Germany in 1980 . . . Whatever they do next they must be ready for anything. We have only a small army. So wherever they go, the 1st Battalion, The King's Own Scottish Borderers, must be fit, venturesome, and adaptable.

Throughout most of its history the Regiment has consisted of the one battalion, as it does today; but in a special sense the Regiment today embraces many old comrades, and the Association through which the Regiment looks after its own, and the contribution its disbanded battalions have made to the great tradition the serving officers and men of the 1st Battalion carry forward. For the Regiment is not only a cavalcade of passing men, it is a spirit.

The young man who joins The King's Own Scottish Borderers may find that the Regiment will be his life. Or he will find that the Regiment has been an influence on his life out of all proportion to the number of years that he actually served in it. He will have become a son of the Scottish Border, with all its Border clannishness, wherever he may have come from, and is heir to the spirit which makes a man mindful that he is a Borderer, 'more especially when in the presence of outsiders, or of the enemy,' that will never entirely leave him.

The Regiment looks forward, for all its long past. The tercentenary of the first call to arms, when the drums beat below the Castle on its rock, soon approaches. The Regiment's allegiance remains, ready for the future, under a crest that is famous in story.

APPENDICES

Appendix I: THE REGIMENT'S BATTLES AND BATTLE HONOURS

The Colours

The Colours were regularized by Royal Warrants of 1747 and 1751, when personal Colours of the Colonel and the captains were abolished. Thenceforth there were two Colours, the King's Colour or First Colour (the Great Union) and the Second Colour, later known as the Regimental Colour. Carried symbolically on pikes, the spearhead was replaced by the Royal Crest in 1858. Until 1857 the provision of Colours was the responsibility of the Colonel of the Regiment.

The Regimental Colour of the 25th Foot was deep yellow, the colour of the uniform facings, which was changed to blue when the Regiment became a Royal regiment in 1805. In those days the Second Colour had the Union Flag in the upper dexter canton. The earliest surviving Colours to have been carried by the Regiment are the ones laid up in the Scottish United Services Museum at Edinburgh Castle, believed to be the stand that was retired in 1805. Both Colours show the Regimental number in Roman numerals within a Union wreath, but when the Regiment became a Royal regiment the words *King's Own Borderers* across the tie of the wreath were recorded in the books of the Inspector of Regimental Colours at the College of Arms.

The earliest of the Regiment's Colours of which there is clear record was the stand received in 1743, and carried in the War of the Austrian Succession and in the Seven Years War. These Colours were buried with military honours at Newcastle in 1763, 'worn out from length of service', when the Regiment returned from the Continent and marched from Kent to Newcastle and Berwick-upon-Tweed, and later into Scotland. The burial place has often been sought. Many successive stands of Colours have served out their time with the Regiment since then, and a remarkable number have found more conspicuous resting places. Altogether, thirteen stands of old Colours and three single Colours have been laid up in Edinburgh or on the Border, or in the Regimental Museum. The Regiment carried its Colours against the enemy for the last time during the Second Afghan War.

The award of Battle Honours, emblazoned on Colours, and appointments to commemorate victories or appropriate feats of arms, developed haphazardly. Many were awarded retrospectively as a result of the deliberations of War Office committees that sat in 1881 and 1909, and in 1910 The King's Own Scottish Borderers were among fourteen regiments to be awarded *Namur 1695*. There was a nice sequel when 2nd K.O.S.B. were marching close to Namur after the Armistice, in December 1918, and the Colour party were sent there for a Trooping ceremony.

The earliest award of a Battle Honour to any regiment was in 1768. The first award to the 25th Foot was 'Minden', awarded on 1 January 1801. The emblem of the Sphinx superscribed *Egypt* was awarded in 1802. *Martinique* was awarded in 1819, the year *1809* being added by authority of an Army Order in 1909. *Egmont-op-Zee* was awarded in 1820.

In 1821, the Colonel of the Regiment, General Fitzroy, applied for *Howe* to be granted as an honour, being the name of the Admiral who commanded the Channel Fleet off Cape St. Vincent on the Glorious First of June, 1794. The Light Company of the Regiment served as Marines in the *Marlborough*, seventy-four guns, in the van squadron, and the Grenadier Company were marines in the *Gibraltar*, eighty guns, in the centre squadron.

Unfortunately, the Commander-in-Chief, the Duke of York, ruled that he 'cannot recommend to His Majesty to permit any regiment to assume the name of a subject as a badge of honour upon its appointments'. The proposal had originated with Lieutenant-Colonel Farquharson, commanding 25th Foot, who had been present in the *Marlborough* when a subaltern. He had cited the award of *Copenhagen*, made in 1821 to the Rifle Brigade, but the answer was that this was no analogy because 'the Rifle Corps did not serve against Copenhagen in the year 1801 as marines, but as a detachment of the land forces specially embarked on that occasion for the purpose of being applied as exigencies might arise in the course of the expedition. (*Public Record Office:* WO.3/71, p. 295).

In 1909, however, the Queen's and the Worcesters, whose predecessors in the 2nd Foot and 29th Foot also had marine detachments serving at Lord Howe's famous naval action, became entitled to emblazon a Naval Crown superscribed with the date. Those who conducted the latter day reviews had apparently followed the principle that 50 per cent of a regiment's numbers should have been present at an engagement to qualify for the Battle Honour, and the 2nd Foot and 29th Foot had more men afloat, about 400 of each regiment, distributed among more ships. (The precedent that a regiment's headquarters should also have been present was waived in the case of Naval actions.) Hence the Glorious First of June is uncommemorated on the Colours of The King's Own Scottish Borderers.

Although there are no Battle Honours commemorating battles fought on British soil, it may be remarked that when the 1st Battalion Trooped the Colour at Fort George, close to Culloden, on the King's Birthday in 1933, it was the first time that a Lowland regiment had Trooped the Colour in the Highlands.

In the following list of the Regiment's battles, the honours that appear on the Colours are shown in capitals.

The War in Scotland:	
Killiecrankie	27 July 1689
The War in Ireland:	
Siege of Athlone	June 1691
Aughrim	12 July 1691
Siege of Galway	July 1691
Siege of Limerick	August to October 1691
The War of the League of Augsburg:	
Steenkirk	24 July 1692
Landen	29 July 1693
Siege of NAMUR	July to September 1695
The 'Fifteen':	
Sheriffmuir	13 November 1715
The War of the Quadruple Alliance against Spain:	
Spanish coast (seaborne raid) — Vigo Bay	September 1719
Renewed conflict with Spain:	
Defence of Gibraltar	February to May 1727
The War of the Austrian Succession:	
Fontenoy	11 May 1745
Ath (besieged)	September 1745
Lauffeld	2 July 1747
Roucoux	11 October 1747
The 'Forty-five':	
Culloden	16 April 1746

The Seven Years War:
French coast (seaborne raids) —	September to November 1757
Rochefort, St. Malo	May to July 1758
MINDEN	1 August 1759
Warburg	31 July 1760
Kloster Kampen	15 October 1760
Fellinghausen	16 July 1761
Wilhelmstal	14 June 1762

The War of the American Revolution:
Relief of Gibraltar	September 1782 to January 1783

The French Revolutionary Wars:
Occupation of Grenada	April 1795 to July 1796
Holland: the Helder campaign	August to October 1799
EGMONT-OP-ZEE	2 October 1799

The Marine Detachments:
Blockade and siege of Toulon	July to December 1793
Conquest of Corsica	February to August 1794
Naval action off Cape St. Vincent	1 June 1794
Naval action off Cape Noli	14 March 1795

The Napoleonic Wars:
EGYPT: capture of Alexandria	August to September 1801
Capture of MARTINIQUE	February 1809
Capture of Guadaloupe	February 1810
Holland: the movement on Antwerp and the action at Merxen (2nd Battalion)	December 1813 to March 1814

The late Victorian Wars:
AFGHANISTAN 1878-80	
Sudan: Suakim	December 1888
Burma: Chin Lushai Expedition	November 1899 to March 1890
North-West Frontier of India:	
Relief of CHITRAL	April 1895
TIRAH	October 1897 to January 1898

The South African War:
PAARDEBERG	February 1900
SOUTH AFRICA 1900-02	

The First World War:
MONS, Le Cateau, Retreat from Mons, Marne, 1914, 1918; AISNE, 1914; La Bassée, 1914; Messines, 1914; YPRES, 1914, 1915, 1917, 1918; Nonne Bosschen, Hill 60, Gravenstafel, St. Julien, Frezenberg, Bellewaarde, LOOS, SOMME, 1916, 1918; Albert, 1916, 1918; Bazentin, Delville Wood, Pozières, Guillemont, Flers-Courcelette, Morval, Le Transloy, Ancre Heights, ARRAS, 1917, 1918; Vimy, 1917; Scarpe, 1917, 1918; Arleux, Pilckem, Langemarck, 1917; Menin Road, Polygon Wood, Broodseinde, Poelcappelle, Passchendaele, Cambrai, 1917, 1918; St. Quentin, Lys, Estaires, Hazebrouck, Kemmel, SOISSONNAIS-OURCQ, Bapaume, 1918; Drocourt-Queant, HINDENBURG LINE, Epéhy, Canal du Nord, Courtrai, Selle, Sambre, France and Flanders, 1914-18; Italy, 1917-18; Helles, Landing at Helles, Krithia, Suvla, Scimitar Hill, GALLIPOLI, 1915-16; Rumani, Egypt, 1916; GAZA, El Nughar, Nebi Samwil, Jaffa, Palestine, 1917-18.

The Second World War:
DUNKIRK, 1940; Cambes, ODON, Cheux, Defence of Rauray, CAEN, Esquay, Troarn, Mont Pincon, Estry, Aart, Nederrijn, ARNHEM, 1944; Best, Scheldt, FLUSHING, Venraij, Meijel, Venlo Pocket, Roer, Rhineland, Reichswald, Cleve, Goch, RHINE, Ibbenburen, Lingen, Dreirwalde, Uelzen, BREMEN, Artlenberg,

North-West Europe, 1940, 1944-45; North Arakan, Buthidaung, NGAKYEDAUK PASS, IMPHAL, Kanglatongbi, Ukhrul, Meiktila, IRRAWADDY, Kama, Burma, 1943, 1945.
The Korean War:
KOWANG-SAN, Maryang-San, KOREA, 1951-52.

Appendix II: THE COLONELS OF THE REGIMENT

Formerly, the Colonel was the Regiment's virtual proprietor, responsible to the Sovereign for its maintenance and discipline. Through a system of 'off-reckonings' he drew an income out of monies made over to him by the Paymaster-General for its recruitment and clothing. Although General rank in the army did not preclude a Colonelcy, the Earl of Leven's absences as Keeper of Edinburgh Castle may have led to the loss of his Regiment, a loss which he felt deeply. He later became successively Major-General of the forces, Master of the Ordnance, and Commander-in-Chief, all in Scotland, and a representative peer, before he fell from favour.

As the 18th Century proceeded Colonels saw less of their regiments. By the time of the French Revolutionary Wars the Colonel's responsibility for the soldiers' pay had ceased, and at the time of the Crimea his responsibility for clothing the soldiers was also at an end, his loss of 'off-reckonings' being made good by a handsome salary. In 1881 the salary was abolished and the Colonelcy became an honorary distinction. To-day, nevertheless, the Colonel has great influence. He is the guardian of the Regiment's ethos, and the selection of its officers is in his hands.

The Earl of Leven led the Regiment in battle, at Killiecrankie, in Ireland and in Flanders. James Maitland led the Regiment at Namur. John Middleton, nephew of the Earl of Middleton, of Seaton, Aberdeenshire, was appointed to the Regiment as Lieutenant-Colonel and Brevet Colonel in 1711. Viscount Shannon had become Deputy Governor of Dover Castle in 1709 and there can be little doubt that Middleton, who was present at Sheriffmuir, in fact commanded the Regiment at that battle.

Viscount Shannon became Commander-in-Chief in Ireland in 1720 and, in the last year of his life, a Field Marshal. Lord Sempill was besieged with the Regiment at Ath in Flanders, when the French allowed the Regiment to march out with the full honours of war. He also commanded the left wing of the Royal Army at Culloden, in which part of the field the Regiment fought. His death in Flanders caused the appointment of 'the gallant Earl of Crawford', who was on the battlefield with the Regiment at Roucoux, but commanding the second line of the British cavalry. The Earl of Home was Governor of Gibraltar when Minden was fought. General Somerset when a subaltern in the 18th Hussars fought at Waterloo.

Of the sixteen Colonels prior to 1882 when the dress of a Lowland Scottish regiment was introduced, nine were Scotsmen. A tenth, Lord Lennox, bore a family name descended from the Scottish Dukedom of Lennox. He was the last Colonel to have served with the Regiment, in Minorca.

James Maitland and John Middleton resigned the Colonelcy. The Earl of Crawford became Colonel of The Scots Greys, and Sir Henry Erskine became Colonel of the 1st Foot, but normally the Colonelcy of the Regiment was terminated only by death. Since the Second World War the appointment is held for a limited period only.

Prior to 1910, the only Colonel to have joined the Regiment as an Ensign was General Napier. After 1910, the only one not to have done so was Earl Haig. Commander-in-Chief of the British Armies in France, 1915-18, his prestige after the First World War was immense, and the nation bought him a fitting home from his kinsman, the 28th Laird of Bemersyde. Thus the Field Marshal lived in the Regimental area, but when in 1923 certain officers requested the Colonel to apply for him to be appointed Colonel-in-Chief, General Woollcombe took the view that only a Prince could be Colonel-in-Chief of a regiment, and resigned to enable Earl Haig to succeed him. General Woollcombe had commanded IV Corps at Cambrai, November 1917, the battle which saw the first massed use of tanks.

Earl Haig had a pair of trews and rounded tunic made for himself, now exhibited in the Regimental Museum. Certainly all his successors, on ceremonial occasions with the Regiment, have followed the nicety of wearing the uniform of an officer of The King's Own Scottish Borderers, with the badges of rank of a full Colonel, whatever their rank in the army. This is so even if the Colonel has retired from the army; for it matters not. He is the Colonel of the Regiment.

Chronological list of the Regiment's Colonels

(S) and (I)·denote Scottish or Irish peerage. Panmure was originally a Scottish peerage, forfeited after the '15 and later recreated in the Irish peerage.

David Melville, Earl of Leven (S)	18 March 1689
Lieutenant-General James Maitland	19 March 1694
Brigadier-General William Breton	15 April 1711
Lieutenant-General Richard Boyle, Viscount Shannon (I)	27 January 1715
late Horse Guards; late Colonel of Marines; M.P. for Arundel, 1708-10; Hythe, 1710-15; East Grinstead, 1715-34	
John Middleton	17 June 1721
late The Duke of Argyll's (H.R.H. The Prince of Denmark's) Regiment; M.P. for Aberdeen Burghs, 1713-39	
Major-General John Leslie, Earl of Rothes (S)	29 May 1732
late 3rd (Scots) Foot Guards and 21st Foot; Colonel, Scottish Horse Guards, 1743-46	
Brigadier-General Hugh, Lord Sempill (S)	25 April 1745
late Scottish Horse Guards; late Colonel, 42nd Highlanders	
Major-General John Lindsay, Earl of Crawford (S)	25 December 1746
late 3rd (Scots) Foot Guards; late Colonel, 42nd Highlanders	
William Maule, Earl of Panmure of Forth (I)	1 December 1747
late 3rd (Scots) Foot Guards; M.P. for Forfarshire, 1735-82	
Lieutenant-General William, Earl of Home (S)	29 April 1752
late Dragoon Guards and 3rd (Scots) Foot Guards	
Major-General Sir Henry Erskine, Bart.	29 May 1761
late 1st Foot (The Royal Regiment); late Colonel, 67th Foot; M.P. for Ayr Burghs, 1749-54; Anstruther Burghs, 1754-65	
General Lord George Henry Lennox	22 December 1762
late 2nd Foot Guards and 33rd Foot; M.P. for Chichester, 1761-67; Sussex, 1767-84	
General the Hon. Charles Fitzroy	25 March 1805
late 1st Foot Guards	
General Sir Henry Campbell, K.C.B., G.C.H.	22 October 1831
late Colonel, 80th Foot and 88th Foot	
Lieutenant-General Sir Henry Somerset, K.C.B.	3 September 1856
late Cape Mounted Riflemen	
General Sir Henry Townshend	16 February 1862
late 24th Foot	
General W. C. E. Napier	23 September 1882
late 25th Foot; late Colonel, 3rd Foot (The Buffs)	

Lieutenant-General S. M. Wiseman-Clarke, C.B.	24 September 1893
late 93rd Highlanders	
General Sir Frederick Forestier-Walker, G.C.M.G., K.C.B.	31 July 1905
late Scots Guards	
Lieutenant-General Sir Charles Woollcombe, K.C.B., K.C.M.G.	31 August 1910
late K.O.S.B.	
Field Marshal Earl Haig, K.T., G.C.B., O.M., G.C.V.O., K.C.I.E.	
	24 September 1923
late 7th Hussars and 17th Lancers; Colonel, Royal Horse Guards and 17th/21st Lancers	
Brigadier-General D. A. Macfarlane, C.B., D.S.O.	30 January 1928
late K.O.S.B.	
Major-General Sir Edward Broadbent, K.B.E., C.B., C.M.G., D.S.O.	
late K.O.S.B.	30 January 1938
Major-General E. G. Miles, C.B., D.S.O., M.C.	19 June 1944
late K.O.S.B.	
Major-General J. Scott Elliot, C.B., C.B.E., D.S.O.	19 June 1954
late K.O.S.B.	
Lieutenant-General Sir William Turner, K.B.E., C.B., D.S.O.	15 November 1961
late K.O.S.B.	
Brigadier Frank H. Coutts, C.B.E.	1 June 1970
late K.O.S.B.	

Appendix III: THE RAISING OF THE REGIMENT

The corps the Earl of Leven raised in Holland was probably broken up in order to strengthen other regiments. *The Melvilles Earls of Melville and the Leslies Earls of Leven,* a family history by Sir William Fraser, incorrectly stated that it fought at Killiecrankie and became the 25th Foot. That this was not so was made clear by Andrew Ross, Ross Herald, in *The Lowland Scots Regiments (Note on the origin of The King's Own Scottish Borderers).* Ross explains that the corps Leven brought from Holland and which garrisoned Plymouth, was given a warrant to proceed to Scotland via Chester, but the warrant was countermanded except for the officers, possibly because of the speed with which the regiment Leven raised in Edinburgh came into existence.

Although 19 March 1689 is the date given for the raising of the Regiment on the Scottish National War Memorial at Edinburgh Castle, and on the commemorative plaque on the Castle Esplanade, the *Acts of the Parliaments of Scotland* show that 18 March was the day the Earl of Leven was authorized to levy a regiment, 'with all expedition'. 19 March was the date of the Convention's report of the event, which appeared in the *London Gazette* a few days later.

It will be seen on p. 6 that the Convention's report of 28 March 1689 stated that men from 'Argyle, Glasgow and the Western Shires' were under Leven's command, a number of whom evidently enlisted in Leven's Regiment. Their identity is somewhat obscure, and Sir William Fraser, in his family history, mistook the Cameronians who had come to Edinburgh from the west for the men Leven raised by beat of drum. However, it was the Cameronian men who were stood down after the arrival of General Mackay in Edinburgh, and not, as Fraser suggested, the regiment Leven had recruited. The Cameronian men received the thanks of the Convention, but it was against their principles to accept payment for their services. After resolving matters of their own conscience, for they would not, at first, serve under officers other than those elected by themselves, they soon formed, at Douglas, Lanarkshire, the foundation of the Cameronian Regiment (Scottish Rifles), as is well known.

In *The Records of the King's Own Borderers* it is said that Leven's Regiment held the Parliament House until the Estates declared William and Mary sovereigns, the *London Gazette* being given as the source. The present author cannot find specific mention of that service, but certainly on 25 March 1689 the Convention ordered that 'the President give thanks to the officers of the Glasgow men for their service in attending the meeting of the Estates'.

It will have been noticed that no Scottish regular troops fought at Killiecrankie. The Royal Dragoons, who were later The Royal North British Dragoons (The Royal Scots Greys), were at Inverness. Dumbarton's Regiment (later 1st Foot, The Royal Scots) was in England, as were also the Scots Foot Guards. The Earl of Mar's Fusiliers, who were later The Royal North British Fusiliers (21st Foot, The Royal Scots Fusiliers), were in the Low Countries.

Appendix IV: APPLICATION OF THE EDINBURGH REGIMENT, 1817

The following communication was addressed to Lieutenant-Colonel J. A. Farquharson, commanding 25th Regiment, from the Adjutant-General. (*Public Record Office,* WO3/381/(34))

Horse Guards
23rd October 1817

I have to acknowledge receipt of your letter of the 25th inst., in which you request me to inform you when and for what reason the Edinburgh Regiment was denominated "Sussex", which appears to have taken place between the years 1780 and 1782.

In reply to which I beg to state that it appears by the Books of this Office that Directions were given on 31st August 1782 that certain Regiments of Infantry should bear County Titles, and that the 25th should bear that of Sussex.

I do not comprehend your application of the Edinburgh Regiment.

Directions were given on 7th May 1805 that the 25th Regiment should discontinue the "Sussex" Title and that it should be styled the 25th Regiment or King's Own Borderers.

I have, etc.,
(*Signed*) H. Calvert, A.G.

Appendix V: QUESTION OF SHEPHERDS' PLAID TROUSERS, 1860

The following communication was addressed to Lieutenant-Colonel A. J. Allan, commanding 2nd Battalion, 25th Regiment, from the Deputy Adjutant-General (R.H.Q., K.O.S.B.)

Horse Guards
3rd November 1860

Sir,

I have received and laid before the General Commanding in Chief your letter of the 27th ultimo, requesting that the 25th Regiment may in future be supplied with Shepherds' Plaid Trousers to mark its Scottish origin, and in intimating to you that no record of a previous application on this subject alluded to by you can be traced in this Department I am to acquaint you that His Royal Highness is unwilling to recommend to Her Majesty the introduction of any new article of clothing for the Army, as much inconvenience is thereby entailed on the War Office.

I am to add that it is considered that the sanction of the Pipers for The King's Own Borderers constitutes a sufficient recognition of its Northern origin, and while giving every credit to you for your object in making this application His Royal

Highness regrets that he cannot consistently with the recent assimilation in clothing recommend the introduction of any new distinctive article.

I have the honour, etc.,

(*Signed*) T. Troubridge, D.A.G.

Note

Sir Walter Scott was the first man to wear a pair of trousers of the small black and white check, described by E. S. Harrison in *Our Scottish District Checks* as the traditional pattern of the plaids worn by the Border shepherds, and the foundation of many of the District Checks throughout Scotland. Sheep and, therefore, shepherds had been introduced into the Highlands in the late 18th Century, perhaps earlier, and the Shepherds' Check became universal.

Appendix VI: THE FAREWELL ADDRESS OF MAJOR F. S. TERRY, 1881

Farewell Address to the Officers, N.C. Officers and Men of both Battalions of the King's Own Borderers by MAJOR F. S. TERRY, *after a Service in their ranks of Twenty-six years* (1881).

SOLDIERS — I wish you goodbye and to each and all Prosperity, Good Fortune, and Happiness. Though now severed from the Borderers I count myself as enlisted for life for such service as may be permitted. A strong fellow-feeling for the old and young soldiers alike has grown up in me, and an experience of many years has produced an affectionate regard and respect for the ranks of the Army as they stand.

I have the fullest confidence that the right spirit is in you, and the ability, to emulate and surpass the grandest deeds of Military History when properly prepared and led as in those great days.

Remember the 8th of October, 1878, when but just returned from a pestilential camp where a tenth of your numbers had been struck down with that fell disease cholera, you responded to the call of the Officer in Command and volunteered for service at the Front before the enemy.

The enthusiasm which you then displayed was of no momentary duration, but carried you steadfastly through the arduous work of two campaigns in a manner which attracted notice and elicited the commendation of the General Officers in Command.

The hope which then possessed us that we should add another honourable distinction to our Regimental Colours has been realized. Henceforth, the word 'Afghanistan', emblazoned thereon will recall to our minds a proud memory of many days of Hardship, Toil, and Danger cheerfully endured in the service of our beloved Queen and Country.

The task is done — From beginning to end I read on your faces that it should be well done and it was so — The living presence in these days of the old stubborn British fighting spirit was clearly shown   The Lion is in you, and will come forth again, and again, when the occasion arises and the call is made.

Strive after efficiency always, and join with me in firm faith that if we do our duty by the present according to our ability, the future will take care of us and prove bright and happy. Press ever forward, Forward, with the work in hand and be loyal and true even to the end. FAREWELL.

FRED S. TERRY, Major

Appendix VII: THE 'LEVEN' OR 'LESLIE' TARTAN

Extract from a letter from the 11th Earl of Leven to Lieutenant-Colonel A. N. Adams, commanding 1st Battalion, The King's Own Scottish Borderers. (The

correspondence is filed at R.H.Q., K.O.S.B., and is reproduced with the permission
of the present Earl of Leven and Messrs. Romanes and Paterson.)

Ashburnham House,
Dover Street,
London W.1.
18th July 1893.

Dear Colonel Adams,

I have been making inquiries as to how to prove any Tartan is legal tartan, and
can find no grounds of any such proof for any tartan. I consulted the Duke of Athol
and others well informed on such subjects without avail.

The best proof of an authentic tartan is its being known in Scotland and sold in
the shops. The Leslie tartan, I believe, has been known and sold for many
generations: the date of its origin no one, so far as I can discover, knows. It is, at
any rate, a real tartan and has been used by the family for generations . . .

Faithfully yours,

(*Signed*) Leven and Melville.

Extract from a letter from Messrs. Romanes and Paterson, 62 Prince's Street,
Edinburgh, c.*1893*.

. . . There is no tartan in existence at the present time as a clan pattern which can
be verified from Books, Prints, or Pictures in colours, as early as 1689, so that in the
absence of evidence of this kind as to its use, the 'Leven' tartan is no exception.

On the other hand, the unvarying tradition of the Tartan, during the century or
more our house has manufactured these goods, and which tradition had been
handed on by those whose recollections would extend to the middle of the last
century, all go to show that the tartan was known as 'Lord Leven's'.

Corroboration of this can be furnished from many old collections of tartan
specimens, where the pattern occurs as 'Leslie' or 'Leven'.

Certain it is that the 'Leven' tartan existed prior to the time when the use of
tartans (proscribed by Act of Parliament in 1747) was restored in 1784.

The pattern has been associated with the Earl who raised the 'Edinburgh
Regiment', in our business traditions, which extend back to the last century.

It occurs in all the early and important collections of old tartan fabrics under its
proper name, and it is impossible to believe but that it is a design of a date as early
as, probably much earlier than, that of the raising of the Regiment in 1689.

The pattern of tartan (of which enclosed is a specimen) is one which has always
been known to authorities on tartans as the 'Leven' tartan. It has also been
associated with the Rothes family and is worn by all the Leslies in Scotland when
they use tartan, but its first association with a name is with that of the Earl of Leven
of 'Leven's' or the 'Edinburgh Regiment', afterwards the 'King's Own Borderers'.

(*Signed*) Romanes and Paterson.

Appendix VIII: 'ADDRESS TO A SANGAR', Belfast, 1975-76

Oh Sangars, curse o' sojer's life,
Whae keeps the guidman frae his wife
And causes mony a hoosehold strife
Tae come tae boil,
Your boredom it wad blunt a knife,
Weel sharp'd wi' toil.

The flair inside ye, hoo it reeks,
While oot the hole the sojer keeks,
Thinkin' days are mair like weeks,
Or so it seems,
Then shuts his ee'n and there he seeks
The warmth o' dreams.

The sojer stands there all alane,
Numb against the wind and rain
That gauns howlin' through the windae pain
That is'nae there . . .
Surrounded by yer wa's o' stane,
He disnae care.

Sae here, ma freens and fellae men,
Juist spare a thocht fur sojers, then,
Whae stand aboot eicht hoors or ten
In every day,
Sae a' aroond is safe ye ken,
Fur folk tae play.

Fur hoors and hoors the sojer stands,
Countin' minutes on his hands,
And dreamin' aye o' distant lands
And their guid cheer,
And wishin' that his hameland sands
Were fine and near.

John Nisbet,
Private, 1st K.O.S.B.

Appendix IX: COMMANDING OFFICERS SINCE 1875 of the Regular, Militia, and first line T.A. battalions and the 1914-18 Service battalions

1st Battalion

(1871) Lieutenant-Colonel J. A. Ruddell
1880 Major F. S. Terry
Colonel J. N. Harvey
1885 Colonel N. C. Ramsay
1887 Colonel G. T. L. Carwithen
1889 Lieutenant-Colonel F. E. Carleton
1892 Lieutenant-Colonel A. N. Adams
1894 Lieutenant-Colonel J. H. Hogarth
1898 Lieutenant-Colonel J. W. Godfray
1900 Lieutenant-Colonel G. N. Mayne
1902 Major M. G. Wilkinson
Lieutenant-Colonel G. N. Mayne,
C.B.
1903 Lieutenant-Colonel F. E.
Wallerstein (York & Lancaster
Regiment)
1905 Lieutenant-Colonel D. A.
Macfarlane, D.S.O.
1909 Lieutenant-Colonel W. D. Sellar
1913 Lieutenant-Colonel A. S. Koe
1915 Lieutenant-Colonel A. J. Welch
1917 Lieutenant-Colonel C. A. G. O.
Murray, D.S.O.
1918 Lieutenant-Colonel W. T.
Wilkinson, D.S.O.
1919 Lieutenant-Colonel A. J. Welch
1922 Lieutenant-Colonel P. A. V.
Stewart, C.B.E., D.S.O.
1926 Lieutenant-Colonel W. T.
Wilkinson, D.S.O.
1928 Lieutenant-Colonel H. J. N.
Davis, C.M.G., D.S.O.
1932 Lieutenant-Colonel C. A. G. O.
Murray, D.S.O.
1934 Lieutenant-Colonel C. S. Stirling
Cookson, D.S.O., M.C.

1936 Lieutenant-Colonel B. C. Lake,
D.S.O.
1939 Lieutenant-Colonel E. E.
Broadway, M.B.E.
1940 Lieutenant-Colonel D. C. Bullen-
Smith, M.C.
1941 Lieutenant-Colonel M. McLellan
1942 Lieutenant-Colonel R. Payton-
Reid
Lieutenant-Colonel F. W.
Johnston
1943 Lieutenant-Colonel R. Payton-
Reid
Lieutenant-Colonel F. W.
Johnston
1944 Lieutenant-Colonel G. D. Renny,
D.S.O.
1944 Lieutenant-Colonel J. F. M.
Macdonald, O.B.E.
1944 Lieutenant-Colonel R. C.
Macdonald, D.S.O. (Royal
Warwickshire Regiment)
1945 Lieutenant-Colonel W. F. R.
Turner, D.S.O.
1947 Lieutenant-Colonel F. M. V.
Tregear
1949 Lieutenant-Colonel J. F. M.
Macdonald, D.S.O., O.B.E.
1952 Lieutenant-Colonel D. H.
Tadman, D.S.O., O.B.E.
1954 Lieutenant-Colonel D. W.
McConnel, O.B.E.
1957 Lieutenant-Colonel J. D. Henson,
M.B.E., M.C.
1960 Lieutenant-Colonel R. C.
Robertson-Macleod, D.S.O.,
M.C., T.D.

1962 Lieutenant-Colonel A. M. Thorburn
1964 Lieutenant-Colonel C. G. Stonor, M.C.
1967 Lieutenant-Colonel R. J. McCallum, M.C.
1969 Lieutenant-Colonel A. D. Myrtle, M.B.E.
1971 Lieutenant-Colonel R. W. Riddle, O.B.E.
1974 Lieutenant-Colonel F. A. L. Alstead
1976 Lieutenant-Colonel M. Thomson, M.B.E.
1979 Lieutenant-Colonel C. G. Mattingley

2nd Battalion

(1869) Lieutenant-Colonel C. J. S. Wallace
1876 Lieutenant-Colonel G. S. Hallowes
1881 Colonel A. S. Cameron, V.C. (72nd Highlanders)
1884. Lieutenant-Colonel N. C. Ramsay
1885 Colonel C. E. Hope
1887 Colonel J. Talbot Coke
1890 Lieutenant-Colonel J. L. Ross
1895 Lieutenant-Colonel E. W. W. Dering
Lieutenant-Colonel H. G. Dixon
1899 Lieutenant-Colonel G. T. N. Hewat
1902 Lieutenant-Colonel C. T. Becker
1906 Lieutenant-Colonel G. de W. Verner
1910 Lieutenant-Colonel C. M. Stephenson
1914 Lieutenant-Colonel E. S. D'E. Coke, D.S.O.
1916 Lieutenant-Colonel D. R. Sladen, C.M.G., D.S.O.
Lieutenant-Colonel P. F. Stevenson, D.S.O.
Lieutenant-Colonel D. R. Sladen, C.M.G., D.S.O.
1917 Lieutenant-Colonel C. T. Furber, D.S.O.
1919 Brevet Colonel E. S. D'E. Coke, C.M.G., D.S.O.
1920 Lieutenant-Colonel E. N. Broadbent, C.B., C.M.G., D.S.O.
Lieutenant-Colonel H. D. N. Maclean, D.S.O.

1921 Lieutenant-Colonel E. N. Broadbent, C.B., C.M.G., D.S.O.
1923 Lieutenant-Colonel J. C. W. Connell, D.S.O.
1925 Lieutenant-Colonel W. T. Wilkinson, D.S.O.
1926 Lieutenant-Colonel L. J. Comyn, C.M.G., D.S.O.
1930 Lieutenant-Colonel R. H. Crake, D.S.O.
1934 Lieutenant-Colonel J. K. B. Campbell
1938 Lieutenant-Colonel T. K. Newbigging, M.C.
1941 Lieutenant-Colonel W. G. Mattingley
1944 Lieutenant-Colonel J. D. A. MacLaren
Lieutenant-Colonel D. W. McConnel
Lieutenant-Colonel R. Caulfeild
Lieutenant-Colonel H. R. R. Condor, M.B.E. (Royal Norfolk Regiment)
1946 Lieutenant-Colonel R. Payton-Reid, D.S.O.

3rd (Militia) Battalion, 1887-1919

(The title Militia was discontinued after 1908)

Honorary Colonels

1893 Lieutenant-Colonel Sir George Walker, K.C.B.
1898 Colonel A. Hume, T.D. (Honorary Colonel late Militia)

(1873) Lieutenant-Colonel Sir George Walker, K.C.B.
1893 Lieutenant-Colonel A. Hume
1898 Lieutenant-Colonel J. K. Maxwell-Witham, C.M.G.
1905 Lieutenant-Colonel C. V. E. Laurie, D.S.O.
1910 Lieutenant-Colonel W. C. Critchley-Salmonson
1911 Lieutenant-Colonel H. W. A. F. Crichton-Browne
1918 Lieutenant-Colonel W. D. Young-Herries

4th (Border) Battalion

Honorary Colonels:

1908 Colonel Sir Richard Waldie-Griffith, Bart., T.D. (late Volunteers)

1933 Colonel The Duke of Buccleuch,
K.T., G.C.V.O., T.D.
1908 Lieutenant-Colonel W. Murray-
Threipland
1912 Lieutenant-Colonel J. McNeile
1915 Major W. E. A. Cochrane
Lieutenant-Colonel G. T. B.
Wilson, D.S.O. (Argyll &
Sutherland Highlanders)
1916 Major W. T. Forrest, M.C.
Lieutenant-Colonel J. M. B.
Sanders, M.C. (Leinster
Regiment)
1917 Lieutenant-Colonel R. Dashwood-
Tandy
1918 Lieutenant-Colonel E. C. Hill-
Whitson
Major P. L. P. Laing
1920 Lieutenant-Colonel E. D.
Jackson, D.S.O.
1926 Lieutenant-Colonel The Earl of
Dalkeith, M.P.
1929 Lieutenant-Colonel M. M.
Thorburn, M.C.
1934 Lieutenant-Colonel C. S. Stirling
Cookson, D.S.O., M.C.
1938 Lieutenant-Colonel G. D. Scott
1940 Lieutenant-Colonel R. A. H.
Kappey, M.C.
Lieutenant-Colonel H. A. Kelly
1942 Lietenant-Colonel J. B. Vans-
Agnew
1943 Lieutenant-Colonel W. A. H.
Maxwell
1944 Lieutenant-Colonel C. L. Melville
(Black Watch)
1945 Lieutenant-Colonel G. H.
Davidson, T.D.
Lieutenant-Colonel J. B. A.
Hankey, D.S.O.
1947 Lieutenant-Colonel C. J.
Ballantyne, T.D.
1951 Lieutenant-Colonel G. H. Rae,
O.B.E., M.C., T.D.
1955 Lieutenant-Colonel J. R. Scott
Noble, M.C., T.D.
1957 Lieutenant-Colonel D. O. Hogg,
O.B.E., M.C., T.D.
1960 Lieutenant-Colonel W. T.
Dundas, T.D.

5th (Dumfries & Galloway) Battalion
Honorary Colonels:
1908 Colonel J. M. Kennedy, M.V.O.,

V.D. (late Volunteers)
1921 Lieutenant-Colonel P. M. Kerr,
T.D.
1929 Colonel A. H. McNeill
1931 Lieutenant-Colonel F. J.
Carruthers
1939 Lieutenant-Colonel The Earl of
Stair, K.T., D.S.O.
1949 Lieutenant-Colonel G. G. Walker,
C.B.E., M.C., T.D.

1908 Lieutenant-Colonel R. F.
Dudgeon, V.D.
1911 Lieutenant-Colonel C. Murray
Kerr, T.D.
1915 Lieutenant-Colonel W. J. Millar,
D.S.O., T.D.
1916 Major W. T. Forrest, M.C.
1916 Lieutenant-Colonel J. R. Simson,
D.S.O. (Highland Light Infantry)
1917 Lieutenant-Colonel A. H. C.
Kearsay, D.S.O., O.B.E. (10th
Hussars)
Lieutenant-Colonel R. N.
Coulson, D.S.O. (Cameronians)
1918 Major G. R. S. Patterson, M.C.
(Highland Light Infantry)
Lieutenant-Colonel F. J.
Courtenay Hood, D.S.O. (York &
Lancaster Regiment)
1921 Colonel A. H. McNeill, D.S.O.,
M.C.
1929 Lieutenant-Colonel A. McC.
Jameson
1934 Lieutenant-Colonel G. G. Walker,
M.C.
1940 Lieutenant-Colonel K. A. T.
McLennan, M.C.
1941 Lieutenant-Colonel T. H. M.
Murray, T.D.
1942 Lieutenant-Colonel W. F. R.
Turner, D.S.O.
1945 Lieutenant-Colonel G. G. M.
Batchelor
1951 Lieutenant-Colonel W. J. M.
Ross, O.B.E., M.C., T.D.
1955 Lieutenant-Colonel A. J. Jardine
Paterson, T.D.
1958 Lieutenant-Colonel C. G. Grieve,
T.D.

4th/5th Battalion
Honorary Colonels:
1961 Colonel, The Duke of Buccleuch,
K.T., G.C.V.O., T.D.

1962 Major-General J. F. M. Macdonald, C.B., O.B.E., D.S.O.

1961 Lieutenant-Colonel C. G. Grieve, T.D.

1963 Lieutenant-Colonel Sir William Jardine, Bart., O.B.E., T.D.

1967 Lietenant-Colonel W. Bruce, T.D.

6th (Service) Battalion

1914 Lieutenant-Colonel H. D. N. Maclean, D.S.O.

1915 Major C. E. Andrews (Highland Light Infantry)
Major R. F. Forbes (Highland Light Infantry)
Lieutenant-Colonel J. C. W. Connell, D.S.O.

1916 Lieutenant-Colonel G. B. F. Smyth, D.S.O., R.E.

1918 Lieutenant-Colonel P. F. Ker

1919 Lieutenant-Colonel E. D. Jackson, D.S.O.

6th (Border) Battalion

1939 Lieutenant-Colonel the Hon. the Master of Napier and Ettrick

1941 Lieutenant-Colonel J. G. Shillington, D.S.O.

1944 Lieutenant-Colonel C. W. P. Richardson, D.S.O.

7th (Service) Battalion

1914 Lieutenant-Colonel G. de W. Verner

1915 Major J. C. W. Connell

1916 Lieutenant-Colonel B. J. B. Coulson
Major C. S. Marsh, D.S.O. (Indian Army)

7th (Galloway) Battalion

1939 Lieutenant-Colonel The Earl of Galloway

1940 Lieutenant-Colonel L. F. Machin, M.C.

1942 Lieutenant-Colonel G. Ilderton

1943 Lieutenant-Colonel R. Payton-Reid, D.S.O.

1945 Lieutenant-Colonel R. D. Sellon

8th (Service) Battalion

1914 Lieutenant-Colonel T. B. Sellar

7th/8th Battalion

1916 Lieutenant-Colonel T. B. Sellar, C.M.G., D.S.O.

1917 Lieutenant-Colonel M. F. B. Dennis, D.S.O.

1918 Lieutenant-Colonel H. P. Hart, D.S.O.
Lieutenant-Colonel H. W. Sutherland, D.S.O.

Appendix X: REGIMENTAL BIBLIOGRAPHY

The Records of The King's Own Borderers or Old Edinburgh Regiment. Edited by Captain R. T. Higgins (King's Own Borderers). Chapman & Hall, 1873.

The Militia Battalion

Weir, Revd. R. W. *A History of The Scottish Borderers Militia.* Printed at the Courier & Herald, Dumfries, 1877.

Weir, Revd. R. W. *The History of the 3rd Battalion King's Own Scottish Borderers 1798-1908.* Printed at the Courier & Herald Office, Dumfries, 1918.

First World War

Gillon, Captain Stair (late K.O.S.B.). *The K.O.S.B. in the Great War.* Thomas Nelson, London, 1930.

Goss, M.C. (late K.O.S.B.), Captain J. and others. *A Border Battalion: the history of the 7th/8th (Service) Battalion King's Own Scottish Borderers.* Printed privately, Edinburgh, 1920.

Scott Elliot (late K.O.S.B.), Captain G. F. *War History of the 5th Battalion King's Own Scottish Borderers.* T.F. Associations: Robert Dinwiddie, Dumfries, 1928.

War Record of 4th Battalion King's Own Scottish Borderers and Lothians and Border Horse. Edited by W. Sorley Brown (late K.O.S.B.). T.F. Associations: John McQueen, Galashiels, 1920.

Second World War

Baggaley, M.C. (late K.O.S.B.), Captain J. R. P. *The 6th (Border) Battalion, The King's Own Scottish Borderers 1939-1945.* Martin's Printing Works, Berwick-upon-Tweed, 1946.

Gunning, Captain Hugh. *Borderers in Battle: The War Story of the King's Own Scottish Borderers 1939-1945.* Martin's Printing Works, Berwick-upon-Tweed, 1948.

Tullett (K.O.S.B.), Captain E. V. *From Flushing to Bremen (The 5th Battalion, The King's Own Scottish Borderers).* Printed in Germany, 1945.

War History of the 4th (Border) Battalion, The King's Own Scottish Borderers 1939-1945. Edited by Major F. H. Coutts (K.O.S.B.). Printed in Germany, 1945.

Korea

MacDonald, C.B., O.B.E., D.S.O. (late K.O.S.B.), Major-General J. F. m. *The Borderers in Korea*, Martin's Printing Works, Berwick-upon-Tweed.

Appendix XI: REGIMENTS ALLIED TO THE KING'S OWN SCOTTISH BORDERERS

1st Battalion, The Royal New Brunswick Regiment. Carleton Street Armoury, Fredericton, New Brunswick, Canada.

2nd Battalion, The Royal New Brunswick Regiment. The Armoury, King Street, Bathurst, New Brunswick, Canada. This regiment was The St. John Fusiliers before the Second World War, and was allied in 1926.

25th Battalion, The Royal Queensland Regiment. Milne Bay Depot, Toowoomba, Queensland, Australia. This regiment was the 25th Battalion, Australian Military Forces, before the Second World War, and was allied in 1931.

5th Battalion, The Royal Malay Regiment. Khota Baru, Kelantau, Malaysia. This regiment was allied in 1955.

INDEX